PLEADING

INSANITY

• • • • • • • • • • • • • • •

PLEADING
INSANITY

ANDREW JAMES ARCHER

ARCHWAY
PUBLISHING

Archway Publishing books may be ordered through booksellers or by contacting:

Archway Publishing
1663 Liberty Drive
Bloomington, IN 47403
www.archwaypublishing.com
1-(888)-242-5904

ISBN: 978-1-4808-0087-8 (sc)
ISBN: 978-1-4808-0105-9 (e)

Library of Congress Control Number: 2013909468

Printed in the United States of America

Archway Publishing rev. date: 6/24/2013

Praise for Pleading Insanity

"This is truly remarkable! I could not stop reading it. He provides such a thoughtful, personal, and, at the same time, scholarly account of what bipolar I disorder is really like. Archer's Pleading Insanity is an invaluable teaching tool for undergraduate and graduate courses on mood disorders. I will assign it in my classes."

—Lyn Y. Abramson, PhD, professor of psychology

"In this very intimate portrait, Andrew offers us something truly unique. He doesn't just describe the painful and destructive course of bipolar disorder; he takes us inside a bipolar body. This embodied report is unflinching and, at times, tough to bear. His writing is a reflection of the actual lived experience of the hell-realm of progressive mental illness. In reading this account, the reader gets a visceral feel for the unfolding struggle, his inevitable decline, the collateral damage to close relationships, and his ultimate return from the edge. This valuable journal includes both the stumbling mistakes of psychiatric treatment alongside moments of touching clarity and profound grace."

—Flint Sparks, PhD, psychologist and Zen teacher

"After reading Andrew's story, my perspective on bipolar disorder has definitely changed a lot. The way it affected and hurt his education, family, and friends was devastating … how a UW student went from typical college kid to psychologically broken was unsettling. I feel Andrew's story to be very poignant and relevant in helping society understand mental illnesses."

—University of Wisconsin–Madison student, 2010

"To see and understand the things he was feeling and going through while being diagnosed bipolar was fascinating. I've had friends with mental illnesses and I've worked with elderly individuals who have had dementia and schizophrenia and some even bipolar, but I don't ever remember them telling me how it felt or the things that went through their minds while having their mental illness."

—University of Wisconsin–Madison student, 2010

"Archer writes of his experiences with bipolar disorder with an impressive raw honesty. His account is inspiring, humanizing, and relatable. Pleading Insanity is a text to be read for personal growth, educational purposes, and literary enjoyment. In the words of one of my psychology students, "I was enlightened by Archer's real-life account.""

–Amanda K. Sesko, PhD - assistant professor of psychology

So these are the three qualities of brilliant sanity: openness, clarity, and compassion. They are unconditional.

—Karen Kissel Wegela

INTRODUCTION

August 24, 1981, was my first day on this earth, and it was the day that my serious genetic predisposition for bipolar disorder began. More than thirty-one years later, I've experienced multiple personal revisions, all with nerves stretched thin in the pursuit of common but persistent desires. At times, I've sunk lower than I thought possible, and at other times, I've soared. I've discovered versions of fortitude previously unknown.

I grew up in a family that hid behind a veil of normalcy. Within our immediate family, the topic—bipolar disorder—was rarely discussed. My father's coworkers, friends, and neighbors were unaware of his illness, which further strengthened his carefully guarded secrecy. Unfortunately, you can't hide from biology. Having a parent with bipolar I increases the likelihood of a child getting it by a range of 10 to 15 percent. I imagine that my parents made Christian, missionary-style love sometime around the holiday season in 1980, and then August came around, and there I was—a tiny new Minnesotan with a little potential problem in my brain.

Because there was so little communication about my father's illness, our family knew next to nothing about the specifics of the disorder. We did not learn about any signs, symptoms, or details surrounding his first documented manic episode at the age of thirty-two. Any knowledge my mother had of his symptoms did not lead her to a worried preliminary diagnosis. However, his sleepless nights, intensive running regimen, insurgency of goals, and flight of ideas were all congruent with symptoms of mania (e.g., decreased need for sleep, excessive involvement in certain activities, and grandiosity).

My father usually expressed his depression and anxieties with anger and emotional distancing. My mother could not hear the muffled tones of his depression when his voice would rise. At a young age, I listened to some of those arguments from an upstairs bedroom, my arms clasping a pillow that absorbed my tears. At the age of six, I did not know that divorce was nearly insurmountable for a marriage that has one spouse with bipolar disorder. If I had, I would have felt a lack of reassurance when my mother tried to console me. She would come into my room, sit with me, and say, "Don't worry; your dad and I are not getting a divorce." I looked at her through rain-soaked-windshield eyes.

I did not ascertain the real stories behind my father's experiences until I was much older. My brother recalled a day in the spring of 1983 when my father walked out of our bathroom without his signature black mustache. My brother didn't even recognize him. I've still never seen him without the Wyatt Earp–style facial hair. Police apprehended my father near Minnehaha Falls in South Minneapolis hours later. He was preaching to a group of senior citizens in the middle of the afternoon. His topics ranged from overblown religious proclamations to Regan, a character from *The Exorcist*. My father's pressured speech and flight of ideas landed him in a psychiatric hospital. The name Regan was phonetically misinterpreted by witnesses and police officers to mean Reagan. After he was brought to the hospital, the Secret Service wanted to interrogate him about his comments, many of which were thought to be about President Ronald Reagan. His psychiatrist, an apparent Hippocrates enthusiast, honored his oath as a physician and refused the Secret Service's requests, based on patient confidentiality. If my manic-depressive father had been speaking about arms deals with future terrorists, or the president's nascent role that produced an eventual recession in 2008, he might now be declared a living prophet. Instead, he was diagnosed with a severe and persistent mental illness. At the hospital, the doctors gave him the antipsychotic medication Haldol, which reliably eradicates psychotic behavior. They also slowly administered lithium, which is known as the gold standard treatment for bipolar I disorder. While in the hospital, he made a beautiful leather wallet for my older brother. For me and my older brother, this simple, tangible artifact was the sole reminder of the event for many years.

Other than his own self-medicating with drugs and alcohol growing up, my father was not treated for bipolar I disorder until this psychiatric hospitalization. More recent dialogues with him speak volumes about the presenting symptoms that we had been seeing for many years. It makes me wonder. How did my mother overlook the signs prior to his hospitalization? She had significant knowledge about psychological disorders from her undergraduate schooling, but this disease is both seductive and deceiving. After caring for two young boys full-time, she eventually got a physical therapy position and immersed herself in her own career. Working enabled her to look past the fact that her husband was becoming ill. In the '80s, information about mental illness was not as ubiquitous or obtainable as it is today. There was little media coverage, and there were few available resources concerning interventions. Antipsychotic medication did not have advertisement campaigns or trademarks that included icons with smoothly paved roads leading up to new name brands. Today, ostentatious commercials for pharmaceutical companies have butterflies or people walking down beaches while negligent descriptions of mental illness symptoms are narrated.

To simplify a little, I will use the term "bipolar disorder" throughout the majority of this book, despite the existence of two types. My father and I were both diagnosed with bipolar I disorder, which requires at least one manic episode. A depressive episode is not required for bipolar I disorder, but such an episode often accompanies the mania. This means that some might describe an individual who has bipolar I disorder but *lacks* a depressive episode using an ignorant vernacular: "That guy is *soooo* unipolar." The basic difference between the two types is that bipolar II disorder requires at least one major depressive episode in addition to one or more hypomanic episodes. A hypomanic episode is a less severe form of mania and often goes untreated. The lack of treatment is usually due to the individual being more organized and productive and less irritable. The diagnostic criteria surrounding bipolar disorder are listed in the appendix of this book.

There are several reasons why I decided to write about my experiences with bipolar disorder. One reason is purely selfish: it is a way of self-disclosing. I hope that this book can be a stimulus for the expansion of awareness in my social and professional networks. Increased awareness creates a built-in safety net in the event I begin to have symptoms. Here is a potential excerpt from a future instant message on Facebook between two friends: "Wow, Archer is acting like a lunatic; we should send him a text." In addition, I can offer deep insight from a personal and professional perspective. I have input in the areas of causation, successful treatments, and interventions with respect to both types of bipolar disorder. My intention is to exhibit what can, will, and should happen when behaviors present themselves, as well as valuable tips about what *not* to do. I believe individuals diagnosed with bipolar disorder, their families, students (in psychology and social work especially), and mental-health professionals will all benefit from this information.

The original title of this book was *Mastering a Mental Illness*. The idea behind the title was that I am constantly in the process of mastering the illness in order to remain stable. I used the present tense because it is not possible to completely overcome the illness. The illness needs constant maintenance and attention. Malcolm Gladwell said that in order to master something, one must practice it for at least ten thousand hours. A decade has passed since I was labeled "bipolar." Diagnostically speaking, I have had the disorder for about ninety thousand hours. However, my therapy (about 250 or so hours), psychiatric and doctor visits (about 50 hours), successful graduate school experience (not sure how to quantify that), and guest lectures on bipolar disorder—minus many years of drinking, drug abuse, and emotional avoidance—do not seem to add up to anything that could be meaningfully described as a victorious conclusion. A lifelong, chronic mental illness takes time, proactive treatment, perseverance through times of instability, and a heavy dose of familial as well as social support.

— 1 —

LIKE FATHER, LIKE SON

Music, sweet music
I wish I could caress, caress, caress
Manic depression is a frustrating mess

—Jimi Hendrix, "Manic Depression"

4/15/05: As I walked out of the Dane County Jail after six-
teen days—fourteen in segregation—with borrowed boots and
blurred vision, my first visitor greeted me outside. After living in
a concrete cage, the feeling of warm sunshine was like the intense
satisfaction you feel from a sip of cool water when you're stranded
in a desert.

My father is one of the survivors. An extremely successful real estate agent, he was the breadwinner in our family. When I was a child, my dad hid most of his mood episodes, or his behavior was subtly nuanced from his regular demeanor.

I do remember him experiencing manic symptoms one night when I was about thirteen. Unable to sleep, he thought he would have a better time in my bedroom, which was basically a pitch-black cave in our basement. He quickly rolled in a makeshift bed, creating a darker version of a *Royal Tenenbaums* sleeping-arrangement scene.

At that point in my life, I recognized aspects of his madness. The effect on me was equivalent to a paralytic state one undergoes when a monster is chasing one during a nightmare. I could not escape the fear as I listened to my typically composed, logical father ramble on, with short periods of self-provoked, maniacal laughter. I pulled the pillow over my head eventually and regressed emotionally to an almost fetal state of being. Morning came, and my father left for work. I cried in the kitchen, telling my mother that the new sleeping arrangements could not happen again.

My father was more animated and embarrassingly funny when he would reach the high end of the pole, also known as mania. No devastating events occurred as a result of his illness other than his initial hospitalization. He didn't read many books about bipolar disorder. Instead, he learned about how to be successful. He practiced goal-oriented daily living techniques that developed into strong internal motivation skills. These adaptive character-istics are not mutually exclusive from today's standard treatment regime for bipolar disorder, but they are certainly unorthodox. My father found the structure he needed by immersing himself in the real estate business, and achievement soon followed. He sold a lot of houses in Minneapolis for nearly twenty-five years. He took lithium. He went to Catholic Mass.

After seeing my father's mania and sharing a house with him throughout my childhood, my attitude toward him set in during high school. I decided I did not ever want to turn out like him. As a parent, he was often emotionally shal-low and distant. As someone with bipolar disorder, he frightened me. To some degree, the comprehensions of his symptoms were intuitive. I was a terrified adolescent with little comprehension of either bipolar disorder or healthy parenting styles. To me, bipolar disorder *was* my dad, and he *was* bipolar disorder. I didn't have access to different experiences, schemas, or other perspectives about this illness. Regardless, I knew I didn't want to go through the ups and downs, instability, or quick temper that characterized his demeanor.

In hindsight, the warning signs for my bipolar disorder were all there. Identifying childhood red flags is becoming a focus in the mental health field to prevent the onslaught of largely adult symptoms. From the beginning, I would cry inconsolably for hours as an infant and small child. I was blatantly dishonest at an early age. "You lied about everything," my mother recently disclosed. I participated in many risky behaviors, including theft on large scales (I'm not talking about pennies from the dish at the counter), drinking, and drug use.

One night during my senior year in high school, I had a panic attack that was induced by caffeine. The attack was precipitated by staying up all night for a homecoming sleepover. Later in the morning, after the anxiety subsided, I found myself in a state of extreme confidence, high energy, and loss of inhibitions. The anxiety in my life at that time was distributed across my exercise regimen, schoolwork, and overall sense of vanity. Perfectionism drove these vehicles, all of which were directed at the hope for peace of mind. Unfortunately, these ideals perpetuated my anxiety and convinced me, despite my being in impeccable physical shape, that my body did not look good. These are all budding symptoms of bipolar disorder but do not meet full medical criteria for the diagnosis.

The warning signs and development of bipolar disorder can be missed because of a lack of information as well as flat-out denial of things in our environment. We miss what is right in front of us, because our attentions are focused on something else. We miss or marginalize changes in the person. We choose not to believe that bipolar disorder could happen to our sons, daughters, siblings, or partners. The illness is too devastating to conceptualize within the framework of someone you love. Passionate cries like "Why me?" or "This can't be happening!" or "This isn't real!" and "I don't deserve this!" echo throughout this text.

I recall talking to my girlfriend outside of our high school one day around the age of seventeen. We were sitting across the sidewalk from the idling bus that would transport our school's basketball team to any number of white suburban high schools in the surrounding area. For the life of me, I cannot remember what provoked the conversation other than intense anxiety and depressive symptoms. We sat for many silent minutes together on a bench with a slotted wood base. I could not look at her directly, because the noxious feelings elevated to the top of my throat. These feelings begged for verbal expression. She was my confidante and definitely my world, especially during times like that.

The tightness in my face told her how wrong something was. When I was finally able to speak, the words came out as splattered shards of glass. I began crying and attempting to tell her that I thought I had bipolar disorder and was "like my dad." I was realizing what I had feared—that I was turning out to be like him. That moment is a very lucid memory for me. At the time, I saw crying not as an expression of deep introspection into one's feelings but as a loss of control that happened only during the darkest of times—the vulnerable times.

In my mind, from up above this scene, there is a physically fit, almost adult figure who is reduced to a small boy. My girlfriend fades away without a response. The boy is abandoned like a left-behind child who has just fallen off of his bike. It was too quiet to cry anymore, and the only escape for me was to crawl onto the bus. I did not know where to go, how to ask for help, or how to heal the pain. I didn't know how to regain my strength. I caressed the tears with my hand to disguise what had just happened. I entered the bus and went to my basketball game. My mind somehow swept away the depressing, frightening thoughts so that I could maintain some form of emotional homeostasis.

When I felt good, I found it easy to abandon my girlfriend for ephemeral dating experiences with other girls or to take her for granted. Despite her being the "it girl" at my school, I thought she was never really good enough for me. I did not know what *good enough* for me was. We stayed together for many years. Staying together made life easier, because she knew everything about me. She was a first for everything during those years, and we shared an immense amount of time together. We told intricate communal lies to our parents so that she could spend adult nights with me. The bond we created at such a young age, in hindsight, disallowed me from developing a strong, healthy ego.

I mention this detail because vulnerability is a key factor in the development—or, more so, activation—of manic and depressive symptoms. Our eventual breakup years later, which led me to develop a depressive episode, gives weight to this theory. A stronger ego or sense of self might have changed my behaviors and thoughts about the breakup. I absolutely needed mental stability to continue to be successful in high school. A shield of popularity and hedonistic behaviors would keep me safe—or so I thought.

— 2 —

VULNERABLE ADULT

The Edge ... there is no honest way to explain it because the only people who really know where it is are the ones who have gone over.

—Hunter S. Thompson

I moved away from home and attended college in Madison, Wisconsin. I was on my own, except for the huge crutch of a longtime girlfriend and a PlayStation (the video race-car game *Gran Turismo* may have saved my life by giving me breaks from calculus homework). I again felt vulnerable. I was out of my high school domain and environmental familiarity. I was deserted within the large student body and created a self-imposed isolation.

I grew increasingly despondent, refusing to try to make friends and clinging to my high school peers who were attending the University of Wisconsin–Madison concurrently. My perfectionistic tendencies (i.e., coping mechanisms for anxiety) evolved with fierce acceleration against the vulnerability. Terrified of the "freshman fifteen," I ate as little as possible, which meant quite a bit, but I was always cognizant of the amount and type of food I was consuming.

Getting up early to work out for an hour before an 8:50 a.m. class was not the freshman norm, but it was what I did. Despite bench-pressing roughly 175 percent of my body weight (or 250 pounds, for those bachelors of arts) and being able to do twenty-three pull-ups, I was terribly unhappy with what I perceived as an unattractive body.

I mention these achievements to paint a picture. I'm narcissistic, but who cares how much you can bench-press? I did. The pursuit of perfection is an exhausting and never-ending process. The beginning, middle, and end result are all the same: disappointment or dissatisfaction and unhappiness, with a dash of continuous suffering. Fortunately for me, this severe insecurity had a prevalent antidote in Madison, Wisconsin. Eventually, I found a familiar, shared, and often communal cure: alcohol. This became a commonality among other students on my floor in the dorm (later I would stand up, and eventually sway, in two of their weddings).

During my freshman year, I had a driver's license (i.e., fake ID) that proclaimed my authority to make purchases at liquor stores and a thirst for connectedness. My socializing had a purpose. The apparent generosity of buying various forms of sugar-filled (Mike's Hard Lemonade was popular at the time) or toxically proofed liquids for my peers powered my notoriety. Listed requests became longer and more convoluted as the weeks passed and more individuals became aware of my access to means. There are few things more daring for a nineteen-year-old than operating a kick-start (usually more like a no-start) moped with a twenty-four-pack of Miller Lite between his legs and a basket full of liquor through streets filled with Madison police officers.

One must remember that the twenty-first century brought an epidemic into the United States and specifically college campuses: Red Bull energy drink and all its glory. Red Bull has since become 5-hour ENERGY's unsuccessful uncle who used to be fun to hang out with before his drinking became embarrassing and creepy. Fleischmann's vodka in plastic 1.75-liter bottles had been around for a while, but the combination took us on a quick ride to neurological shutdown. It was great. The concept of blacking out all weekend and then having a rigid, self-imposed schedule for working out, completing schoolwork, and eating during the week made perfect sense then. I can now comprehend the hypocrisy in that form of thinking. Now I understand how alcohol prevented my feelings of vulnerability. Although I was *with* other people during those late nights, I wasn't presenting who I was. In her book *The Gifts of Imperfection*, Brené Brown states that vulnerability "is a risk we have to take if we want to experience connection." A constant state of intoxication is a clear route to superficial relationships.

Somehow the balance of perfectionistic goals, the ability to turn off the anxiety temporarily with massive quantities of alcohol, friends, and a somewhat mentally stable girlfriend allowed for two semesters on the dean's list and a costume that hid what was lying beneath. Everything was perfect. After a summer at home, in the fall of my sophomore year, it was finally time to reach the last point of teenage autonomy: getting an apartment. Four of us shared a small box that was an upstairs two-bedroom apartment. The size did not matter to us, because the apartment was equipped with six or seven amazing views of the belligerent Breese Street during Wisconsin Badger football games. The draw to our new place of residence was the flat-roofed garage. It acted as an overhead theater to the gluttonous stage of binge drinking and carnivorous eating below. The sea of eighty thousand midwesterners was a staggered Million Man March for Caucasians. There was an impeccable line-of-sight vista into Camp Randall Stadium, which was a drunken football toss away. We could warehouse at least eight people uncomfortably inside the slouched apartment and, barring collapse, another twelve on top of the garage.

I distinctly *do not* remember blacking out while traveling back and forth between the apartment and the garage on one of those Saturdays—a trip that included a potentially fatal climb over a break between the fire escape attached to the apartment and the garage roof. The blackout occurred around one o'clock in the afternoon. A couple hours later, as I was told, I spent time on my roommate's desk chair (sorry, buddy) with my girlfriend before waking up at nine o'clock that night. There's nothing worse than a same-day blackout that bleeds into a wretched nighttime hangover. Always aware but somewhat enabling (e.g., paying for partial tuition and rent, giving me access to a car, etc.), my mother would scold me about this childish behavior. I assured her that "everyone drinks this much in college."

Slowly, influenced but not pressured, I began smoking more marijuana. Using marijuana acted as an avoidance mechanism to combat my depressing and ever-shrinking living environment. As a reminder, there were four guys living in a two-bedroom tree house. The night prior to the first day of spring semester classes came with an unconventional double date. My roommate, his girlfriend, my girlfriend, and I decided to make some "special" brownies. This was our first time baking to get baked, and we soon realized that you do not need an eighth of a gram of marijuana to make the magic happen. I remember saying to my apprehensive girlfriend, "You can't get too high," as she attempted to persuade me into slowing my ingestion of our culinary delight. Not long after my five brownies, while watching *The Big Lebowski* on DVD, my mind began to race. I felt as if everything were in slow motion. This feeling was largely due to the thoughts that were attached to every detail of the movie, which I had seen about thirty times prior. The sensation felt like something out of a science-fiction movie, such as *Terminator 2*, where the robots size up every human with detailed and swift analyses. They scan the shape, age, sex, and body movements of every human they come across and process the information with lightning speed using some sort of infrared sensors. My brain connections sped uncontrollably, and a feeling of fear quickly came over me.

After one of our other roommates drove us to each girlfriend's separate apartment, I was certain I would never sleep. As I lay in bed waiting for my girlfriend, who was also high, to join me, my eyes slowly adjusted to the darkness. The situation was reminiscent of a National Geographic video recorded at night, where one can still see the lions hunting some hopeless wildebeest. Basically, I could see her, and she could not see me. I witnessed the familiar "I can't see a thing right now; I hope I don't hit anything" walk. This in turn prompted me to say something like "It's okay" or "Come this way," but the words did not register with her, because she assumed I could not see her, as she could not see me. At least that's how I read it with a head full of THC. I think she was both annoyed by the drug and the event and somewhat frightened of me as well as my behaviors.

The next day, we stepped out of an excessive Chipotle lunch and into the chill of the January air. Downtown State Street was alive with equal parts liberal adults and hungover college students who were ill prepared for the commencement of the spring semester.

Parallel sidewalks trap State Street's narrow road. The straight three-quarter-mile strip begins at the outer edge of campus and ends due east at the state capitol building. On that day, this heterogeneous organism was divided by slow-moving police cars and apathetic city buses with blatant disregard for oblivious pedestrians. Earnest panhandlers and slow-moving out-of-state families disrupted the ambience. These barely animate objects had strollers and actively turning heads, and they observed places like Jamba Juice as if they were cultural representations of the city. At that time of day, in the last of the presemester days, State Street was as active as Manhattan but not quite as odorous (i.e., less urine and circulated air). This was the epicenter for thirsty Madisonians, as one could spit in every direction and hit an active bar.

I told my girlfriend that I thought the way my mind had operated the previous night was probably a lot like mania. As I uncomfortably looked at her and described the racing thoughts, schools of students traversed the single-file impasse our conversation created. The people moved both east and west along the sidewalk with swift intention and the flexibility of diverted running water. I would soon find out that a chemical-induced high from brownies is not the same as mania, but there are some faint similarities. During the commencement address to the 2005 graduates of Kenyon College, David Foster Wallace popularized this little existential anecdote:

> There are these two young fish swimming along, and they happen to meet an older fish swimming the other way who nods at them and says, "Morning, boys. How's the water?"

> And the two young fish swim on for a bit, and then eventually one of them looks over at the other and goes, "What the hell is water?"

There is a fundamental difference that is easily confused between being high on a drug and experiencing mania. When one is manic, it is very difficult for the individual to comprehend the "water" he or she is swimming in. The individual just feels great while in an oblivious state that is filled with wrath and bizarre behaviors. The person is frequently unaware of the potential consequences of his or her condition. There is no reflection or foresight. This reality greatly contrasts the usually more temporary experience of using drugs. More often than not, even if one is stoned out of his or her mind or tripping off of mushrooms to the point of psychedelic hallucinations or visualizations, the individual can usually step back (i.e., reflect) and think, *Holy shit, I'm really fucked up right now. That building looks like it is melting right before my eyes. I'm really high!* This type of reflection is analogous to the understanding of "This is water." There is a cause-and-effect connection whereby the person can understand that the drug is causing his or her environment to change. With mania, all too often, the person is unable to uncover this dissociation from reality or realize just what he or she is "swimming" in.

I speculate that the brownie night had an even more profound effect on my girl-friend than it did on me. Not long after that, she decided she wanted to end the almost-five-year courtship. I was at the infamous College Library on February 12, 2002, when she called me crying. In an idiosyncratic turn of events, she pleaded with me to allow her to end the relationship. I was in good spirits at the time and was confident that a break would be just that. Thinking it was nothing more than a temporary phase for her, we broke up. Her own battles with depression and anxiety preempted this change. I recall being comfortable with the breakup happening. I went back to my desk in the quiet study area and finished scrutinizing the dry, dull information for my accounting quiz, thinking the break would last only a couple weeks at most. This chapter of the book concludes here, but soon after the breakup, the first chapter of my life ended with a dramatic shift in my perspective. I would feel as if everything I knew had been lost, and rebirth was a consequence. I was naive and unfamiliar with this new environment, which was filled with too much independence. Had I been asked during that time, surely my response would have been, "What the hell is water?"

— 3 —

ON THE ORIGIN OF SYMPTOMS

An American monkey, after getting drunk on brandy, would
never touch it again, and thus is much wiser than most men.

—Charles Darwin

After a couple weeks had passed and I had finished enjoying being single,
I called her. She declined to meet for lunch. She said she was not ready. A
slow, paralyzing shock wave pierced through every vein of my body. The
reality that we might not get back together set in. I was devastated. I felt as
if I had reverted to an insecure fifteen-year-old child who had never learned
the ups and downs of adolescence because of the protective shield that a
steady, stable, and intimate relationship had provided. My social invincibility dissipated with the thought of being alone. Prior to the breakup—for
the first time—I had fantasized about spending the rest of my life with her.
Some call this "marriage" or stretch it to "an eternal commitment." *This can't
really be happening!* is just one of many negative thoughts I had. My drinking
got worse. My anxiety levels skyrocketed. My business school classes were
intolerable. My only focus was getting back together with her, and it bound
me to an internal place of desolation. The obsession grew. I would study in
the business school library, knowing that she sometimes did, hoping to run

into her. There were no Facebook pokes in February of 2002 and no circular green icons representing online presences and potential chat mates to cling to. Crying, which had once been a foreign emotional reaction for me, happened frequently. One trip to Steenbock Library led me to write a lengthy e-mail to my ex-girlfriend; tears rolled down my cheeks with each key I pressed on the keyboard. I made sure my emotions poured out soundlessly, hoping to avoid making a scene in front of the strangers in the small computer lab. I have no idea what I wrote in that e-mail, but I imagine desperation, longing, and defeat were within the lines. Below is part of a clinical note from my therapist after an assessment in early 2006.

> First relationship (5 years) may have ended as gf wanted to explore other relationships when they got to college and she broke it off. They never discussed what happened and A [Andy] was unable to get closure. She was shy and internalized feelings as well.

I kept all of the "internalized feelings" hidden as I sunk into an abysmal, clinically depressive state. It took years to habituate the loss of this profound relationship. Even though the pain is gone now, I continually learn from failed relationships as I experience the nuances of dating that I missed during those growing years (i.e., ages fifteen through twenty). Not long after the breakup, I had a whole new experience during spring break.

In March of 2002, five of us embarked in a large, old, Suburban to our oasis: spring break in Panama City, Florida. Our transportation let out a thick black cloud from the muffler when the driver reached fifty miles per hour. From the passenger's perspective, it appeared that the smoke monster from the television show *Lost* had escaped from our vehicle. This conspicuous dark fog we were producing was less than settling for the driver and, I am sure, cars approaching from the rear. Somehow we made it to the promised land. This trip was a good thing for me—or so I thought. Drinking incessantly and smoking marijuana as we went from bars to the beach to random hotel rooms was a daily occurrence. I would awake before my roommates, filled with energy. Immediately, I would go on an extensive run across the beach despite experiencing an alcohol-induced blackout only hours prior. I felt amazing. I was completely uninhibited around girls and did not have the insecurities or fear that I'd left behind in Madison.

One example that stands out was my interaction with a girl named Laura. It took every ounce of me to start talking to her by the pool outside of our hotel room. Leaning up against a fence, my friend smiled in the background as if to cheer me on and say, "Yeah!" We exchanged phone numbers, and this girl became my destiny. Despite the expansive and rapid thought processes that were taking place, she was the center of my spotlight. I missed a call from her, and she passed out early or something later that night, so the stars were not aligned, as our crew had to set sail the next day.

The high of spring break wore off as I transitioned back into school. Not long after, I began having insomnia. Despite limited sleep, I would not be tired the next day. In one class, during a class discussion, there was a specific moment when I said the word *bullshit* within the context of my comment, which elicited laughter among the small group. Up until that point, I would rarely talk in class, let alone take the risk of doing something as radical as using a curse word. I felt empowered as I looked over at the girl who was my semester-long secret crush. She expressed amusement with a smile and curious eyes. These are little, segregated, retrospective incidents, but collectively, they assemble a clear puzzle of a manifesting mental illness. Read that sentence ten times fast.

— 4 —

ABNORMAL FAMILY MATTERS

Bipolar I disorder is diagnosed if the individual has had a manic or mixed episode. This is noted as "a distinct period of abnormally and persistently elevated, expansive, or irritable mood, lasting at least 1 week" (DSM-IV). The person usually does not need as much sleep, is more talkative, has increased goal-directed activities, etc.

—excerpt from my Psych 441 final exam, 5/5/05

To put it concretely, *mania* is the "excitement manifested by mental and physical hyperactivity, disorganization of behavior, and elevation of mood" (merriam-webster.com). These fourteen words can be extrapolated on through the subjective stories I aim to describe. The definition is not diagnostic in nature, but my narrative is both a classical depiction for the criteria of bipolar disorder, as well as a detailed account of the depths of mania. My experience with mania is that it reveals itself at a slow pace and is a continuous extension of one's personality or social presentation, except the person is grossly uninhibited. The gradual onset makes it difficult for friends and family to pick up on the mania, especially before the diagnosis is made. Some of the behaviors develop into what is analogous to a child's growing need for autonomy. Expressions of grandiosity, combativeness, risk taking, and defiance of authority—or, more so, parental advice—seem to merge with mania and what can be called the behaviors of the "outer child." I craved vocal intercourse and attention from everyone. My speech became pressured—or, from other people's vantage points, I was excited and more talkative. I exhibited no aggression or orneriness; rather, I displayed euphoria and optimism as my mood elevated. Overall, my social fear of the seeming conglomerate that the masses of the University of Wisconsin–Madison represented had suddenly dissolved. I no longer suffered from the belief that I would be alone for the rest of my life due to the devastating aftereffects of the breakup.

I have no memories of anyone asking, "Are you all right?" during that stage. My writing improved as the ideas poured onto the pages for my Scandinavian literature course and the flood of dopamine pooled in my synaptic cleft (FYI: that course could elicit a depressive episode among the most balanced of the balanced; it's nothing but darkness and existential prose). For clarification purposes, this gap, or cleft, is a minute space that allows the concentration of neurotransmitters (in this case, serotonin and dopamine) to be raised (leading to a higher mood, as when you have sex or eat dark chocolate) and lowered quickly. I recall sitting on the grass of Bascom Hill before class one day and gathering the nerve to attempt a flirtatious conversation with a young female student. Apparently, my opening comment about a small child being able to fit into her rather large backpack did not spark romance in her eyes. Afterward, I called a friend and ranted about the situation and whatever other exciting things I was doing, and he responded with laughter. Unlike someone experiencing depression in terms of behavior, I feared aloneness, as sitting with my own thoughts was not an option. Movement or action needed to occur at all times. I felt akin to a shark—stillness meant sinking. My mind was swimming with prodigious and creative ideas. There was wonder and excitement all around. Everything was a fun adventure as my confident mind temporarily relinquished the previously rooted pessimism.

Soon thereafter, I started to gain insight into what was going on with me. As my mood started to fluctuate, my anxiety and insomnia increased, and my ability to focus was diminished. I contacted my dad when I realized what might be happening to me. I called and told him I was having trouble sleeping. He asked me directly if I was experiencing racing thoughts. Comparable to a deer in the headlights, I was mentally blinded by his question. My next breath felt like a life span. I was suspicious that he was aware that the fears from my childhood were becoming a reality. Racing thoughts were prevalent—especially at night—and were a big contributor to my insomnia. I recall talking to my roommate from my bed across the room more than ever during nighttime exchanges, which previously had been short in duration. One of my most sorrowful and guilt-infused lies was my response to my father's question about racing thoughts: "No." Little did I know that my as well as my parents' growing concerns were shared with increased trepidation by my older brother. I found that out years later. He was going to college in Fargo and apparently he had a vocal confrontation with my parents. He had a strong belief that "Andy is manic." My parents heard his pleas but did not validate them as I continued to decompensate. My close relationship with my brother, along with his firsthand experience of my dad's manic episodes, fueled his intuition surrounding what he believed to be an imminent danger.

A couple days after I spoke with my dad, my roommate and I went on a long and fast run. No energy drink can compete with mania. However, I was quickly overwhelmed and had to hide a full-body cry by going in the shower. The water pressure drowned the sounds of confusion and despair.

I'd finally had enough and decided I would call my mom. Ashamed that I had withheld the truth from my dad, I chose to broadcast to her the news that would change my life dramatically. I drove my Jeep Grand Cherokee to the library parking ramp, and before I could get the words transmitted through my ketchup-bottle-sized cell phone, tears and gasping breaths of terror erupted. I did not have to say anything; she knew. This episode was not a new depressive wave; it was the distinct feeling of knowing my life had been infiltrated by an illness that had no quick fix—and one that would last a lifetime. Loss of control is a fear that all humans face. That fear is why parents struggle as their child leaves for college and why three vodka tonics and a side of Xanax are needed for some to fly in an airplane. My autonomy was suddenly broken, and I was helpless.

My parents and I decided that I would leave Madison in order to receive care in Minneapolis, where I could gain respite at my parents' house and see a doctor. A friend agreed to go with me and then take a bus home at the end of the weekend. Later that night, still in Madison, I watched a movie with her, and I talked through the entire movie, giving what could have been the director's commentary. There was no conservative construction of thoughts or filtration system—only stream of consciousness, brain to tongue. She looked at me in a different way that night but secured the liquid in her lower eyelids. She was a psychology major and an overall brilliant individual. She clearly knew that something had changed and I needed help. She was not judgmental, nor was she turned off by the events that led to my state; instead, her face was sunken in sadness. Perhaps it was an expression of her knowledge in regard to just how hard, devastating, and draining the future years would be during my recovery.

The drive home was fun, and I did not have a care in the world. My speech was rapid, and there was but a mere breath of silence during the four-and-a-half-hour weave across I-94 West to Minneapolis. We played a game to see who could be the first to spot the Subway restaurant signs that were posted on the blue exit signs along the way (ten to twelve of the franchises at least). Despite constantly telling stories, I was more than capable of dominating this game (perhaps my prescription contacts played a factor). Multitasking does not adequately describe how fast my mind was working, and surprisingly, it was working in a fairly organized manner. The fluidity of thoughts and heightened perception allowed for space and time to sit idly in the background.

Upon our arrival, my mom greeted us with a face loosely mirroring that of someone who had recently lost a loved one. I, however, was full of task-oriented energy, so conversation in the kitchen was not an option. Next stop was the basement office and computer room with my friend, who helped me register my classes online for the upcoming fall semester. As I type this, I realize that some may view this detail as an irrelevant part of the picture; however, it was then, in addition to registering for my mundane business school classes, that I signed on for abnormal psychology with the same friend. This choice was a catalyst that led me to eventually fulfill my dream of working as a psychotherapist.

— 5 —

OUTER CHILD

There is a particular kind of pain, elation, loneliness, and terror involved in this kind of madness.

—Kay Redfield Jamison

Meriter Hospital 3/12/05: They moved me to a completely empty room next door (probably because I said something about hurting myself) with a suicide smock, light blanket and a thin mattress fit for a lenient dog. The floor was cold and the vehement pounding of my fists on the door merely fevered the hostility in my mind. The poor nursing student (watchman) had to listen to my onslaught of pejorative discourse. I cried that night.

The outer expressions of mania can frequently be attributed to feelings of impulsiveness, self-centeredness, and a desire for instant gratification in the "now." Havoc on relationships comes swiftly as the child metaphorically slams doors and runs off through seemingly adult avenues, such as drug and alcohol use, extremely uninhibited social interaction, and loose financial expenditures. In general, some believe the "outer child" is born from an individual who lacks resolution in the area of previous or present fear of abandonment. The person experiencing mania, much like a teen-ager, yearns for absolute autonomy and resists authority (e.g., parents, friends, mental health professionals, treatment in general, etc.) with an "I'm not sick" or "There's nothing wrong with me" mind-set. Rigid think-ing allows the mania to take over one's psyche, leaving the individual at a childish or even infantile level of self-awareness and acceptance of his or her altered state. There is a sense that the mania is largely a cry for atten-tion, and it may include past reflections that surface antagonistically at the speed of light. This concept of mania, which is applicable to depression as well, should not be confused with popular or analytical psychology's no-tion of the "inner child," which is used to explain remaining effects of one's childhood as well as the strong emotional memories that are warehoused from earliest recollections.

Being at home was a trip back in time to my childhood, and I reclaimed my appreciation for the little things in life. A rebirth opened my eyes to complete fulfillment. I loved my mom's cooking and let her know it—even if it was Kraft macaroni and cheese. Conversations flowed, albeit with me being the instigator and dominating presence. Everything was fun. Food tasted better, and my senses seemed heightened overall. I had never felt so creative, and my grandiose ideas were so sensible and concrete to me. If you ask children what they want to be when they grow up, their responses rarely are an office manager, clerical worker, investment banker, or janitor. Their imaginations and fantasies create real opportunities to become a baseball player or movie star. We do not call this grandiosity but instead a hope or a dream. With mania, a person believes his or her goal-oriented, ostentatious ideas as much as a boy pondering his opportunity to become the next LeBron James. I will return to my idea of how a bipolar individual's behaviors when episodic (e.g., manic or depressed) reflect an expression resembling that of a child.

My two younger siblings were not able to comprehend or even care that something was different about their brother. I spent all of my time with everyone in my family. I helped my younger brother with his photography homework by going to Nine Mile Creek and giving brilliant advice about simple forty-five-millimeter shots. My dad and I went to the recreation center at my old high school, and he rebounded as I shot baskets (back when I was actually still participating in the sport). These memories do not feel as if they are from my college years; I had a pleasant developmental transformation to a child who wanted to be taken care of and have constant attention and instant gratification. Part of my respite was daily, vigorous Ping-Pong matches with my younger brother and occasionally a friend who came by the house. I would eject copious amounts of knowledge and stories at every instant of the game, often making my brother laugh, all while consistently ensuring precise contact and placement of the ball. Usually, I removed my shirt as well, because the mental anxiety was like a furnace for my body. I think my brother beat me once out of the hundred odd games we competed in. I do not say this to brag, because currently he can kick my ass. His arms now reach across the table, and his stature is an intimidating road block for the small, flashing white spheres. Much to my content, the grasshopper has become the professor. Unfortunately, this family assimilation that occurred in 2002 was starkly different from the experiences in 2005.

The nights were hard. As if I were a child, my mom stayed in my room and talked to me in the late evenings until I was tired enough to fall asleep. Soon after I returned home that week, I had an appointment with a primary care physician. Dr. L., MD, looked at my condition with a familiarity that resembled the first time a seventh grader observes algebra. He decided to prescribe Zyprexa (an antipsychotic and mood stabilizer) as well as Trazodone (a mild antidepressant used primarily for insomnia) for both mood stabilization and to help me fall asleep. The medication helped to some degree, but one night, I awakened from a nightmare—similar to what a fever dream feels like. I was terrified. My legs were tight, my body was restless, and I was unable to return to a baseline level of comfort. I experienced a surreal feeling as I literally crawled on the floor to my parents' bedroom door. I was paralyzed with fear and immense anxiety. I felt as though I needed to get to my parents' room, which was a matter of feet from the guest room I was sleeping in. I was so scared. I remember feeling the way I had as a lonely child walking downstairs into the ominous basement. I was never sure what those shadows would bring and was too afraid to find out. It did not make sense then and does not now. Once I reached their room, my eyes filled with tears reminiscent of a six-year-old who was sick and could not sleep. When I arrived, my mother consoled me. With my mother patiently waiting in my room with me, I did go back to sleep. From that point on, I was convinced the episode had to do with a specific medication I had taken—Zyprexa. This incident led to my reservations about the antipsychotic drug. The truth is, there was probably no connection between ingesting Zyprexa and experiencing the fear I awoke to that night. On a sidenote, the successful distribution of this little pill marked "Lilly" would years later face a full-scale class-action lawsuit (and lose badly). This lawsuit was prompted by findings that a clear side effect of the medication was intense weight gain that frequently led to type 2 diabetes in virtually all long-term consumers.

On March 26, 2002, it became official. Accompanied by my parents, I visited Dr. S., MD, PA. I did not know then but clearly recognize now that seeing your father's psychiatrist for a mental health assessment is probably not the ideal clinical intervention for an objective mental health assessment. Of course, my parents were just doing what they thought was best. Certainly I do not harbor resentment over how they handled the situation. Perhaps this literature will make others aware of the importance of objective treatment. This objectivity, of course, includes the presence of family and their valuable information. I think this information can alter the modes of treatment one initiates in his or her challenges with bipolar disorder.

I recall attending the appointment wearing a white T-shirt purchased from *The Onion* (a satirical newspaper publication) with simple black writing on the front: "I'm Like a Chocoholic but for Booze." I recall choosing the outfit for a specific reason, but I know not why to this day. I guess I wanted to convey a strong message to the doctor. However, he never commented on it, and I am sure his aged, cataractous eyes couldn't even read it. My dad was not enthused by my wardrobe decision. Looking back, it feels comparable to walking into church with a shirt that says "I'm Like a Whore but for Priests." The clothing choice might have related to the all-too-often misogynistic hierarchy, sexism, and exclusion of individuals within the structure of parts of the modern Christian church or just an angst-filled, outer-child expression of mine. It also represented my perverse sense of humor.

Dr. S. was an old man who could have been friends with B. F. Skinner or Carl Jung for all I know. Compassion and people skills were not his strong points. Most of the information communicated to him was from my parents. He obviously knew that my dad had bipolar disorder and had been successfully prescribed and treated with a daily dose of 1200 mg of lithium for almost twenty years. Instantly he prescribed for me—not surprisingly—1200 mg of lithium as a mood stabilizer. Lithium is nature's lightest metal; in the early 1900s, before it was used as a treatment for bipolar disorder, it was added to tonics and other beverages. For this reason, during my manic episode in 2005, I drank 7UP instead of alcohol at times. The brief clinical trials revealed that the substance had no significant effect as a liquid sedative. Because the medication is derived from lithium aspartate and lithium orotate, which are minerals, lithium cannot be patented. Is this why bipolar disorder is predominantly being treated with the larger pharmaceutical companies' medications (e.g., Abilify, Seroquel, Zyprexa, Zoloft, Wellbutrin)?

In addition, he gave me 0.5 mg tablets of clonazepam (brand name Klonopin) but made sure I knew that this benzodiazepam (i.e., antianxiety medication) was very addictive and that one could build a tolerance to it quickly. Based on our discussion, I perceived that this antianxiety medication was to be used with extreme caution. What do you imagine that did to my anxiety? Despite my need, I rarely took the medicine. A drug I should have been eating like Pez until I was stabilized—in my opinion—became a frightening yellow pill that was not to be touched. Despite genetically inheriting bipolar disorder from my dad (no fault of his), ultimately I had anxiety and depression predisposed to me from my mother's side of the family. I am much more like her than my dad in terms of biochemical and even physical makeup (hell, she's five foot two, and I'm the shortest in my family out of the remaining four). The maternal family tree has subtle branches of largely untreated anxiety and depression. My evidence is anecdotal and based on interpretation, but the origins of my condition are clear to me as a mental health professional.

Despite my father outweighing me by about sixty pounds, I was fed 1200 mg of lithium, and I avoided the clonazepam. To be fair, one must know that it is not solely the amount of lithium one takes but, rather, the level in one's bloodstream that makes the therapeutic difference. This is one reason for regular blood checks. Another erroneous part of my treatment plan: psychotherapy was not even mentioned during this process. My residential treatment was basically being shut in a suburban home with no mental health providers. If you can sense the undertone of disdain for this process, it is because what I know now gives sanction to both a wish I could go back and amend some of the variables as well as share what those alterations could have been. A least-resistant approach would have included this: a meeting with a psychotherapist immediately to process what was happening as well as psychoeducation about bipolar disorder and the medications I was prescribed.

Years later (8/22/07)—in the context of my treatment—I would write the following about the effects of therapy:

> After coming down from the manic episode in 2005 (spring), therapy has changed my life. The more structured based therapy that I have received through _____ has especially benefited me. Seeing a therapist was never something highly encouraged during my treatment for bipolar disorder until then [...] Given the choice, I would have included cognitive-behavioral therapy as the nucleus of my treatment for bipolar disorder as soon as I was diagnosed.

In addition to therapy, I would have prescribed clonazepam for a short period of time.

Twelve hundred mg of lithium is not a huge amount, but going up slowly is not a terrible thing, especially when an individual's behaviors are in no way physically destructive or escalating.

The clonazepam and 900 mg (as opposed to 1200 mg) of lithium would have been a good initial trial. I currently take 1050 mg of lithium and have done so since 2002.

Another intervention—especially when students are diagnosed—is to give a *short trial* of a stimulant medication (e.g., Adderall, Ritalin, etc.) once the individual comes down from the mania. The depressive phase, which I will focus on in subsequent chapters, can make it difficult for the person to come back online cognitively and finish out the semester. One will often struggle with concentration and overall attention deficits because of the strain placed on the brain during the manic episode and the slow-motion feeling experienced during the depression. Doctors primarily prescribe these drugs for individuals with attention-deficit/hyperactivity disorder (ADHD), but they can be helpful for bipolar disorder if used with caution.

In addition, family therapy is a successful adjunct to the treatment for bipolar disorder. Regrettably, this was not considered by my family in 2002 or after the 2005 tragedy.

Along with prescribing my medications, Dr. S. sent the following letter in scribbled handwriting to the University of Wisconsin–Madison (I would take incompletes in all but one of my courses; I returned for the final exam of one, because the professor stated that I had to despite my condition):

4/26/02

To whom it may concern

Andrew Archer is under my care and will need time off from school for 4 to 6 months to recover.

Sincerely,

Dr. E. S____, M.D.

— 6 —

HIGHER POWER LINES

The person in whom Its invisible agony reaches a certain unendurable level will kill herself the same way a trapped person will eventually jump from the window of a burning high-rise. Make no mistake about people who leap from burning windows. Their terror of falling from a great height is still just as great as it would be for you or me standing speculatively at the same window just checking out the view; i.e. the fear of falling remains a constant. The variable here is the other terror, the fire's flames: when the flames get close enough, falling to death becomes the slightly less terrible of two terrors. It's not desiring the fall; it's terror of the flames. And yet nobody down on the sidewalk, looking up and yelling 'Don't!' and 'Hang on!', can understand the jump. Not really. You'd have to have personally been trapped and felt flames to really understand a terror way beyond falling.

—David Foster Wallace, *Infinite Jest*

A graph can appropriately depict what happened during the spring of 2002 in terms of my illness as follows:

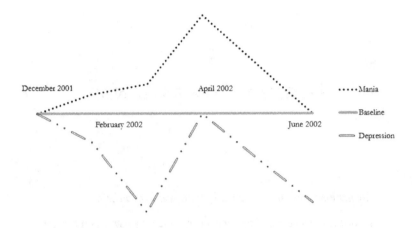

Basically, mania and depression do not work as separate entities. No spider or bat attacked me, and I didn't instantly put on a costume in order to fly everywhere (that would be cool, and I could probably make out with a girl upside down). As an alternative, in this case, the mania slowly increased (represented by the dotted black line) during the depressive episode, and when the depression began to lift (represented by the jetting dashed gray line), then the mania progressed at an increased rate. With bipolar disorder, especially when it is not treated, the episodes are comparable to the rubbing of two stones (one depression and one mania stone) against each other. Eventually, the sharper stone wears down the other. To continue the metaphor, anxiety acts as the energy that moves the stones. One can have anxiety about the end of a relationship (such as I did), and the feelings of loneliness, lack of control, and hurt all lead one to ruminate these negative thoughts into a dark state. In my case, this rumination led to a severe depressive episode. However, the same mechanism works with mania. If I meet a woman and fall in love because "she's the one," anxiety can come in the form of obsession, fixation, and euphoria that leads to mania. The obsessive ruminations act the same way as with negative thoughts, but the extreme optimism and confidence lead to mania as opposed to depression. This is why a cognitive balance to events in one's life (I will give advice and examples of this at the end of the book) is essential when dealing with bipolar disorder.

In the spring of 2002, I was eventually cutting like a diamond rather than a dull stone. As the depression lifted, the mania began rising. I did not wake up one morning and all of a sudden become manic; the two states of mind overlapped. The graph I will later share of my 2005 episode looks much the same, except the intervals are extended in each direction (i.e., there is a great severity of symptoms). This brief explanation should shed light on the misconception that someone with bipolar disorder is either up or down in the drop of a hat. Alternatively, there is a progression—and often overlap—of symptoms and mood states.

In my family, normalcy was a constant picture of our life. This ideological framework made it difficult to share or understand where our family system broke down. There were breaks when there were tragedies, but someone must have read James Joyce, because the phrase "pull yourself up by your bootstraps" is not far off from how it was growing up. Do not get me wrong— my family and especially my friends were very supportive during this time, but I do not recall a lot of conversations regarding my future, the illness, or, more importantly, that everything would be okay. Statistically, I was screwed, but nobody wanted to talk about the battles to come. My family had a desperate internal need to feel normal during this time period.

Unfortunately, in reality, *normal* does not exist. It is an abstract concept that is constantly shifting within individuals' environments and, more importantly, their perceptions of themselves within those environments. Not to get too philosophical here, but I think this point is extremely valuable. There is a sudden feeling of abnormality when one is diagnosed with a mental illness (e.g., pessimism regarding the future, a new conceptual reliance on medication that is often dreadful to take, and the stigma of a scary label), so logically, that person grabs hold of the idea that he or she needs to be "normal" again. A mind-set geared toward feeling this unachievable state of normality will make it difficult for that individual to cope with having bipolar disorder. I have become a "normal" person within some of the confines of the illness, but I will never be normal in the same way as someone who does not have the disorder.

For example, it is not "normal" to monitor your exposure to the sun because it can precipitate or cause a manic episode to develop. For this reason, despite living in dark parts of the Northern Hemisphere, I cannot use light therapy, as many do, for seasonal affective disorder (or SAD—such a fitting acronym), which causes individuals to have depressive symptoms, most commonly in the winter.

In the same way, it is not "normal" to make sure that you are properly hydrated because the medication that you are taking (i.e., lithium), which has saved your life, can also kill you. Death occurs when the amount of lithium in your blood reaches a toxic level and causes kidney failure. Therefore, because of the dangers that dehydration could cause, part of my "normal" life is being cognizant of how much salt I eat and my level of perspiration. My thyroid and kidneys are monitored, as well as blood levels, to determine the range of lithium in my body.

There is a laundry list of these different things that roughly 98 percent of the population does not deal with, but for me, without the knowledge of these precautions and the legitimacy of these concerns, I can quickly become "abnormal." *Normal* and *abnormal* are words I do not find to be important; rather, they can often debilitate an individual who seemingly falls from one extreme to another. The subjective terms are not substantiated in my world. The summer of 2002 was a fight that led me to question what exactly normal was for me.

I started going to work with my dad, who was rehabbing, or remodeling, a house in South Minneapolis, Minnesota, that summer. I could not make sense of my thoughts or the world as I had before. *What happened? I should be in school partying and finishing out a successful second year in college.* I had been an exceptional student my whole life, and the thought of enduring incompletes was devastating to what was left of my ego. My grade (temporarily incomplete) for the semester was suspended, and I was allowed to complete the work over the summer without penalty. The work with my dad gave me something to do and provided structure for the day. However, it was also monotonous and, thus, mindless work, which allowed me to ruminate over how bad life was. I dreaded everything. There was a future, but it was scary, and the disappointing past fueled my depression. Anxiety is worrying about future events and that depression is being mentally stuck in the past. This simplified explanation is accurate to some degree. In addition, mania merges the past and future into an almost unified state, whereby the present occurs at such a seamless rate that time completely dissipates from reality. As you slide out of this rapid momentary thinking, it makes perfect sense that you would become depressed. When your thoughts go from the usual thirty-five miles per hour to one hundred miles per hour, returning to even a rate of sixty-five miles per hour makes you feel as if your thoughts are stuck in mud. We have all experienced getting off the freeway after many hours of driving and slowing down to thirty miles per hour inside of a town or on a slower road. Traveling seventy-five miles per hour for three hours and then driving thirty makes you want to slam your head through the windshield because it feels *so slow*. I spent that summer in a purgatory that felt as if I were driving slowly through small towns.

My metaphorical windshield-slamming moment came when working at my father's property. I remember him yelling at me for doing something that was incorrect in his mind. Whatever it was, it certainly was not significant, nor would it have usually upset me, as I have felt the penetrable wrath of my father's discourse before. I was painting on the roof of the house at the time and probably brushing the "wrong way." It was a small one-story home with a triangular roof, or an A-frame, that included a small window peeking through a lifted, angled area. The electric lines ran so close to the house that I had to be vigilant in order to avoid touching them (I don't recall a worker's compensation clause or hazard pay during my employment). Nevertheless, after already holding in tears during that hot, bright, sunny day, his words set me off. With recessed eyes, I stood for several minutes, thinking about what would happen if I were to just leap from this perdition and grab the snakelike series of cords with both hands. I so desired emancipation from this pain that death was a serious and alluring alternative.

Mania causes chaos among the individual's family, social network, and community at large, but depression destroys the individual and nullifies his or her sense of worldly optimism. A person with bipolar disorder rarely kills him- or herself in a deliberate manner during a manic episode. Suicide is much more likely to occur when one is hopelessly depressed or dying from a chronic physical illness. During mania, judgment can become so impaired and concurrently delusional, even psychotic, that suicide can result. Believing you will save the world if you kill yourself by drowning in a lake is very different from being completely aware of cause and effect. My depression felt like an inflammation of my brain pressing against my skull. It pushed against my forehead similar to sinus pain, except the constant pressure begged for release through tears. The intense feelings were always on my mind but somehow just barely tolerable. I had faith in Catholicism, which in turn had faith in a hell that invites suicides with open arms. What kept me on the roof that day was my belief in a higher power, or possibly, the metaphorical building was just not hot enough to jump from.

In clinical terms, this episode would be called an incidence of intense suicidal ideation bordering on suicidal intent. The impulsive thinking to act on this suicidal fantasy illustrates that I could not have been completely defined as depressed. My brain was still adjusting from the mania. The anxiety fueled both the depressive symptoms and the previous manic ones, which resulted in residual impulsiveness from the mania and latent depressive symptoms. This tipping point is a scary place to be with a mood disorder (the lines of the above graph for depression and mania were still in motion). In regard to bipolar disorder, I speak from highly personal as well as clinical experience. I believe the episodes and extreme moods do not have swift, distinct starting and stopping points. There is a clear difference between depressive and manic episodes, but the transition or convergence of the two can lead to death. One has a despondent desire to end his or her life, along with the energy to carry it out.

This complexity makes the disorder even more difficult to treat. Many individuals go on trials of antidepressants during a depressive episode. However, for some, including myself, these medications can backfire in the sense that they precipitate a manic episode. If you do not have bipolar disorder, this can happen but rarely does (i.e., antidepressants causing a substance-induced manic state). To me, this suggests that during severe episodes, there is a rubbing together of two forces (as with the example of the stones)—depression and mania—whereby the sharper or stronger emerges. If you feed the depression enough of an antidepressant (this could be in the form of taking a medication, regulating sleep, or exercising, for example), then it can soften the stone in order to return to a homeostatic, or stable, baseline state. However, too much of an antidepressant can trigger a manic episode by giving strength or movement to that stone. This is why my pleas for an antidepressant were denied by my psychiatrist in 2005 after a manic episode. Continuing with the metaphor, stones of course need energy to move, and this movement comes in the form of life events (e.g., breaking up with a girlfriend, drinking, using drugs), one's environment (e.g., stressing over school, living in a small dump of an apartment, taking an amazing spring break trip), and, more importantly, the resulting anxiety. There is a forward process where a person's reaction to these events and relationships with others leads to the episode. This includes not sleeping, feeling a sense of hopelessness or persecution from others, or regaining an inflated self-confidence. No one gets manic inside of a vacuum.

— 7 —

I Cannot Swim

Once a person has had a depressive or manic episode, self-confidence is eroded. Knowing that both mania and depression can recur, many people experience fearful anticipation, while they also look back and recall how painful and difficult the mood disorder was ... These disappointments can color future perceptions as well as future potential for success.

—Nancy C. Andreasen, *Brave New Brain:*
Conquering Mental Illness in the Era of the Genome

In May of 2002, I returned to Madison to complete one final exam, attend the Mifflin Street Block Party, and pack my belongings for the duration of the summer to live in Minneapolis. This would provoke anxiety in most people, but it is safe to say I was beyond my comfort zone. It was terrible. The exam went fine, but as a good walking mental illness would, I refrained from drinking at the block party altogether. Abstinence at the Mifflin Street festivities was sort of like going to a swimming pool and staying out of the water. There were no swimming trunks involved, but there was a pool filled with drunken assholes, attractive girls, and lots of police officers who did not give a shit what people did outside of urinating on or near them (this was in

2002, and since then, the party's reins have been shortened and tightened). The possibility of running into my ex-girlfriend also caused intense anxiety as well as a confusing sense of hope in seeing her. *Is it possible that we will get back together?* I was still holding on tightly to an abstract or even nonexistent possibility of a reconciliation that would ultimately free the shackles of my hellish depression. The reunion would not come until the fall of the following school year, with unremarkable results.

I spent the summer working at the same job I had had the previous few years—Après Party and Tent Rental. I was set to become crew chief, which was a highly sought-after position. It basically gave one authority and large-vehicle-driving responsibilities and was a step above most other employees. My promotion did not happen, because I was afraid of the stress that came with the extra responsibility. In spite of the sinking feeling in my stomach the day I decided to speak with my manager about my employee status, I entered the cluttered warehouse office.

There were archaic-looking printers that spit out three-layered, perforated, esoteric pages of itemized receipts and instructions. Coke cans were frosted at the top with regurgitated chewing tobacco, and there was a lack of No Smoking signs. This allowed for soot-filled ashtrays and dense, asthmatic air. Fortunately, a close friend of mine who also worked for the company accompanied me to the office for my first of many eventual public disclosures. I recall taking the magical yellow antianxiety pill before the occasion. I told my manager about the diagnosis, and his response was a mixture of understanding and a loss for words. He smoked with the pensive nature of Don Draper—a character from the television series *Mad Men*—in an office culture that had similar themes of smoking, drinking, sexism, and homophobia.

That year, 2002, was different. Insecurity was a constant as I tried to discover just who I was—or, more importantly, who I had become. High levels of anxiety not only created but also resulted in these existential themes. My eating issues were back. I calculated the size of my lunch, and I would eat it meticulously—as slowly throughout the day as possible, fighting urges to devour it, despite being hungry all the time. In addition, I isolated myself from friends and did nothing but cry myself to sleep each night. The hunger for food and the recession of social connections were both previews of my time spent in jail during the 2005 episode. Not only was I dealing with a mental illness, but I was also tackling a strong psychological addiction to alcohol or, more so, peer socialization and the closeness of a girlfriend. The use of alcohol often leads to social and intimate connections. Intimate connections had been and needed to be my antianxiety medication. I went cold turkey from alcohol and other drugs the day I returned home to my parents' care in the spring of 2002 until I could take it no more—about a month. Most of the summer was fused with heavy drinking and a constant search for a girlfriend. The twentieth of each month was a painful reminder of the monthly anniversary that I had once celebrated with my ex-girlfriend. We would always spend that day together on a date and exchange gifts. It was just one of many routines or structured events that were previously a large part of my life. I was stuck in a past that I misperceived as "normal"—hence my consequential depression.

My twenty-first birthday came in August of 2002. I went to a friend's wedding reception with my brother and some other people I knew on the eve of the epic day. Additionally, a woman I was infatuated with was my escort (not that kind of escort). At the stroke of midnight, I downed shots of liquor with my older brother to go along with the other drinks I'd consumed. My blackout started to take shape when the groom's brother, a good friend of mine, broke into "You've Lost That Loving Feeling" by the Righteous Brothers. I have a faint memory of swaying like an uneasy pendulum with the girl and no memory of making out with her in my friend's car during the ride home. Fueled by alcohol alone, I vaguely recall getting in my car, which was parked outside of my brother's apartment in Uptown, a trendy area proximal to downtown Minneapolis. I also felt it necessary to bring the cooler full of alcohol, as I would surely need to drink more. My memory of driving down I-35 West that night is a blur. I do recall thinking it was hilarious to drive ninety miles per hour in the fast lane of the freeway, an area heavily trafficked by police. I cannot imagine what my companion's sober eyes were saying at that point (fine, she was a couple years younger than I).

By extraordinary means, we arrived at the party in Bloomington about twenty-five minutes away. Upon our arrival, shots were delivered and then soon laid out on the table in front of me (literally—I threw up all over it) as I passed out. Detox probably would have been an appropriate intervening measure, as I am sure my blood alcohol level (BAL) was in the .30 range— nearly four times the legal limit for driving. Instead, I slept it off, awoke, and drove a friend home. I drove while suspended in a drunken yet hungover, euphoric state from the prior night. This inexplicable sense of normalcy had a temporary positive effect on my mood and aided in my disregard for the encapsulation that the afflicting illness had over me.

— 8 —

OMINOUS BELIEFS

*They are unable to differentiate their selves from the illness
and to decide which is "real." The stigma of their interpersonal
experiences further shapes their confused self-definition, and
as a result they fail to experience coherence and consistency in
their identities. An adolescent who develops bipolar disorder
may experience a particularly severe arrest in psychological
development, acquiring self-efficacy and dependency problems
that endure into adulthood.*

—Jacqueline Corcoran and Joseph Walsh, *Clinical Assessment and
Diagnosis in Social Work Practice*

The fall of my junior year at the University of Wisconsin–Madison was a
frightening time. I feared not being able to compete with the rigorous demands of the business school—or, more specifically, juggling finance, mar-
keting, and another calculus class along with abnormal psychology. I hated
it. I sat by myself in large lecture halls, marveling over how the students knew
so many other people, and I doubted that my social network would ever expand. This was my "wonder year," and I spent it much like the introspective
character Kevin Arnold. His presumably typical suburban American family

in *The Wonder Years* had resonated with me growing up. At school, I felt a constant, self-induced pressure to influence or win over a potential Winnie Cooper. You can imagine the melancholy that would follow, but abnormal psychology kept me sane. The personal familiarity of the course content as well as sharing it with the same friend who had driven home with me the previous spring during the crisis gave rise to excitement for each lecture. The class was difficult, but I was interested as well as engaged in the material. Of course, being diagnosed with a severe and persistent mental illness does not necessarily translate into regurgitating knowledge of lecture material via correct answers to fifty multiple-choice exam questions in a curved class (a certain percentage of students are allowed As, Bs, Cs, etc., based on a determined interval or bell curve from the test scores). I studied my ass off and received a C+ on my first of four tests. The first examination preceded my trip to Las Vegas with my brother and his friends, so I was somewhat distracted and then eventually disappointed.

Las Vegas is the city of sin, but religion aside, it is also not the perfect sanctuary for bipolar disorder. The structure-free environment encourages gambling, drinking, and self-induced insomnia—not exactly the pillars of recovery from a mental illness. Having intense anxiety often goes unrecognized until after the fact. For example, the twenty-dollar buffets allowed me a complete lack of eating boundaries. The food was not even pleasing to the senses, but it filled the void inside of me in a temporary way. I had no control over how much I ate. Even seemingly simple aspects of life, such as appetite, are grossly affected during depressive episodes. Feeding oneself is a developmental process learned as a young child, but at that point, my lack of self-regulation needed someone to prepare my meals. I felt physically sick throughout the vacation until I convinced the group to go to the Hard Rock Café for dinner on the last day of the trip. The meal was light, and then

I participated in a game of War in the casino. The player and dealer each flip over one card from a randomly assorted deck, and the high card wins. If the cards match (e.g., two aces), then a "war" begins, whereby three additional cards are dealt, and the final card is flipped over. This game is a completely absurd competition to wager money on. There is no skill or way to predict the cards unless maybe you can count cards in a six-shoe deck. However, without the help of Rain Man, I still managed to take the house for thirty-five big ones. The female dealer attempted to get me to keep playing, and I responded by saying, "Are you kidding me?" I took my money and started drinking. After the previous two days of GI track inflammation and extreme discomfort that surely were comparable to a bad pregnancy, my journey to intoxication began. Midday drinking is never a skillful approach to living. My thinking is this: if it is not dark outside, you should not be drinking. Dispersed bottle caps of Heineken in the hotel room paved our way to the illuminated streets. One-dollar beers on the Old Strip degenerated our brains to levels beyond nursing-home care. Circus Circus would have been more bizarre had I been at all coherent. The same goes for the strip club that is not ingrained in my long-term memory.

My flight was at six in the morning, so I had decided earlier in the day that I would pull an all-nighter. Somehow I made it to the shuttle at 3:30 a.m. and then to the airport, check-in, security, and my terminal successfully even though I was teetering between drunk and blacked-out drunk. Ostensibly home free, I thought a little siesta would be appropriate. I awoke in a panic. I had missed my flight, and "Andrew Archer" was being called over the intercom system. Temporary paralysis set in. I did not leap from my chair and sprint to the counter for customer service. Not unlike a PC awakening from the hibernation setting, it took about thirty seconds for me to comprehend what had just happened, along with what my actions should be.

The moments felt slower, perhaps akin to President Bush's reaction shown in the video where he is reading with children when the news of 9/11 was whispered into his ear. Eventually, the mental cursor stopped spinning. *Fuck me. What the hell should I do?* I would have to buy a new ticket for sure. *Fuck!* Still drunk, I went to speak to the airline representative. I looked at the woman in the same way a child would look at his teacher when asking for help after wetting his pants. My expression was composed of confusion, fear, and embarrassment, exacerbated by my wrinkled airline ticket. She somehow completely understood my situation. With a graceful and sympathetic smile, she handed me my new voucher, and I was placed on the next flight. My itinerary did not even skip a beat. Apparently, in Las Vegas, this type of mishap occurs on a regular basis. My belief in a higher power was never stronger than at that moment. However, running into my friend and his dad (he had the rights to the condo we were staying in) before leaving was more than awkward.

Both the stress of school and sharing a new apartment with four other individuals with girlfriends perpetuated my depression. I still had a strong belief in Catholicism, and my father sent me a Christian version of *Reader's Digest* every couple weeks. It was a daily prayer tool, and each miniature magazine rested on my nightstand. Prayer was a nightly exercise, as sleep would not come. Desperation stimulated my desire for religion and God to heal me. A crucifix, a symbol of my childhood, was mounted above the bed. The cross, which my parents had given me as a gift for my confirmation into the Catholic Church, prominently hung in a way that enabled me to direct attention to my past. It would also speak or convey nonverbally to a potential girlfriend that "I'm Catholic and afraid to tell you that as well as other things about me, and I feel guilty when I have sex with someone I don't plan on marrying."

In hindsight, what I needed was intensive psychotherapy during that time. What I received were thoughts of suicide (i.e., suicidality) and an outlook of hopelessness. I believed there was no possible way that things would ever return to how they had been. This is what I now comprehend about depression: the fundamental aspect of depression is that your mind is incapable of conceptualizing what it is to feel good. It is less about feeling shitty and more about not knowing what unshitty feels like. To put it in another way, a brain that is afflicted with depression has no sense of a future brain that is not depressed. It is analogous to a child who asks his parents if they are close to their destination during a family road trip. More often than not, the father states, "You just asked me five minutes ago!" Children suffer through car rides because they have no concept of time. Depressed people feel miserable because they have no concept of when not feeling miserable will arrive. They believe they will never *not* be depressed. A person might rationally know that he or she will prevail or get over it, but the belief is what clogs the brain. A child on a road trip might say, "We're *never* going to get there!" In the case of depression, the *never* is the hopelessly depressed person talking, and the *there* is what the depressed person cannot fully understand.

In my small room, at night, unable to sleep, the contemplation of death swirled through my unstable mind. The suicidal thoughts quickly turned to a plan. My psychiatrist knew of my depression (not the levels of my drinking), but the infrequency of psychiatric sessions (about one every three months) and my secrecy about the mental decompensation that was occurring made it easy for the symptoms to go unnoticed. He did prescribe Seroquel to help me sleep. Seroquel is a newer antipsychotic medication that is now found to have mood-stabilizing effects for individuals with bipolar disorder. The medication did work. The first time I took it, I remember walking through my apartment and dropping something out of my hands with no cause other than that I felt as if my brain were shutting down. Zombie-like is the only way to describe the feeling. This course of action did not interest me or bring about optimism in any domain of my life. The lithium had seemed to dull my cognition, but that effect was also due to the agonizing depression. My mind quickly converted existentialism to apathy and then to despair as I began to consider the lethality the bottle of medication contained.

Lithium reaches toxicity in the body easily, which is why it is important to get a minimum of three to four blood levels drawn per year, especially when the medication is first initiated. A toxic level causes kidney failure and possible death. I know this now and knew it then. I filled my prescriptions a week early in order to get the most out of my health-insurance coverage. I had plenty of lithium (thirty to forty times my daily dosage) as well as leftover antianxiety and antipsychotic drugs. Certainly, by my recollection, it was enough to kill a person many times over.

My plan was simple. There was a lock on my door, and all of us in the apartment usually kept our doors shut during the day. With five other roommates coming and going, I assumed it would not be difficult for me to lock myself in my room before retiring to bed, and I figured it would be late into the next day before anyone discovered me. Jack Daniel's would give me the courage to follow through with the consumption of lithium as well as other medications. I might have prepared suicide notes, but it is hard to say what was going through my mind. One thing is for sure: I wanted out. I could no longer swallow the pain of everyday life. Simple and once-absentminded activities had become dreadfully burdensome. Constant ruminations invaded my every decision. My self-esteem had long ago bottomed out. I cannot say why I did not enact this plan, but I am sure that believing in an afterlife or a just God as well as knowing that suicide was a mortal sin (defying the fifth commandment that states "Thou shall not kill") were inhibiting agents. However, the overriding factor that prevented me from suicide was a fear of failure—not the guilt of how my family would feel or the potential looks on my roommates' faces when they found my body. Interestingly, this fear had been a pervasive influence in my daily life. It led to perfectionism, unhealthy dependency, and insecurity (remember, I am also a psychotherapist, so it probably led to overanalyzing). The theme—or, more so, the genesis—of my illness is related to this fear. Ironically, my fear of not accomplishing that particular feat (i.e., death) and the ramifications (e.g., being put in psychiatric hospital, worrying my family, dropping out of school, etc.) were what stopped me.

Months later, I found out that a friend from grade school took his own life after a period of insomnia, erratic spending, and countless letters written to be read at his funeral. His roommate found him hanging inside of his apartment with a belt secured to his neck. He had an intense personality, so the violent manner in which he chose to die did not surprise me. I met with his roommate. We had lunch, and I disclosed my own illness, as I wanted to know more about what had tragically happened. It was clear to the roommate and the man's family that he had had untreated bipolar disorder. His death produced one of the largest visitations in Bloomington, Minnesota, history; the line of lamenting faces wrapped around the funeral home. With strained eyes, I stared at the body of my former friend, whom I had once envied so much. The stale air, the meticulous position of everything in the room, and the rubbery appearance of his face made him seem like a character from a wax museum. His casket was just another object to study. I realized how close I had come to being the one lying motionless in my finest suit. An emotionally hollowed parade of individuals intermittently studied the particulars of their shoes during the slow, painful approach to view the empty vessel. I do not intend to speak for everyone in attendance, but I could empathize with his pain. I knew the kinds of torment he had been through and the desires to act on it that he and I both shared. His nickname was Superman, and unfortunately, it appears he was never able to reveal his hidden identity. To this day, I cannot help but think of him when that Five for Fighting song with the matching title comes on the radio. These lyrics especially resonate:

> Wish that I could cry,
> Fall upon my knees,
> Find a way to lie
> About a home I'll never see.

Sometimes it is easier to not make your pain heard. Secrecy and depression go hand and hand but also work against one another. The fewer people you tell about your feelings or symptoms, the worse the depression gets, and when it reaches the point of no return, the secrecy makes it harder to reach out to someone. Frequently, individuals who are depressed take their own lives when they are finally breaking through the cocoon of hopelessness. Antidepressants often precipitate suicides, because they give people the mental energy or motivation to finally carry out their desires. An antidepressant can be the subtle push to the apprehensive child teetering on the edge of the deep end of the swimming pool. Just the right amount of mood elevation gives individuals their control back. Regaining control can be an empowering moment, as they extinguish their fears and emancipate themselves from the pain, but sadly, it can also lead to their death. There is no known cure for bipolar disorder by any stretch of the imagination, but suicide can be a light at the end of the tunnel that a mental illness so often represents. This sense of deliverance can come from many different sources for many different people struggling with a mental illness, and unfortunately, that incident was not the last time I considered suicide.

— 9 —

FORMER LIFE

Being certain means that you aren't worried about being wrong.

—Brian Christian, *The Most Human Human*

March 2005: *I saw pills being snorted frequently, including antidepressants and Adderall. At an after-party one night with a large group of people (filled with unfamiliar, perspiring faces), a mirror was passed around with a trail of white powder that inevitably leads to one's pleasure center. An invitation to another flood of dopamine sat before me.*

We have all heard the expression "time heals all wounds," and with depression, there is some truth to this age-old proverb. Even with no intervention, the episode usually passes over time. In my case, I was prescribed Lexapro, a medication that is an antidepressant, or a selective serotonin reuptake inhibitor (SSRI), and also has antianxiety properties. Other examples of SSRIs include Prozac, Zoloft, Celexa, and Paxil, to name a few. Somewhat apprehensively, my psychiatrist prescribed Lexapro despite the possibility of it precipitating or igniting a manic episode.

For someone with bipolar disorder, an antidepressant can often begin the process of increasing one's mood in a positive direction. Ideally, this happens in a slow and moderated manner, much like starting a campfire. In my case, it was as if the idle coals were sprayed with a bottle of lighter fluid. SSRIs, to put it simply, work by tricking the brain into closing its doors on returning serotonin. When most of the receptor's doors are closed, one is left with a serotonin party, and everyone is invited. The neurotransmitters are suspended in the synaptic cleft, which often increases one's mood. The euphoric feeling, or "runner's high," that people experience during long runs occurs when the brain produces endorphins. Endorphins function as neurotransmitters along with norepinephrine, serotonin, dopamine, and others. The result is a reduction in pain and stress as well as overall psychological well-being.[1] This high does not last long, because most of the neurotransmitters go back inside the little doors. My neurotransmitters were similar to friends who refuse to let the party die despite it being four in the morning, the host processing recyclable materials, and faces stretching in horse-sized yawns.

By late winter or early spring 2003, my depression had lifted, which immediately brought about my concerns of mania. If I was not depressed—or, even further, was happy—*I must be almost manic.* This was my mind-set or the direction of my thought processes at the time. Spring break was one of the catalysts for this mood change. Sun, irregular sleep habits, no schedule, and heavy drinking are textbook ingredients for mood elevation for someone with bipolar disorder. Mania never reared its ugly head during that spring break, and I ended my hiatus from dating. I got involved in what quickly

---

1 Secretion of norepinephrine, dopamine, and serotonin reduces feelings of depression. More of the neurotransmitters are discharged and are manufactured at a greater strength during exercise, which explains the case of the runner's high. Runners and habitual exercisers statistically have increased moods, less depression, and less anxiety. Unknowingly, my marathon training was a self-contained, self-imposed form of medication.

turned into a serious relationship, which felt really good to me. I was no longer alone, and my girlfriend truly understood my disorder in an intimate way. Oh, and also, I was having sex for the first time in over a year. What could be better? Now that I was experiencing what I thought was the answer to my problems (i.e., a girlfriend), the single life quickly roped me back in. The relationship had renewed my feeling of independence from the shackles of bipolar disorder and returned my sense of self-worth, my confidence, and the optimism I had lost. The prospect of living with four single fraternity guys while having a girlfriend was also a factor in my decision to rerelease myself into the wild during that summer (2003).

My senior year of college (2003–2004) was the most gluttonous and glorious experience of my life. By association, a new, large, and appealing social network surrounded me (and I am not just talking about the Facebook pilot program that hit our campus). Being included in the Greek system instigated a feeling of connectedness I had not encountered in college up until that point. The best part about it was that without a formal induction, the $1.50 tax per friend, as I calculated it, did not apply to me. My new roommates did not introduce binge drinking; they promoted and perpetuated an already unhealthy activity that allowed me to meet crowds of girls as well as hang out with various new groups of guys. I felt like one of the cool kids again. During the years prior, I had felt like the new kid in school, but this new existence alleviated my adolescent discomfort. My desire to intensify or just maintain that state of mind kept my outlook positive; I saw the glass as more than half full (usually of Jack Daniel's and Coke). We would drink excessive amounts of whiskey before going to the bars, where we would drink more and then start having shots of potent liquor. Our apartment was in the vortex of downtown Madison, meaning we could not spit in any direction without hitting a bar or liquor store. This in turn meant that we always had

"A-bars" (i.e., parties after bars closed for the night) at our apartment, and it was not uncommon for the events to last until four or five in the morning. These events happened at least four times a week, and I am not sure how I was able to get any schoolwork done. It did not matter; I felt "normal" again, and I would do whatever I could to escape another depressive episode.

In order to reduce my anxiety, I started doing long-distance running. This gave me another avenue for a high, especially when I began training for a marathon that was to take place that spring (2004). The exercise kept the anxiety somewhat at bay, along with the constant drinking. The obsessive-compulsive nature of my training as well as the meticulous documentation of it (the program called for anywhere between twenty to forty miles per week) was also a protective factor for my mood. I did not have any signifi-cant depression during that school year, but I was running at a hypomanic state during much of it. As I was training for the marathon, a somewhat healthy undertaking, I continued drinking, as well as smoking cigarettes and pot more and taking nonprescribed ADHD drugs for studying. One incident of partying sticks out in particular. I have no idea where I was or what happened, which is partially due to how long ago it was but most likely because it was a blackout night—not a rare occurrence that year. The next day, with alcohol swimming in my bloodstream, I tackled a nine-to-ten-mile run with ease. The run consisted of a stroll through the winding roads of the Arboretum with what I can only assume was a mind full of pleasant reflection from the debauchery that had occurred not many hours prior. I remember this vaguely, because one of my friends called that day to reminisce about the fun night and said, "You ran nine miles—are you insane?"

I was destroying my body in many ways. None more so than during spring break of 2004. The whole crew of roommates set out to drive to South Padre

Island, Texas—a fifteen-hundred-mile drive from Madison, Wisconsin. We stopped in San Antonio at a Sam's Club in order to get "a little bit" of alcohol for the trip. Keep in mind that although there were only five of us, we could drink for fifteen. Three 1.75 liters of Jack Daniel's and three twenty-four packs of Miller Lite, one would think, should have been enough for the five- to six-day trip. The Jack Daniel's was gone by the fourth day, and the beer was gone soon after that. We took our drinking to a whole new level, which is hard to believe, because the height of drinking we had reached in our weekly activities back in Madison had been beyond alcohol abuse. I blacked out almost every night during that week in South Padre Island. In general, I did everything to the extreme that year. Bipolar disorder usually does not permit this, because there is an increased sensitivity to behaviors of excess. Somehow neither a manic nor depressive episode manifested during that school year. I had a fear of being treated differently and a need for my roommates to see me apart from the illness. Therefore, I only disclosed that I had bipolar disorder to my very close friend I shared a room with. It was not until one year later that the others would find out about my illness under the worst circumstances. In 2005, despite others' insistence for me to seek treatment, mania would not resign its tight grip over my psyche.

—10—

MENTAL EXERCISE

*According to the cognitive theories of depression, the way
people typically explain events in their lives, their cognitive
styles, importantly affects their vulnerability to depression.*

—Lyn Y. Abramson, *Cognitive Vulnerability to Depression*

Summer of 2004 picked up where the end of the spring semester had left off, except three of the roommates moved back home for the summer, so it was just my close friend and me leftover. This just meant the same behavior but more space to pass out in. I completed the marathon on June 19, 2004, but not without some of the most severe pain of my life. My grandiosity and miscalculations made me erroneously believe I could pace myself for a three-and-a-half-hour finish. I was on pace for the first half (1:48), but around mile nineteen, I completely shut down. I was forced to stop and try to stretch. Dropping out was a preferable option at that point, but I kept going. Barely able to lift my legs above ground, I crossed the finish line only to witness the calf muscle in each of my legs shrivel into a large raisin with involuntary compression. The cramps went on for quite a while, as I had foolishly thought that drinking too much water during the race would slow me down by making me need to stop to go to the bathroom. I realized later that

I did not urinate for approximately a five-hour time span. Dehydration and running do not go hand in hand, but I felt proud of myself for completing a goal that took so much commitment. The first thing I did afterward was take a bath filled with cold water and several bags of cubed ice. The celebration then began that afternoon as I numbed my brain on Jägermeister and Red Bull cocktails. I cannot tell you how much I drank or the number of cigarettes I smoked on that hazy night.

I realize now that both marathons as well as my drinking habits have been endless, self-defeating, and pointless pursuits. This type of behavior bled into the relationships I had at the time. After a breakup with a girlfriend that previous spring (2004), I instantly pursued a former coworker who had just ended a long-term relationship. I had already laid out in my mind how the courtship would begin and quickly solidify. I meticulously worked through this template in my mind—including the details of how I would meet her, what I would say, and how best to get her back to my friend's apartment before the closure of the weekend. However, unlike depressive longing, my obsessions were self-assured, and foresight was met with extreme optimism. Because extreme confidence bridged the gap into hypomania, I had an underlying level of anxiety, causing an extreme sense of urgency for this preplanned agenda to take place. The one treatment that worked best for this anxiety was alcohol. Using a borrowed car, I ventured to Chicago one July weekend in 2004. I stayed with a friend but then met up with the object of my desire the second night. I felt instantly in love. I had liked her before, but the solidification of our mutual feelings sent floods of dopamine through my brain (perhaps a relationship high). I had not felt that way about someone since the five-year relationship with my first girlfriend. The connection between my alcohol dependency and view of intimate relationships is so clear throughout the narrative that I may need to write another book.

My happiness with this individual led me to believe that I wouldn't need to drink so much, because I had a girlfriend. That was not the case. She came to visit me in Madison a couple weeks later in August, and on one of the nights, I blacked out during a bar-crawl event. It did not matter to me that I knew little about her. At that moment, she was it for me.

The school year prior, I had won a Kaplan study course for the Graduate Records Examination (GRE) in a raffle, so seeing as how I wanted to go to graduate school for psychology, I decided to start the class that August before the 2004 fall semester. Unfortunately, working two part-time jobs, taking a full load of classes, and studying for the GRE was more than I could handle. I stopped coping with my stress with any healthy activities and depended on my girlfriend to take care of me in almost a maternal way. At the end of those long days, I would collapse on her collegiate-dorm-room-special futon bed. Within the inviting security of her studio apartment, she would tenderly brush my hair with her hand. We coalesced in a deeply heartfelt way. A year later, I wondered how I could have messed up so badly.

The stress and anxiety I carried eventually weighed so much that my mood sunk into a deep, abysmal depression. A night at the medical school library with my roommate was a significant moment, because I recall fighting back tears while on the opposite side of the table from him; he was immersed in medical doctrine that I will never understand. He knew—and had known from the beginning—that I had bipolar disorder, but just as my mania was an outward demonstration, my depression was a concealed state of mind. Mania is the thrill of your first bike or puppy as a child, mixed with an overdose of candy, while depression sends itself to its room without dessert. I left the small study room before my eyelids could overflow with tears. The feeling was similar to the physical discomfort and terror you feel when you know you are going to throw up but are unsure if you will make it to the bathroom in time. I called one of my good friends from an inconspicuous, isolated wing of the medical school and cried uncontrollably. That moment only knows the words that came out of my mouth. My compassionate friend collected the fragments of undigested and masked feelings that I had held inside for so long. I had hit rock bottom but again was functioning remarkably well.

I did not call my girlfriend because, despite our being together for several months, she did not know that I had bipolar disorder. The disclosure was an overwhelming fear to me because of the stigma attached to the disorder (even though she was studying sociology). I had been conditioned to bury this dangerous evidence of my secret and believed exposure would result in rejection. I would take my medication in her cupboard-sized bathroom before going to bed. With the faucet running, I would delicately unscrew the key-chain pill holder and tap out 600 mg of lithium. She would soon discover something was terribly wrong when, in the spring of 2005, outside of Hair Forum, she confronted a euphoric ex-boyfriend with a freshly buzzed haircut atop what no longer resembled the face of sanity. Her disjointed petition to make sense of the situation still rings in my ears: "Andy, *are you on drugs or something?*"

The weekend before the GRE in October of 2004, I tried to study, but my anxiety was so intense that I could barely focus. During a practice examination on the computer, I stopped to take a break outside on our second-story balcony. I smoked a cigarette at a time when I did not smoke unless drinking alcohol. I felt so stressed that I thought smoking would help. Standing outside with the dark sky and cool fall breeze, I looked over the wooden edge of the balcony to the concrete driveway below. I analyzed and internally speculated as to whether I could survive a leap from that altitude. This memory, in a disturbing way, conjures up the image of that right-angled corner of the balcony comprised of unsteady wood. My thoughts were passive measurements of the situation from a mathematical perspective or mind-set that only the rote learning of a strenuous test could produce: *If individual A stands twenty-five feet in the air and leaps at a twenty-three-degree angle (holding all other variables constant), what distance X will individual A land from Y?*

This Pythagoreanesque attempt at a math problem is a poor example, but what is frightening is that I was so apathetic during my observation on that dark night: *If I stand up on the railings and take a swan dive, will it all be over?*

Depression always seems bad, but it is hard to realize just how far down your mood is until after the fact. A few days later, I completed the GRE beyond my expectations (unfortunately, it would prove unnecessary, because the score was not needed to get into the social work master's program at the University of Wisconsin–Madison) and went out to celebrate with my friends. I blacked out to a walking unconscious level as two of my friends were arguing politics (one on the far left and the other a moderate right). This was near the approaching reelection of George W. Bush. Apparently, my girlfriend followed as I abruptly left Brocach Irish Pub unannounced to go I am not sure where. This story was told to me, so that gives a relative picture of the level of my intoxication. My girlfriend put up with that shit all the time.

This episode was a mild awakening, and I turned to my psychiatrist for help. Not for my real problems—alcohol dependence and anxiety—but for the depression. He put me on a trial of Lamictal (the generic form is called Lamotrigine), an anticonvulsant that often works as a mood stabilizer but can also have antidepressant components for individuals with bipolar disorder. Lithium works as a metaphorical ceiling for preventing mood escalation (i.e., a manic episode), and Lamictal is the floor that ensures one does not slip through a black hole in the ground (i.e., a depressive episode). Lamictal was my wonder drug. It made a night-and-day difference. My eyes reopened. The Lexapro attacked the depression, so the addition of Lamictal made for an unforeseen kindling effect in terms of my increasing mood. In November of 2004, as my change in medication was taking place, my girlfriend and I took a trip to Chicago. In the wake of me getting us into a car accident en route, I blew off my girlfriend during what some would call a "bender." I blacked out during a Ryan Adams concert and did the same the following night of the weekend trip. I felt nauseated on the drive back to Madison, and we barely spoke. I knew she was upset, but certainly, I thought, she would not end things. When we returned, she broke up with me. No judge or jury. I was guilty and knew it. Nevertheless, I pleaded with her, but it did not change her mind. The breakup would normally have been more devastating, but my mood was on the rise. It is embarrassing now to recall my lack of maturity despite my age at the time—twenty-three. Ultimately, my drinking prompted the conclusion of our relationship.

I became uninhibited in the classroom and felt good overall in the month following those events. I had gotten my nose pierced not long before, which may have been related or a precursor to the symptoms of an escalating mood, but it is hard to say. Certainly the piercing was an outward expression of some kind. My ex-girlfriend contacted me a couple weeks after the breakup, and we reconnected briefly. In spite of this, I was already enrolled in a three-week Spanish Immersion course in Oaxaca, Mexico. The trip took place during the holiday break in order to fulfill my foreign language requirement to graduate after the 2005 spring semester. *I can complete a whole semester of Spanish in three weeks while being in Mexico?* It was not a difficult decision. That choice—or, more so, the actions I took while on the trip to Mexico—would come with grave consequences. If ever I said, "Mexico was insane!" during that time, then I was all too accurate.

—11—

NEURAL PASSPORT

Cause I feel just like a map
Without a single place to go of interest.

—Ryan Adams, "My Winding Wheel"

For those who are not well versed in the medical criteria for a manic episode, I will interject descriptions from the symptom list during the narrative in hopes of helping the reader make sense of the events from a diagnostic perspective. This information is also listed in the appendix in the back of book. Spring break in South Padre was a cakewalk compared to the extreme debauchery that took place in Oaxaca, Mexico. The night before departure, a group of friends and I went to a Bloomington, Minnesota, tavern and drank heavily until closing time. This did not stop me from having a female acquaintance come over to my parents' house until three in the morning. I believe I slept two hours that night, despite my early flight in the morning ("decreased need for sleep"). In spite of the sleep deprivation and a prior night of heavy alcohol consumption, I felt amazing during those early hours. This disjointedness between my amount of sleep and my mood would continue to rise.

Mexico was nonstop self-gratification and risk taking. The small school that our group of University of Wisconsin–Madison students attended along with some American students from other universities offered various forms of classes (all in Spanish), including salsa dancing, within the small confines of this intensive educational milieu. A friend and I decided to drink five to six beers before what was the third or fourth salsa class. As there were only three men in the class, the females had few partners to choose from. The women saw an immense improvement in our dance skills. Apparently, Corona has a powerful effect that loosens the infamous stiff-white-guy dance syndrome. I had a revelation of sorts when the salsa instructor defined *cienega* for me, as not surprisingly to many, I was listening to a lot of Ryan Adams music during the trip (more specifically, his former band, Whiskeytown). My music of choice was depressive, sorrowful songs—nothing upbeat. "La Cienega Just Smiled" was a favorite of mine, and I took the opportunity to gather some meaning of the title. The instructor stated that the word meant "swamp." Instantly the song's significance changed for me. A dark, insignificant, metaphorical swamp can also be perceived as a beautiful environment filled with life underneath. This dualistic viewpoint and unsubstantiated understanding of mine would intensify in the coming months, coinciding with manic symptoms.[2]

Living with native Oaxacans at a homestead was fascinating. As symptoms were brewing, I decided to ask in in my broken Spanish-English combination—also known as "Spanglish"—if it would be okay for five girls and a couple guy friends to come over every day and sunbathe on their roof. Instead of studying the language and culture, we listened to Whiskeytown and worked on coloring our

---

2   The album *Gold*, as a whole, was written in Los Angeles, California, and the song was certainly related to or inspired by La Cienega Boulevard. I found this information out about a year later. Revelations and subsequent fixations often stem from being misinformed, and with mania, revelations are daily experiences.

pale Wisconsin winter bodies. I never took the siesta that Mexicans take after the large dinner meal at around one o' clock in the afternoon ("feels rested after only three hours of sleep"). Sleep was not on my to-do list, even though sleep is an important variable in preventing episodes. Almost every student went out as a group to drink each night. Some individuals drank responsibly, while others with reckless abandonment (I was in the latter of the two categories). One of the nights, I found Domino's pizza on the table when I returned early in the morning (the family I stayed with kept hot food out for hours at a time, refrigerating very little). It was amazing. Unfortunately, I awakened to find bedmates in the form of several whole pieces of pizza. My host mother never said a word (or the translation of words was lost), because I, of course, did not do the laundry.

On New Year's Eve, which spilled into the late morning of 2005, after visiting many bars and riding in the beds of trucks as well as other strangers' cars ("excessive involvement in pleasurable activities that have a high potential for painful consequences"), I returned home and decided to camp out on the roof. I smoked a cigarette and then woke up just in time to make it to the mandatory orientation meeting. Being hungover became part of my daily process until it was so insignificant that that state of being became normal. Moments before I had fallen asleep that night, I had spoken into my twenty-four-hour-a-day diary (i.e., my MP3/digital recorder). I carried what now would be considered an antiquated MP3 player. The recording device captured audio all the time, including my ongoing journal. This device is still in my possession. It also includes unethically recorded therapy and psychiatric sessions that I secretly documented months later. You have not lived until you have heard your delusional voice speaking with the intense pressure ("more talkative than usual or pressure to keep talking") that an unfiltered, manic mind creates. I needed full coverage of this trip in an obsessive way, so the device went everywhere with me.

In addition to acting as the class clown ("inflated self-esteem") and show-ing no respect for our *professora* (this includes asking her out for a drink at the end of the trip) or her educational strategies, I also undertook many risks where bodily injury easily could have occurred. On a trip to Hierva el Agua, an area located on a mountaintop filled with scenic views and naturally formed swimming pools, I decided to scale down a steep slope and then climb back up. The photograph I have suggests a slip could have been deadly or, at the very least, a major inconvenience.

A bridge-like beam across a dry aqueduct in my neighborhood provided me with another climbing opportunity. This feat would have been a bit more reasonable during the day, but it was something else to tackle at one in the morning with a brain drenched in mescal (a smoky-flavored liquor similar to tequila that has a taste akin to what I imagine battery acid is like). A "friend" and I gracefully climbed over a twelve-to-fifteen-foot wire-pronged fence in order to get onto the structure, which was approximately thirty to forty feet above the dry concrete ground. The structure was wide enough for one ("sexual indiscretions") but pH bal-anced for two (sorry, Mother).

Renting a motorcycle in Oaxaca was no chore for me, as all I needed was identification. Of course, driving in a foreign, non-English-speaking city and participating in its vehicular traffic was synonymous to running with the bulls ("high potential for painful consequences"). In both cases, a helmet is usually absent. Traveling with a passenger on a small bike (125 cc engine) was also fairly risky as I attempted to go up steep inclines with winding roads while avoiding the street dogs that were attracted to the motorcycles (the clutch had to have been in horrible shape upon return).

Physical danger was not the only odd risk-taking behavior I partook in. My spending habits were grossly over budget ("unrestrained buying sprees"). This tends to happen when one purchases large quantities of drinks at bars every single night and useless souvenirs by day. In the classroom, my major project included a presentation on Las Posadas, a yearly nine-day holiday, usually celebrated by Catholic Mexicans, beginning on December 16 and ending on December 24. It celebrates the trials Mary and Joseph suffered before finding a place where Jesus could be born. I used a traditional holiday song, which I rapped to the accompaniment of Cypress Hill's "Insane in the Brain." Not a person who prides himself in rapping or stage presence ("inflated self-esteem"), this was quite a leap for me. The obnoxious display included a huge piñata named Zorra that I had purchased from a store despite it not being an item for sale (the sale took little convincing). The name translates to both "fox" and "prostitute." In addition to the piñata, the presentation involved a radio for my iPod to play the song and an elaborate costume that consisted of a hooded sweatshirt and sunglasses ("attention too easily drawn to unimportant or irrelevant external stimuli").

The presentation was actually not that horrendous, but ironically, our usual instructor was out sick that day. Her replacement was a rigid middle-aged woman who did not find my antics amusing. I wonder how that affected my grade. During the end of the trip, I recall a congregation of students from the various programs having drinks and coffee together. I had a conversation with a student in which I talked in an incessant yet articulate manner ("more talkative than usual") about my work with individuals who had severe and persistent mental illness (referring to my job with a community support program in Madison, Wisconsin). I felt like an expert ("grandiosity"), and my overflowing confidence in the knowledge transcended any feeling I had ever had. In this surreal way, I became conscious of where my mind had gone and could be going. My brain was flooded with thoughts ("subjective experience that thoughts are racing") and conversation without limits or finality ("flight of ideas"). It hit me in that moment that I was experiencing hypomania (probably closer to mania), but the thought left as quickly as it came. It is fair to say that I was experiencing symptoms of mania at that point, which I have noted, along with traces of manic symptoms from the aforementioned weeks. Racing thoughts, a decreased need for sleep, hypersexuality, impulsiveness, and euphoria were all present, to name a few. The alcohol at night kept some of these symptoms at bay while exacerbating others.

I feel too good. Don't worry about it. Inhibition is a thing of the past.

This was a crucial moment, as I still had insight into my disorder, believed I was experiencing symptoms of hypomania, and realized there could be a problem. However, the mania had gotten a step in front of me at that point. This was the crucial moment, the highest point of the roller coaster before the descent into jarring chaos, the climax of the story—the "don't open that door" or "look behind you" part of the movie, when there is still hope for the victim. I believed I was dealing with hypomania, when in fact, I had crossed the line; a full-blown manic episode had begun. This is the pivotal "if I could go back in time" moment. I had reached the tipping point. If I had taken action based on this recognition—that my mind was beginning to exercise unbridled energy—I might have prevented what was to come. The hopeless mood of the fall repressed any notion of manic symptoms to come. I sought medical help only when the trip was winding down, because I became physically sick. In the middle of a morning class, I excused myself and threw up for the first time in years. I was frightened, because I was not hungover. I had been drinking for three weeks straight, so a hangover did not come easily at that point, and I most likely had not gotten food poisoning. What concerned me was lithium toxicity. What should have concerned me was my escalating mood and my severe levels of drinking. I contacted my psychiatrist and my parents, lied about the amount of drinking I was doing, did not see a doctor, and then slept for about fourteen hours. Unfortunately, this episode came the night before the final exam. I was unable to study ("distractibility") other than one to two hours right before the exam; whatever focus I had was lost. The teacher offered me more help than she probably should have during the test, and afterward, I had a conversation with her. The other students were gone, and I explained to her the best I could in Spanish about my psychological condition. In hindsight, from a positive perspective, this disclosure was quite an accomplishment. I explained the dehydration process that can occur and the consequences of toxicity in the body from lithium as well as my overall fear; the words poured out with sobs. She sympathized with me. This scene represents a mood fluctuation that can occur within an episode. I was not depressed but was crippled with anxiety, which was fueling the soon-to-be-boiling mania.

After cutting down slightly on my alcohol consumption (partially due to my drained bank account), the last days soon turned to nights of insomnia. The final evening before my flight, I was finally feeling better, but I got only three hours of sleep. My friend picked me up at the Dane County Regional Airport in the nightfall, minus my bag of everything I had had in Mexico, which the airlines had temporarily lost. This inconvenience did not concern me. Classes did not start for a couple of days, so my thinking was "Let's go out [to the bars]." I had a tan, an elevated mood, a soaring ego, and many stories. Back on US soil, my world was void of structure and lacked any negative consequences, which allowed me to disregard everything except things that brought me pleasure (socialization, drinking, drugs, and sex).

—12—

Hyperbolic

We are informed by our memories, not controlled by them.

—Francine Shapiro

Upon my return to Madison, I continued the streak of going out every night. I had no concerns. My course load was light, I would graduate in a matter of months (not that I had any idea where I would work), and, most importantly, my mood was in the sky. During that time, I managed to continue working part-time at two jobs and going to class (some of the time). Filling my down-time was easy; I went out with lots of different girls and always moved in the direction of places crammed with socialization ("increase in goal-directed activity … socially"). It seemed that I got along with everyone. My confidence and uninhibited style were fitting during periods of drinking as well as going out with new people, as they were traits equated with a gregarious person. No one saw a disorder or maladaptive decisions; people perceived my behaviors to be indicative of an outgoing personality.

My parents, especially my mother, grew concerned—not with the unseen, rising mania but with the amount of alcohol I was drinking. When I was pandering for money from my parents during a weekend back in Minneapolis in the middle of February 2005, my mother and I had an argument about the state of my drinking with sounds louder than the usual dissonance. Frustration and disappointment flooded her eyes as she told me I was an alcoholic—a visceral criticism only a frightened mother could conjure. Looking back, I would not disagree with the statement she made at that time. However, my irate retort was a response to the perceived degradation of my character. I was impervious to her concerns, as nothing could holster my bulging confidence. I left with a friend, who was driving me home late that Sunday night. I took over the wheel halfway through the dark trip on I-94 East. Soon after I started driving, my speed reached the upper nineties. A police officer pulled me over and gave me a ticket after clocking me at eighty-two miles per hour. The ticket by no means discouraged me, but my mother's words lingered in my mind, and I harbored the idea that I was now the repudiated son. I sent an e-mail to a close friend with an attached letter that I had sent to my parents. Both documents are below, with the e-mail to my friend appearing first. I removed the names and added some clarifications, but I otherwise kept the documents as they were originally sent.

Wed, 16 Feb 2005 10:13:40

Where have you been? I called you when I was at home. This was hours before my parents had an intervention with me. Spouting claims of alcoholism, which were warranted under the circumstances, however my mom cut my life into small pieces and then blended those pieces in [and] served them to our dog. Whatever that means. To sum this up I attached the letter I sent to them, bc I think you will enjoy it. I am pissed that you called [friend's name] but not me. As punishment you will have to hear about my lifestyle. It is something close to yours back when you were willing to makeout with my blacked-out _____. No offense, it is a lot of fun. Currently I am hooking up with a past hook-up, going on dates to the zoo with a girl that has a boyfriend in Chicago, talking to a 20 yr old that used to have cervical cancer (?what?) who gives me free tanning, making out with the ex-novia [ex-girlfriend], talking to a girl I made out with in Minneapolis a couple weeks ago, crazily attracted to my roommates-girlfriend's-friend, who in certain social circles, goes by "big tittied Hanna." Decided in a moment of clarity (i.e. pot smoke) that I would not go down the path already traveled (ex-novia), but instead enjoy my whorish lifestyle as it is my last semester here in Madison. My semester is such a joke it is ridiculous. I have no dinero [money] however, which makes things difficult. I start back up at my real job at _____on Monday so I won't be trippin' off the flows for loot.

Keep it real.
Andy

Dear Mom and Dad,

I regret the incident that occurred on Sunday afternoon. More and more lately I have felt detached from our family in general, but especially from the views and lifestyles that the two of you embrace. This is no fault of yours, however if our communication skills were both improved and assumptions were deemphasized, I know our relationship would be a lot healthier. I agree that my drinking has increased recently (which I have made changes in order to remedy this), however there are reasons behind this that can easily be put into a large category such as "alcoholism." Since our "discussion" on Sunday I have not had a drink, even while going out several nights with my friends to the bars and turning away drinks.

Whether you guys choose to accept the fact that large amounts of drinking in college occurs for the vast majority of students or not, many of those people go on to be successful without a substance abuse problem subsequent to college (i.e. _____, my roommates, _____, _____, etc. etc.). The point that I am trying to make is that these success stories should reduce the anxiety that you feel for my situation. It is true that none of these people have a diagnosed mental disorder, but I have never used that as a copout. I was very offended by the comments made about the potential that could have been achieved in various aspects of my life. At this point in my life I have very few regrets and am very content with who I am and how far I have come. The disaggreement [disagreement] we had could have been avoided had I been more specific with you on where my money is going. I have other expenses than alcohol (utilities, groceries, medications, books, clothes, etc.). A realization has come to me and that is the fact that the reliance for your support has increased when it should be decreasing. It will not be necessary for you to give me anymore spending money. If you could still help me pay for my rent and medical bills for the remainder of the year, I would appreciate it. My cell phone bill will now be sent to my apartment since the billing address has been changed.

It is unfortunate we both did not have more time to discuss my trip more in-depth as well as my career ambitions. Mexico was exactly what I needed, and it changed my outlook on minorities, since I was one for 3 and a half weeks. Thankfulness was felt for living in America and having the opportunities that I have and have had throughout the course of my life. The opportunities that Madison has given me both academically and the philosophical viewpoints that I have heard during my stay here has changed my previously conservative views. The diversity of students from all over the U.S. enables one to meet and explore new ideas from various testimonials. Unfortunately, a lot of this liberal ideology contradicts with the beliefs that you two instilled in me. I hope you trust that I am making good decisions and following my heart, because I know that I will be successful and that my goals are in sight.

Our hopes and faiths in life seem to divert more and more lately. During the course of my illness, I have learned that the decisions I make and my faith in religion do not help to change the chemical imbalances that occur in my brain. Looking back at my life, I can see the ups and downs that have occurred are do [due] to transitions and stressors in life, and that faith in God alone do not alter these events from happening. It is true that the decisions I make and the lifestyle I choose will have an effect. However, living in fear of having an episode will cause you to do that; live in fear. My outlook, which now has become cognitively positive will allow me to live with this persistent disorder. The point is that my days in Minneapolis are probably limited as well as my time in the Catholic Church. The segregation and arrogance of one religion discourages me from affiliating with a religious sect, instead I try to help people whenever it is possible and keep my opinions and beliefs open, because I am still learning and growing. I want to find out about the world on my own and have strong convictions for what I believe in. It is important to explore other religions that you were not born into by geography or family.

My accomplishments and directions are solid (see resume) and the networking I am doing now can only continue my success. My professor for mood disorders is world renowned in her field (Major Depression) and I encourage you to google search her on the web (Lyn Abramson). This is an upper level class that looks at major depression and bipolar disorder, so you can imagine my knowledge and interest in the class. Two years ago I attempted to get in to Prof. Abramson's lab, but my GPA was not quite high enough. However, I have made her aware of my interest to work in her lab after graduation for a paid position, which she was very receptive towards. She also encouraged me to drop her name in an email to professors at the University of Minnesota as well as another one of her colleagues that I had as a professor. Experience with a professor this well distinguished would ensure a ticket into just about any graduate school program that I desire.

My plan after a year off is to go to graduate school at a place that offers a PsyD program. This is very similar to a PhD program; however it cuts out most of the research aspect and includes much more real-world application and therapy. This is a doctorate program, which means when I complete it I will be a clinical psychologist! Programs that I have begun looking at are the Argosy Professional Psychology School, which has a location in Eagan, Minnesota as well as downtown Chicago. These schools are independent of a university, which basically means they are very expensive. Some schools that are not independent, which appear to be good fits for me are the University of Georgia and four schools in California. The benefit to the California schools is that their program is basically the same as a PsyD, but you finish with a PhD. After grad school, I plan on writing a book, but that is a long way off and probably will happen after I am established in the field.

I hope you agree that my future is very promising. Despite being clinically depressed and having suicidal ideation, I was able to do very well on the GRE, which will help my chances for graduate school. My only request is that you have some compassion for what I deal with, especially because when I am very depressed I do not usually where [wear] it on my shoulder and it is much easier to isolate myself from relationships than to reconnect when I am feeling that way. Even though I had many doubts about graduating college, the day is vastly approaching. My mood is good and I have never had so many friends and

co-workers before in my life that care a great deal about
me. I wish you guys the best and hope to hear from you
soon.

Your son,
Andrew

I wrote the above letter in the vein of deep conviction; it is surprisingly coherent and organized. The language contrasts the soon fiery combativeness
that my speech would project at my parents. It is interesting that I signed the
letter "Andrew," because I would not go by my given name until five years
later as I started a new career practicing psychotherapy. This last month,
during my writing process, was the first time I had read the digital letter
since creating the original document. Finding the letter was like opening a
time capsule. This extensive response to my parents contains chilling parallels to my current beliefs, aspirations, and career; the words make the hairs
on the back of my neck rise. The comment about my future is eerie: "After
grad school, I plan on writing a book, but that is a long way off and probably
will happen after I am established in the field." The message is also littered
with grandiosity: "Experience with a professor this well distinguished would
ensure a ticket into just about any graduate school program that I desire."
The truth was that I barely knew my professor and had only just started
an undergraduate course with her as the instructor. My favorite part of the
letter, if I may inject humor, is the time-stamped modernity of the piece: "I
encourage you to google search her on the web." The suggestion to acquire
information about an individual is now simply put: "Google her."

It is evident that I was in denial about my drinking as well as my spending habits, but it is also true that alcohol was not the main problem. Unfortunately,

no one knew what the problem was. I think it's important to note that it must have taken a lot of courage for me to write the letter. Challenging my parents' beliefs and talking about mental illness were two things that did not occur in my family. To take it a step further and tell them how I felt about the Catholic Church in a mildly pejorative manner must have brought fire to their eyes. If nothing else, this letter is a relevant testimonial during a specific time period when my religious beliefs and ideologies first started to deviate from my family's status quo.

With mania, most people do not remember what they did or the series of events clearly, if at all. The mind is so disrupted that it is hard to do so, especially when neurons are firing at lightning speed and the brain is overbooked with neurotransmitters. My case was different. I remember most events—and maybe too much. The sequence of events is not entirely clear, but the major incidents are. What happened in the following two months—March and April—of that fateful year of 2005, I do not wish upon anyone.

—13—

999,999 Little Pieces

I wanted to use my experiences to tell my story about addiction and alcoholism, about recovery, about family and friends and faith and love, about redemption and hope.

—James Frey

4/6/05: My face evaporated into the mattress, so my sense of sight was gone, but I could feel the pressing bodies as they seamlessly removed all of my clothing and handcuffed me. For a long lasting moment, the impression of adulthood and autonomy was stripped from my mind.

A friend of mine, an MTV *Road Rules* "star" (my description), was asked to go to a bar in Iowa for a promotional event one weekend that spring. I am not sure if he asked me to go along or if I requested, but either way, I was headed to Nowhere, Iowa, on a weekend night to bump elbows with some reality TV notables. The setting was to be a mediocre hotel, and then the promotion was at a gay bar. My friend, another *Road Rules* participant, and Ruthie from *The Real World: Hawaii* were the celebrity representatives. On the way to Iowa from Madison, Wisconsin, driving in our friend's Jeep Grand Cherokee, I smoked pot the entire two-hour or so drive. I remember talking constantly, but I have no idea what about. Bowl hit after bowl hit resulted in me getting out of the car upon arrival at the hotel and spilling my guts in the parking lot.

I have seen clinical diagnoses in reports about cannabinoid hyperemesis syndrome, which basically just means that too much pot smoking will make you vomit. My recollection is this: I was really, *really* high. At the level I was at, my anxiety caused a physical reaction. My embarrassment wore off quickly as I told my friend to find a cleaner parking spot. We were treated like royalty in the small town. Hotel personnel could not differentiate me from my friend in terms of stardom, so that trip was my three hundred or so minutes of fame. We went to the bar and met the other MTV members, who, as I recall, had been there for a significant amount of time. Prior to my mild alcohol intoxication, I entered into the "perfect body" competition. I have always had quite a bit of stage fright, so this was out of character for me, especially being high as a kite and not at all drunk. I think I took off my shirt, which was tame compared to the behavior of other contestants, and did not have the votes, despite my friend being one of the judges, to make it past round one.

All of us consumed cosmic portions of alcohol at the bar. By the end of the night, I was working on a girl who was not sexually attracted to men (grandiose, perhaps?). When we returned to the hotel, it was like a scene out of the *The Real World*; everyone was drinking alongside the indoor swimming pool and acting out of control despite it being well past after hours. I was using a one-hitter (small pipe) to get high and also drinking. Ruthie (please do not sue me) had a quintessential Ruthie moment when she drank a significant amount from a large plastic vodka bottle. When it came time to eat (at approximately three or four in the morning), everyone decided to go to a Perkins or a Denny's, but it was not clear how we would be transported there. This was not a problem, because I decided to take the thirty-minute "foot bus." After my long walk, I arrived to find the group finishing their food, and Ruthie was on the phone with her girlfriend. They were fighting, and Ruthie was upset and crying. We were all belligerent and surely making a scene. I did not black out that night, because I had the foresight to drink a little less, knowing that this would be a memorable occasion. Once back at the hotel, I tried to convince Ruthie to let me stay in her room, but to no avail. When you are manic, hooking up with a gay celebrity of the opposite sex is not out of the realm of possibilities. After all, Ruthie and her girlfriend were fighting. Instead, I slept across from my affectionate male friends who occupied the other queen-sized bed (so much for a conservative political career). We headed back to Madison fresh off of a four-hour night of sleep.

My mental health continued to decline—or, put in other words, my mood began to skyrocket. Around this same time period, one morning, after a week-day night of partying, I awoke with some free Miller Lite gear acquired from a promotional event at a bar in downtown Madison. Among this junk was a Miller Lite water bottle (a cheap version of a Nalgene bottle, a type of bottle that was prevalent at the time on campus). For some reason, I felt I had to fulfill a desire to make a statement about the irony of drinking water out of a bottle that advertises beer to my morning Mood Disorders course. I earnestly walked to the psychology building carrying a Miller Lite beer can with pink lemonade inside of it; an unlit cigarette was in my mouth. The bizarre connection or argument in my mind was the hypocrisy that it was acceptable to cart around a water bottle with Miller Lite stamped on it, but people's perception of someone walking with a beer can was different. Parts of that argument make a little sense, and I am talking about small pieces. These little pieces of legitimate understanding of the world, as well as new, positive, or constructive ideas that arise, coalesce with the grand schemes that full-blown mania acts to inflate. This is how the disorder gets overlooked by friends and family. The symptoms are relative to each individual's personality, and the illness polarizes those attributes. Entering a "perfect body" competition at a bar with an audience consisting of mostly gay individuals is not implicitly insane. However, for a conservative, insecure, and crowd-shy person (i.e., me), it was the opposite of my usual presentation. I walked into the classroom pretending to be drunk, slaloming through desks, intentionally bumping into some, all while sporting a cigarette in my mouth as well as what appeared to be a full beer in my hand. After a minute or two, I stood up and explained myself and even made accurate associations with the course material that happened to be projected in the front of the room (yeah, the instructor was still using a projector with transparencies for notes). I grabbed the transparency and pretentiously announced, "I'm going to integrate the material from the semester." One member of the class in particular was outraged with my presentation. He scowled and said, "Sit down, man; I want to hear the lecture!"

My professor, who had extensive notoriety in the field as well as a vast knowledge of mood disorders, looked terrified. She did not show signs that one exhibits when physical danger is approaching, but she had the facial expression of someone who knew she was in the presence of an individual suffering from a manic break within his bipolar disorder. At the risk of sounding hyperbolic, I believe my peers felt the same tension experienced by other students victimized in the classroom. There is an element of fear and betrayal when someone who belongs to the group and on the surface fits the norm transforms or explodes in such a disjointed manner as I did. In my classmates' minds, I likely could have been part of the twenty-first-century Trench Coat Mafia, carrying handguns on my person. People who appear to be suffering from a mental illness can be scary, but I think deep down inside, the scariest people are the "normal" ones who act exceedingly out of character when we least expect it. The instructor excused me from the classroom and asked me to wait outside. Asking a person suffering from mania to wait in one place is like asking a fish to stop swimming. However, I managed to wait out the time until class was over.

At the end of the class, two of my friends and I spoke with the professor. I was adamant that the beer can merely contained pink lemonade, which was my sole defense for the actions I had taken. I found it upsetting that the instructor appeared to not believe me, and I eventually poured a teaspoon of the liquid into my hand. I was like a child offering an explanation that only made sense to him in his underdeveloped world.

Right now, I am back in that classroom. A feeling of mild discouragement comes to mind despite the self-assured presentation at the time. I am smaller in that memory now as I look back and examine the faces of my two friends and professor. They look back, arranged in a semicircle, as I drift farther from the planet.

The contents of the beer can were not the cause of their immense distress. I agreed to call my psychiatrist and gave verbal consent for my instructor to speak to him. During the call, one of the most composed and eloquent faculty members at the university displayed trembling hands as well as inhibited speech—or, more so, thought deregulation. She expressed her unease to both the psychiatrist and me. Subsequent to that absurd morning, I eventually went to my psychiatric appointment. Surprisingly, my psychiatrist did not come across as overly troubled. He did say that he had been "getting a lot of calls" about me. Unfortunately, with confidentiality laws, he could not speak with any of my alarmed friends or family without releases signed by me. This relates to a lesson since learned that I will discuss later in the book. The stringent nature of the confidentiality laws creates a thin line between life and liberty in the preponderance of mental-health-crisis interventions.

My psychiatrist gave me a prescription for Zyprexa, the very drug that, in my mind, had precipitated the frightening panic I'd awoken to three years prior. The psychiatrist also prescribed Seroquel, an antipsychotic drug similar to Zyprexa, to decrease the unbridled mania I was experiencing. I am quite sure I was off all of my medications at that point, and I was certainly not going to take anything that would slow me down. Comparable to a defective Toyota car, the gas pedal was stuck, and the option of hitting the brakes was not of interest to me. The psychiatrist knew this. He requested an order for a blood draw to assess what my lithium level was and most likely to confirm his suspicion that I was not taking any of it.

After a sleepless night, I went to the Meriter Laboratory to get a blood draw. I had not been taking my lithium, but knowing my level would be very low (a therapeutic blood level is approximately between 0.8 and 1.2), I put about 600 mg of lithium down the hatch just before the blood draw in an attempt to boost the amount in my system. All this last-minute spurt of lithium accomplished was an unreliable blood draw (I do not know what the number was, but it was probably well below 0.8). If the blood draw had been high (above 1.2), then standard laboratory protocol would have been to notify me in order to rule out lithium toxicity. At the next appointment with my psychiatrist, I walked in and placed a string of objects on the table, including a pack of cigarettes and who knows what else (I was trying to display something out of character from my normal presentation, which he already was well aware of). This rebellious act was analogous to the risk-taking behaviors of teenagers who subconsciously want to get caught. They dance around the rules that aim to contain their desire for ultimate autonomy.

Unbeknownst to my doctor, I recorded the session on my MP3 player, and I recall asking the psychiatrist what the number three meant to him. I encouraged a stream-of-consciousness response, and he mentioned the three lobes of the brain as well as the Trinity in the bible. Throughout the session, I postulated that my diagnosis was in actuality bipolar II disorder (see the appendix). This remark implied that I was experiencing hypomania (feeling a decreased need for sleep, multitasking, and accomplishing more than usual amounts of work, which is usually accompanied by a limited desire to get treatment) and not the more harmful and out-of-control mania. The reality of the situation was that I was completely manic, and my unsubstantiated diagnostic appeal was rejected. I was like a child with bronchitis insisting, "No, Mom, I'm not really that sick. I just have a cold. Please let me go outside and play!" I could not stay on task and had breached the point of delusional thought processes as well as a certain denial of my illness. In addition, I was not on medication, or was not treatment compliant. In hindsight, I wish someone had put a straitjacket on me, placed me on a gurney, shoved a wooden spoon in my mouth, and administered an insulin shot to produce a hypoglycemic shock—as they did in the good old days. This might have avoided the *One Flew Over the Cuckoo's Nest* state that would ensue.

The graph below depicts the direction my mood moved, beginning in October of 2004. As the depression lifted, the mania followed suit. It is

important to note that the depression and mania did not move independently. One slowly took over the other. By March of 2005, the mania had
reached heights that could not be contained.

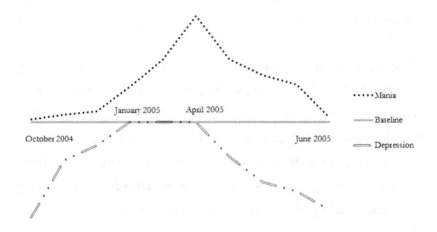

—14—

STUDENT DISORGANIZATION

*There's a truism, at least in the United States, that every person
has one novel in him. In other words, one autobiographical novel.*

—Jonathan Franzen, *Farther Away*

I allocated my time and a small amount of innumerate energy to a student organization that I wanted to establish. I shared the proposal with my roommate, and he agreed it was a good brainchild. The name would be Innovated Student Psychology, or ISP. During a short bus ride home from the downtown Madison area to our apartment near Camp Randall, in a matter of seconds, I constructed the mission statement based on the acronym HEALTH: Honest & Educated Accounts of Lifestyles, Therapy & Histories.

The idea was born. Eventually, on Facebook, I started a group for the potential student organization, which I was sure would take off in much the same way that the now-ubiquitous social-networking website did (grandiosity). The Facebook group's description included the following:

> [ISP] is an outlet for individuals seeking a no pressure,
> uninhibited environment involving psychological issues

concerning young adults. It is not an intimidating group, which allows individuals to give or take as much as they would like from each individual gathering. Everyday issues such as depression, mental illnesses, and relationship problems, which the public has false stereotypes about, will inform members. The purpose of this advocacy is to create a trickle-down-effect, whereby, members will inform other students through everyday conversations. A minimal goal is to at least inform all of the students at the University of Wisconsin-Madison, so that every student is aware that a group exists, which consists of students who know first-hand about and have experienced the same stressors.

Located under the section for "office" within the Facebook group, I notice now that I listed "wherever I am." The group page goes on to declare the following:

> There will be weekly meetings involving discussions regarding personal experiences of the individuals in relation to psychological topics (i.e. depression, suicide, mental illnesses, relationship problems, etc., etc.). In addition, advocacy in social circles and throughout the university, both individually and collectively, in order to encourage a safe, anonymous, environment for students to talk about people's issues.

What I had surmised was more than a rudimentary proposition for students who wanted to share their discomfort of mental illness while avoiding the bureaucracy and stigma of seeking treatment. In addition, from my perspective, the syntax of the description does not appear to be insane in any shape or form. Perhaps this is why bipolar disorder has survived the evolutionary process of natural selection, or survival of the fittest. From Winston Churchill's mobilization of individuals, to Ted Turner's business investments, to Edgar Allan Poe's creativity, to Vincent Van Gogh's innovation (studies have shown they all appear to have had a mood disorder), it is evident that inspiring leadership qualities and seductive, appealing characteristics frequently result from this illness, and this connection has stood the test of time. However, when I scrutinize my behavior through the lens or context of what I was going through ("distractibility, inflated self-esteem"), it is easy to see the unraveling of my psyche. Despite massive amounts of confidence, achievements would not come as a result of this episode. I worked on the group into the late hours of the night ("increase in goal-directed activity, decreased need for sleep") and often when I was drinking or smoking pot ("excessive involvement in pleasurable activities"). My pot use increased during that period, and because marijuana is a stimulant, it kept me up all night and precipitated the amplification of my anxiety. The ISP group *did* have potential for a positive on-campus intervention. However, the creator was not organized enough to handle the task. I made hasty attempts to contact the office for student organizations in order to get university approval, but I never followed through.

Against the better judgment of my roommates, impulsively, I got my first tattoo. I engineered the drawing at around three or four o'clock in the morning at College Library (this information is based on the log-in and post times for when I was finishing up the online Facebook group: 4:33 a.m. on March 9, 2005). Below is the "intricate" design (made on a piece of scratch paper with a pen) for the resulting tattoo. If you look closely, you can see the scattered phone numbers and arrowed connections on the back of the page. I had become delusional and obsessed with numbers in general.

Several years prior, I had contemplated tattooing the universal symbol for psychology (the three-pronged, trident-shaped Greek letter *psi*) on my arm, but I never gathered the nerve to follow through with it (several years later, in a sane, voluntary manner, I had it tattooed on my back). Instead, I now displayed a dedication to a student organization that did not formally exist—a brand on my wrist that had originated from a delusion surrounding the "magic number," three. The organization was no further off the ground than when I had conceived the idea for it, yet my grandiosity perpetuated more impulsive behavior. This decision that lacked any serious introspection would go on to haunt and embarrass me over the next four years. The indelible brand was a constant reminder of what had happened in the fateful year of 2005 before it was eventually covered up by a lotus flower in 2009. How do you explain something like that to a person without stating that you were out of your mind when it happened? I would grapple with that question during periods of existentialism through a plethora of therapy sessions in the years that followed. I did not want people to believe the tattoo was an authentic representation of my decision-making process. I felt that in order to dispel this preconceived notion, I would have to reveal the fact that I had a mental illness to every passing inquirer.

The following night, for whatever reason, I went back to the same tattoo shop to get a green-and-yellow *N* tattooed on my upper forearm, along with reflected numbers at three corners of the letter. The *N* represented the North Star and also the North Stars, the former Minnesota hockey team that now resides in Dallas, Texas. In addition, my inspiration was that one always knows where he or she is directionally oriented from the North Star. My fascination with the reflective properties of numbers (e.g., 2 and 5, 8 being two 3s put together, etc.) and letters stemmed from Dan Brown's book *Angels and Demons*. The placement of the tattoo—at the intersection of the bicep and inner forearm—was such that I could initially pretend the bandage for the tattoo was actually a bandage from a lithium blood draw, as it is the same spot where blood is drawn. The tattoo was ludicrous and revolting. I talked incessantly to the artist throughout the procedure and felt absolutely no physical pain. The only known picture of the tattoo was on my cell phone that I intentionally dropped into an ice-fishing hole on Lake Mendota.

The ISP and North Star tattoos, from my perspective, were outward and concrete visual expressions for others to see into my madness as I continued to rebel against who I was and wanted to become. I had the state of mind of a young boy who believed he would become a baseball player when he grew up, so I viewed the ISP's success as assured rather than a pondered reflection. The tattoos were out-of-character, dramatic changes in my personality that indirectly signaled that something was wrong. However, my brain was not thinking that way. Mania is meant to be seen and heard like a protest against the status quo, unlike latent depressive symptoms, which seek solace in dark, internal isolation.

—15—

DEVOLVING MIND

Hypomanic or manic individuals usually have an inflated self-esteem, as well as certainty of conviction about the correctness and importance of their ideas. This grandiosity can contribute to poor judgment, which, in turn, often results in chaotic patterns of personal and professional relationships.

—Kay Redfield Jamison, *Touched with Fire: Manic-Depressive Illness and the Artistic Temperament*

Although the ISP group[3] started as a fairly good and inventive idea, my lack of coherent commitment to it was quickly evident. As you will see, the regres-

---

3 In December of 2005, I received this message on Facebook regarding the ISP group, and my reply follows:

[Name of Person]

I just found this group while doing a random search and I was wondering if these meetings were still going on or not …

December 24, 2005 at 1:48 a.m. • Mark as Irrelevant • Report • Delete Post

Andrew J. Archer

The group never really took off, based on my own mental health and of course going to jail for a few weeks. Sorry dude.

February 3, 2006 at 10:42 p.m. • Delete Post

sion of the main flyer coincided with my mental deterioration. The date at the top of the initial flyer was 3/7/05 at 3:07 a.m. It read as follows:

Innovated Student Psychology

H.E.A.L.T.H.

Club

Honest & Educated Accounts of Lifestyles, Therapy, & Histories

~non-pressured, uninhibited discussions involving various psychological issues concerning young adults~

Are you interested in discussing **stress, depression, mental illnesses, relationship problems**, and other *psychological* issues *anonymously* with various **college students?**

Join us for an hour to explore the endless possibilities of our collective minds. Through these shared experiences we will all have a better understanding of ourselves. <u>There are no participatory obligations or fees.</u>

1st Informational Meeting (7:00pm) March 10th

Psych Building Rm 105

For Questions, Call or email Andy Archer at 608.658.4515

ajarcher@wisc.edu

Not long after, I made the following fliers, which illustrate what was happening to my mind:

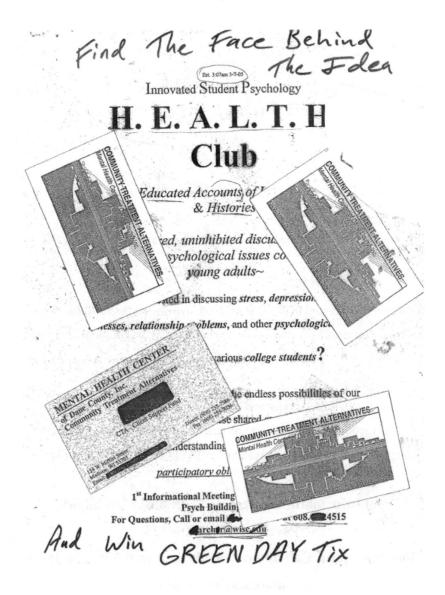

Green Day was coming to play a show in Madison, which is where I heard on the radio that they were giving away free tickets. I am not sure how I figured I would get those tickets, but the important part is the grandiosity. The belief that everyone was aware of this group and, furthermore, had an interest in tracking down the person who had created this abnormal poster (especially just to win tickets to see a mediocre band) was not realistic. Soon my ostentatiousness went deeper. From my perspective at the time, I believed that not only would the ISP group spread socially and digitally in viral fashion but also that I could somehow make money from it (perhaps I hold the same sentiments for this book). The organizational framework for ISP became similar to a pyramid scheme. I wrote the following—ironically, on a Zyprexa notepad—at my former job and left it for all to see:

At this same employer, with my anxiety at such an elevated level, not only was I smoking cigarettes in my boss's car (a big no-no) during work in the community, but I also questioned stopping at a liquor store. It was midday, and the drive to the store came with the intention of slowing my racing mind. When I arrived at the liquor store, I found a client I had been attempting to locate. This coincidence of course was some kind of a sign to me, and I did not purchase the coveted Jack Daniel's that had lured me there. I told a co-worker whom I was close with what was happening (no one at the job knew about my preexisting condition). I made another emergency appointment to see my psychiatrist. As my boss dropped me off at my psychiatrist's office, he asked if my part-time position should be given to another worker (not a firing situation), because it was clear that I would not be able to continue at the moment based on my mental health. I did not give it much thought and agreed that someone else should take the job.

—16—

Flight of Ideas

[Virginia Woolf] talked almost without stopping for two or three days, paying no attention to anyone in the room or anything said to her. For about a day what she said was coherent; the sentences meant something, though it was all nearly wildly insane. Then gradually it became completely incoherent, a mere jumble of dissociated words.

—Leonard Woolf

The psychiatry appointment ended with a prescription from my doctor containing clear instructions: take the Zyprexa and lithium, get some sleep, and follow up with him the next day. I did the latter but continued to resist treatment. My psychiatrist stated frankly that if my mood did not stabilize, he would need to send me to the hospital. Why was he not more aggressive or earnest about this?

The following morning, as my meandering had increased to the drifter level, the next journey was to the west side of Madison. I quickly decided upon the venture in order to pick up a few things after a long night of not sleeping. I made the trip on foot as well as public transportation. I was in no hurry. I headed to the West Towne Mall after picking up a mouse to feed to my pet snake, which was on a trial of Lexapro (the same SSRI that I was taking) at the time because of some perceived depressive symptoms. I mean, Christ, the snake would not get out of bed and exhibited a poor appetite; this was an *obvious* intervention. At the mall, I set the small box that contained the rodent down as I spoke with a worker inside the pit of worthless items (hermit crabs, lotions, etc.) that was the atrium. The next thing I knew, a disheveled-looking man had the mouse on his shoulder. This would have frightened anyone. It was like a Halloween hayride only scary. The man looked like a smiling pirate crossed with a serial killer from a low-budget film. I apologized to him under the assumption that the mouse had escaped from the box and somehow leaped on top of him. As I took the white fur ball from his shoulder, in a flash, he struck me with a quick, methodic whisper and wide eyes: "Wantsomecrack?" He walked away, and my curiosity followed. After all, I figured, I could at least use a ride home. He obliged, and then we drove in his girlfriend's convertible back to my apartment, both smoking his Marlboro Red cigarettes as he discussed the drug trade. If you have never met a person addicted to crack (I hope you have not under similar circumstances), then you may not know that an individual's appearance suffers as a consequence of the drug. He was a short-statured man who resembled the guy from those *Police Academy* movies—Bobcat Goldthwait, the individual with the weird, raspy voice. There were sporadic holes in his mouth, where teeth had previously resided. The man was extremely thin and had long, grayish, unkempt hair. His skin was stretched, smoky-colored, opaque drapery that held on to his dying skull.

We arrived across the street from my apartment, in the parking lot outside of the Madison Public Library on Monroe Street. He proceeded to take out a glass crack pipe in broad daylight. I was more enchanted than nervous as he loaded a small piece of what resembled coral. There was something exciting about the process that is not easy to articulate. The high for me did not come from freebasing crack cocaine with the gentleman but from the anticipation of his experience presented in front of me. The high was the knowing that I would soon have a story beginning with "You're never gonna believe what I saw today!" The fire approached the inside of the pipe and then dramatically arced to connect with the rock material inside the pipe. The onomatopoeic sound of crackling coals in a fireplace, which is the genesis of the drug's name, broke the dense silence of the Marlboro air. Thankfully, I did not partake, but I did slightly inhale (à la Bill Clinton) the long trail of smoke released in my direction from his eroded mouth. I am not sure that it did anything, because this was not an intimate shotgun that we shared, but the feeling stretched beyond any placebo effect. He left me with a crack rock larger than I have ever seen on the show *Intervention*. I stored it inside my filled prescription bottle of lithium that was quickly collecting dust. One night, unsuccessfully, I did try to freebase part of the rock according to his instructions. I had trouble sleeping (not surprisingly), so I thought I would give it a try. Not exactly a cool glass of milk at the end of the night. I really did not know what I was doing, so I am thankful it did not get me high[er]. Eventually, I gave the crack to a friend, warehousing it from me but maintaining access to it in case we wanted to experiment in the future.

I know that people were looking for me during that time period, and I was not answering my phone and was constantly on the move. A friend was going to California to visit Berkley that same day, so naturally I thought I would go with him. I had set my sights specifically on going to San Francisco for quite some time. He did not believe this to be a good idea, but my credit card was not opposed. I went to the airport in a taxi and accidentally left my old cell phone, which was not even connected to a phone service, in the back of the cab. It was like one of those freshly twenty-first-century Sprint phones that might as well have come in a case. Well, it was not that old and big, but using it was basically like holding a baseball stadium minibat to my head for each call. At the time, I used the phone to access numbers that were still stored in the device and then used pay phones. I did not want to be tracked or "on the grid," so to speak. Paranoia was setting in, and I felt the best way to handle it was a clean getaway and new life out west. I went to the airline counter and attempted to purchase a ticket (last minute, of course—I had no knowledge of kayak.com back then) with the demeanor of someone going to catch a matinee at a movie theater. Apparently, someone had told the Madison Regional Airport to expect an individual in the grips of mania who was a flight risk. Airports monitor such situations through what are known as welfare checks—not to be confused with the monetary compensation that individuals who are truly unable to work receive as assistance from the state and federal government. The duration of the manic episode at that point was both frying my brain and leading me in that direction as a future career (in a state of catatonia while filled with antipsychotic medication and drooling atop a disability check). A police officer took over for the woman at the counter. Officers questioned me outside while I smoked a cigarette, fearless of authority at that point. Just to momentarily hark on the point of how mania manifests as an extension of one's personality, I was not flailing my arms and spouting conspiracies about the government during this incident. Despite the abnormalities in my behavior from a friend's or family member's perspective, there was nothing the police could do or even necessarily see that was outside the realm of possible "normal" behavior. Many have taken a last-minute trip to California. More so, I knew how to remain calm and keep my mouth shut around the officers. The content of the conversations is unclear to me, but they were definitely not letting me get on a plane to California. Instead, I was granted a police escort to my psychiatrist's office.

At one moment during the psychiatric visit, I went to the bathroom—something I never did during the twenty- to thirty-minute sessions. A man walked into the facilities after me, and I was sure my psychiatrist had sent him. *He's following me and knows my entire situation,* I thought. This frightened me. After the session, I walked down three floors of stairs to the basement, thinking there were some sort of secret underground happenings. This belief was fueled by my paranoid delusions as I captured footage of my trip to the basement with my phone.

Looking back, it is hard to remember what happened next and what happened after that. The events are fairly clear, but the order is not. The chaos that my friends, family, and I were experiencing in separate time frames, chunks, and contexts relates to the cluster of my own memories, which undermines the ability to compose a precisely documented narrative. Piecing together the time frame of events during a manic episode is much the same as organizing feathers in a tornado. The recollections come to me at different points during this writing experience, and I want to write about all of it, but going after one thing ultimately leaves others behind. This is not going to be a perfect reflection. The inconceivable year of 2005 was more like a perfect storm that would have been hard to prevent or ultimately derail. I will just focus on what got knocked over. Up until now, I have been telling a rather linear, historic recollection of the events. However, when I remember the events that occurred as I became sicker, the story gets harder to follow or retrieve from memory, but I will try to do my best.

Throughout that period, there was no structure in my daily life. Impulsivity was the norm rather than an occasional occurrence, so when my brother and friend ostensibly came to visit (actually to take me home), my impulsiveness continued. They arrived late on a Friday, and one of the antics I pulled, which I thought was funny, consisted of lighting nearly a whole pack of cigarettes in my mouth, smoking them briefly, and then extinguishing the cancer sticks in a glass of water. Not crazy enough? I then proceeded to drink the entire glass of smoky water with a "Ta-da!" smile on my face. What a welcome. Their fears had become a reality, and action was all they had. I am sure they were worried for my life or, more conservatively, my well-being. They told me that they wanted to leave that evening (it was already around ten thirty at night), and that was certainly not part of my plan. Instead, I went alone to buy cigarettes (after the magic trick, the rolled tobacco product was deemed unsmokable), which led me to a bar ironically named Lucky's on Regent Street. At that point, I knew that alcohol would slow me down, so I drank a more subtle sedative: 7UP. I chose 7UP because I had recently found out lithium was initially part of the recipe for the soft drink when it was launched in 1929. The diametric soft drink made by Coca-Cola included cocaine from coca leaves around the same time period. Today, Diet Coke and coffee are by far my drugs of choice.

Eventually, my brother and friend picked me up, but we did not make it far. As a guest speaker for my former graduate school course in the spring of 2010, I explained, "This is how not to handle someone that is manic," in reference to my older brother and friend's attempts to bring me home. These two incredible individuals were merely doing the best they could with limited resources and knowledge of how to intervene. At the busy intersection of Regent Street and West Washington Avenue, I challenged the plan by starting to open up the front passenger-side door and window. I was in no mood for a four-and-a-half-hour car ride back to Minneapolis, Minnesota. Heading east on Regent, the car pulled over on the southeast side through the intersection. There was a struggle, and I punched my brother in the face as I fought off my best friend, who was in the middle of the backseat. In an instant, the open window was my escape route. I took off diagonally across the roads, narrowly missing oncoming traffic in two directions. For me, escaping confinement was a life-or-death situation. According to my brother's and my friend's accounts, they feared they would witness my death at any moment, sure that I would be struck by a car.

I ran to a nearby neighborhood of clustered but somewhat segregated apartments that were probably oriented closely to the shape of the BlackBerry logo. It was there I pulled my first fire alarm. In my mind, the alarm would act as some kind of diversion. Meanwhile, unbeknownst to me, my brother was calling the police to report the assault that had just occurred (in hopes of getting me hospitalized), and police soon picked me up in a parking lot that enclosed Blockbuster, Kinko's, and other businesses—at the same intersection I had fled from. Needless to say, I was not happy with the police officer's kind gesture to bring me to the hospital, as I was handcuffed and placed in the backseat. I spoke belligerently in Spanish with fire spraying out from my mouth. Many people have experienced an enhancement in their foreign-language skills while drinking at the bars, which is largely due to a lack of inhibitions. My mind was sober, but my zero inhibitions and my streams of manic thoughts most likely aided me in recalling what little Spanish I knew. My manic brain could not see the restriction it faced (i.e., hospitalization) as an instrument for safety or security; instead, the hospitalization felt like an involuntary imprisonment, and it fostered discontent toward my brother and friend for their deceptive actions.

—17—

CONTAGION

There's nothing to do here
Some just whine and complain
In bed in the hospital
Coming and going
Asleep and awake
In bed at the hospital

—Cold War Kids, "Hospital Beds"

After being checked into the hospital's emergency room, I was taken to a small room where I was put in a gown and handcuffed with one wrist to a gurney as the police officer held security post at the door. The cooperation between the officer and me was a radical shift from minutes earlier, when I had unleashed a barrage of expletives during the car ride. The police officer waited with me, but he was not much for conversation. We talked about motorcycles a little, and I believed he was hinting at selling me his as well as the possibility that I would soon ride with him and his friends. When you are experiencing mania, everything is possible—nothing is out of the question. My mood soared, and my status rose to an indigo-colored threat level (more like a kaleidoscope of colors) as I was guarded and assessed for danger.

The young, seemingly inexperienced resident psychiatric doctor came into the room eventually and asked some questions. The end result, in a sense, was that I was mildly coerced into signing a voluntary admission into the hospital. When you have your wrist shackled to a bed and a large police officer pacifying you with his eyes, competency and legal representation do not cross your mind. Instead, a subservient reticence came over me as I quietly agreed to their demands with my signature on a document. As I will explain later in the book, they did not have enough merit for an involuntarily commitment to the hospital, because at that point, I was not (at least on paper in the court system) a threat to myself or others. I should note that I wish people would have coerced and broken rules even more in order to confine me, so in no way am I upset by the admission to the hospital. Laws and procedures need to be altered in order to ensure the safety of the individual and emotional sanctity of friends and family. Knowledge is power, and from my perspective, the more people who are aware of my mental illness, the better, because the knowledge offers me both a safety net as well as spotters for early intervention before my mind is completely lost.

Time stood still, but my spirits were high. After a brief wait, a disgruntled mid- to later-aged woman—wearing a forehead wrinkled with discontent over the intake she had to do at one o'clock in the morning with an oppositional prick—sat down with me. I was condescending and sarcastic and did not consider the process in any serious or mature manner. The most ridiculous part was my disclosure—or, rather, my blatant medical perjury—that I had pertussis, which is commonly known as whooping cough, a highly contagious bacterial infection that causes an uncontrollable, violent cough that lasts several weeks or even months. I had experienced whooping cough about a year and a half prior. The fact that my mother and sister had come down with it the previous fall gave weight to the diagnosis when I informed the woman that "I may have gotten it from being in contact with them." A week prior, I lied of my whooping cough symptoms—to a University Health Services physician—which were entered into the medical system. Such an illness is of course disconcerting to a psychiatric staff on a communal unit where individuals are coming in contact with each other on a daily basis. The workers did not appear to believe that I was sick, but it was a good excuse to keep the potential contagion quarantined.

I do not recall getting settled in the hospital early that evening, but I probably slept, as there was nothing else to do. I fostered an affinity for one of the nurses, who appeared to get my sense of humor. Others were extremely displeased with my behavior and blatant disrespect for them. A major barrier— and I mean this literally—was the four surrounding walls of my room. I was not allowed to leave, because of the possibility that I did have pertussis and the imminent danger of an outbreak. After the first day or so, I admitted that my whooping-cough story was not true, but at that point, they needed a test result. I was not the boy who cried wolf; rather, I was a child inside the manic exterior of a wild canine. Consequently, the hospital staff forced my visitors to wear Michael Jackson-esque (RIP) surgical masks when they came to visit. Unfortunately, I was like an infant being dangled over the edge of a balcony (keeping with the Michael Jackson reference), because the fragility of my mental health was at risk of plummeting further at any moment. Visits were only allowed inside the doorway, so physical contact or affection was forbidden. I showed my drawings and other nonsensical workings in the hospital to my friends. For the first time, they were subjected to concrete evidence for the dualistic reality of my mind—a normally composed, organized individual who had become stricken with madness.

systolic = 162   11am 3/12/05
diastolic = 100

Bassakwards

Coffee black and one 1 egg white.
The devil in the blue dress serve me. an
an $e = mc^2$ early lunch. It has a link
to something that un diablo laughs @. The
symbol is an alligator, similar to the frat
by craze; i.e. polo shirt. Sausage was the
one thing my stomach did not like. Lids keep
you scarred for life, and trying something
for the first time, opens up new windows/
doors to fly through. Threw this learning 1 or 7
can reach their teen-spirit (Nirvana).

The changes in words with different spellings and the use of numbers for words were absolutely intentional (e.g., *four* versus *for*). I believed this style of writing was brilliant in some way. I can only surmise that the last part, stating "1 to 7," was related to a Likert scale, which is used for many different psychological measurements. The pictures follow along the lines of my obsessions as well as delusions surrounding numbers and also double meanings or exchanging phonetically alike words or symbols in language (e.g., English versus Spanish, letters versus numbers, etc.).

The middle section of the drawing below is a large picture of an eye with a dart going into it, which I traced from an actual dart. The eye is also a spaceship, and it is shooting rays into Wrigley Field (relating to a girl from

Chicago, Illinois, I was smitten with). The American flag elements and bizarre collage speak to a mixture of Andy Warhol and Van Gogh, only the work lacks artistic talent.

My ramblings and pictures developed during the isolation appeared, to me, to be colored with genius. This grandiosity as well as euphoria continued despite my compressed environment. I bragged to my friends that the hospital had given me a telephone to call for "room service" whenever I wanted. There was even a full menu. Milk shakes and scrambled eggs are two menu items that come to mind. This royal treatment was a harshly different reality from the elaborate cuisine I would soon enjoy in jail.

The hospital was a respite for me—or, more so, the overbrewed mania. In terms of the treatment of my mania, my hospital stay was actually counterproductive in a sense. The structure or constraint forced me to slow down, sleep, and eat, but there was not enough time to allow for stabilization, and there were no therapeutic interventions (e.g., group, family, or individual therapy). Ultimately, my batteries were recharged, because even though I accepted the medication, the stay was too brief to make a difference. The period in the hospital consisted of phone calls, drawing, coloring, and writing. I keep coming back to this theme—and will continue to do so in the upcoming chapters—but I strongly believe that a childlike behavior is awakened and expressed during both manic and depressive episodes. Does the brain regress developmentally? Is the capacity for cognitive processes limited due to the overwhelming stimulation in other parts of the brain during a manic episode? When one's cognitive processes seem so limited during depression, does one regress and interact in an immature or infantile way? The answers to these questions mystify me, but there is evident attention-seeking behavior during delusional and irrational periods of sickness on both ends of the pole.

There were also hours filled with flinging playing cards one by one out of a deck transversely from my bed to a basket on the floor. The nights were living nightmares. Feelings of entrapment, both physically and systematically, instigated paranoid thoughts and harsh reactions to the paraprofessionals and nurses. One night, I decided that a fork I had hidden would be a good tool to use in breaking open the narrow window in my room (I was on at least the third floor) in order to emancipate myself from the perceived prison (and possibly the world). For some reason, I still have the bent utensil that was to be my checkout key. In a way, the object is a metaphorical tool that always spears these memories. The utensil and other archives that have been filed in a box for years have become the talismans that magically summon the lucid memories that assemble this story.

I helplessly dug at the division of the foolproof windows while looking at the dark Madison sky and anticipating an intrusion to my plans by the staff. Someone inevitably caught me in the act, and my response was less than cordial. He or she moved me to a completely empty room next door (probably because I said something about hurting myself) with a suicide smock, a light blanket, and a thin mattress fit for a lenient dog. The floor was cold, and the vehement pounding of my fists on the door merely fevered the hostility in my mind. The poor nursing student (watch guard) had to listen to my onslaught of pejorative discourse. I cried that night. Wrapped in the blanket like an abandoned child, seconds felt like hours before the night swept me into a deep sleep.

The anger I felt was real, but anger is actually a mental and often behavioral response to a constellation of other feelings. If one imagines an iceberg floating out in the ocean, one can see that buoyancy permits it to float. From one's perspective above the water, the iceberg looks massive. However, the dark ocean actually confines approximately 90 percent of an iceberg's mass. As anger is a secondary emotion, people habitually mistake their feelings as solely anger, and their visible reactions (throwing things, yelling, swearing, making severe facial expressions, etc.) are comparable to the top of the iceberg. Recognition of the activity below the surface is the hard part. I was angry, but in reality (or my disconnection from it), there was an existential crisis occurring. I was feeling terrified and lost as well as abandoned, imprisoned, hopeless, sad, and completely powerless. The iceberg analogy is something I learned in graduate school, and I frequently use it in my practice as a psychotherapist. My dry-erase board often has an adolescent depiction of an iceberg that aims to dispel the misunderstanding. Anger manifests from a constellation of feelings (the part of the iceberg below the water); it is not a feeling independent of others (with global warming, the metaphor might soon have to change). My immobilized state in the hospital would soon be altered. Drifting out to sea was my desire, but my head would not stay above water for much longer.

—18—

VOICE OF REASON

The statistics from the thirty writers and their families, compared with the thirty controls and their families, are quite amazing. Thirteen percent of the writers were bipolar I, 30% were bipolar II, and 37% suffered from major depression. Thirty percent also suffered from alcoholism.

—Nancy C. Andreasen, *Brave New Brain: Conquering Mental Illness in the Era of the Genome*

After three or four days and a pertussis test with a negative result, a jury of doctors, nurses, and administrative faculty assembled to meet with me to review my problem as well as any improvement and to collectively perform a present-day assessment. I knew that if my appearance was anywhere near insane, my chances of being released under my own volition would be slim. The content of that meeting escapes me, but just prior to entering the room, I said to myself, *Talk slowly, and be calm*. Essentially, I was preparing to lie. This behavior escaped the boundaries of morality because I felt persecuted and needed out. I know now what it must be like to enter a parole hearing. It was my day of reckoning. The meeting took place in a large room with a chair close to the door (meticulously placed there for me). There was sunlight streaming in from the large windows on the adjacent wall, and a blurry cast of white coats with spotlight eyes pointed at me as the inquisition began. My memory is of a group of faceless authoritarian shapes with glowing halos from the bright sunshine. This was just one more entity I was about to fight, and losing was not an option.

After the conference and their assumed deliberation, they agreed upon a discharge, as I was not a threat to myself or others. This decision partially included my adamant argument against an extension of the visit. My parents picked me up, and I was as happy as could be. This was the first time I had seen them since our falling-out a month prior. Our first stop was State Street, which was crowded with a diverse assembly of individuals. On the weekends, State Street was the place to be for consumerism, particularly at any of the thirty coffee places. Students walked with their heads down as they sent important text messages through the eyes of expensive sunglasses. State Street, which stretches four to five blocks, is filled with local businesses, plenty of bars, and the unfortunate impact of globalization. I needed to get cigarettes and then show my parents the student union. *Nothing is wrong, and isn't it great that I am out of the hospital?* This was the depth of introspection I must have had at the time. I was carefree despite everything falling apart around me. My parents had only been to Madison briefly one time before, so I figured this was as good a chance as ever for them to become slightly acclimated.

At the student union, I set up shop just outside the opening to the Rathskeller, a common area for students to congregate. It includes a bar and an amazing view of the expansive Lake Mendota landscape. At that point in time, the lake was covered by a thick sheet of ice. I was there not to enjoy the food and beverages but to share some information on my ISP work as well as some other random books, including one I had written around the age of twelve.

It was a tale of a young penguin leaving his mother to go on an existential journey and follow his dreams. In the story, the main character, Pete, has a desire to fly like other birds despite his biological limitations. After consulting with his mother, he embarks on a mission to discover how to fly.

Ultimately, after encounters with a variety of diverse arctic animals, he discovers through a dream that he is not limited in life because he cannot fly. Rather than flying in the air, he realizes he was meant to *fly* below the water's surface. Actually, I am pretty impressed with my accomplished literary work from grade school, but seeking publishers at this point is not on my agenda. At the time (March of 2005), a Pulitzer Prize did not appear out of the scope of reality in my delusional world. Unfortunately, the book sustained some water damage, as I carried the book around everywhere I went. On the topic of writing, Jonah Lehrer spoke with National Public Radio (NPR) in March of 2012 about creativity and his book *Imagine: How Creativity Works*. The author reported that "people who are successful creators—especially writers—are anywhere between 8 and 40 times more likely to suffer from bipolar depression than the general public." He goes on to say that ideas "pour out of you" during the manic episodes and that the period of productivity is then "followed by this dismal low period when maybe you're a better editor." His suggestion is that the depression and manic symptoms tend to mimic the natural swings of the creative process. Fortunately for my childhood self, the penguin book represents the creative process (i.e., a question, a subsequent struggle, a pause, and a moment of insight) rather than psychopathology.

Once my parents reached a tolerance threshold, they went to their hotel to get settled in. I met up with my roommate, who was bartending at the student union, and also saw a friend I knew. I did not participate in the midday drinking, but I probably would have benefitted from it as a temporary tranquilizer. Instead, I committed a maniacal antic in which I threw my cell phone at the outside brick wall of the Memorial Union as a joke to impress people. The friends who were with me appeared to think it was funny at the time. (Sidenote: Days later, in a delusional state, I purposely dropped the phone into an ice-fishing hole enclosed by an icehouse built by the engineering students at the university. At the time, I thought that the phone would someday be discovered in some sort of archeological dig and that because it was so important, well, who knows?). Interestingly, the phone's digital screen was shattered from the impact of hitting the brick wall, but phone calls still came in. As the microphone was broken, the caller could not hear me, but as with everything else, this was my reaction: *No big deal.* My friends were less enthusiastic about me throwing the phone and alerted my roommate. His appropriate, visceral reaction was a strained "What the fuck are you doing?" I did not believe his remarks of concern were channeled from the other friends, and I stated that they were having a good time with me and had exhibited no concern. This incident further strained the relationship between me and my friend with whom I shared a room in the apartment.

My parents shacked up at the Campus Inn, but I refused to stay with them. I ran into an old friend (former roommate from the days of South Padre Island) on State Street later that day, and he quickly became troubled by my behavior. My parents, my friend, and I went to dinner at Chipotle that night, where I acted out the letter I had sent to my parents a month prior, but from a new character's perspective. This time around, it was antagonistic and suggestive of an abusive, alcohol-addicted parent speaking to the family. The rebellion was met with lowered eyes. I let them know how I felt about their parenting style, their religious beliefs, and whatever else was on my mind. With unbridled, pure inhibition, I practically spoke through a bullhorn as I vilified their very existence. My mother did not last long before leaving the restaurant. It is not clear how much she cried as a result of what I had said versus what she had witnessed. The transformation would have shaken anyone. In my mind, the event was at one table inside Chipotle. This egocentrism is an accurate representation of how I was feeling. I did not give a shit if my parents were embarrassed (let alone my poor friend who was dragged into the situation), and I refused to lower my voice despite the confused patrons around us. The same voice that was causing such chaos was beginning to wear itself out. The incessant talking eventually took its toll on my vocal cords.

The manager of my former employer, White Horse Inn, was not thrilled or compassionate about my supposed laryngitis when I stopped over to get my schedule. I quit and proceeded to the schedule posting in order to pin my own propaganda to the board: Innovated Student Psychology (ISP) information. That night, my parents invited me back to the hotel despite my blatant resistance to their accommodations. When my parents phoned an on-call psychiatrist, my friend acted as an intermediary for me to communicate with the individual. I had indeed started to lose my voice from smoking and talking, so I wrote down my thoughts on a piece of paper, and he relayed the information to the psychiatrist. I have no idea what the content of that discussion was other than that the rational psychiatrist made a valid attempt to get me to take some medication. His recommendation was for me to take some amount of Seroquel in order to sleep. I informed my parents that I would take the medication when I got home; they of course suggested that I take it immediately. That was when I began to feel the power being taken away from me. The room was getting smaller. My friend and mother stood in front of the door, and my father was sitting near me on one of the beds in the small hotel room. They pleaded with me to take the medication, but I resisted. When I asked to leave, they refused to let me. It did not take long for me to decide to call security. I called security several times, stating that they were preventing me from leaving the hotel room. *It's time to make a move.* Now, one must understand the strength and tenacity of me at that moment while filled with extreme agitation. I was a wild beast that had metabolized the sedation from a tranquilizer and was now awaiting the opening of the cage door that prohibited its freedom. Despite my friend's six-foot-three-inch frame and my short-statured yet tough-ass mother, my 150-some-pound body turned into the Incredible Hulk. I managed to penetrate the barricade, run down the many flights of stairs, and exit the hotel. To prove a point, I popped a pill or two of Seroquel as if to say, "See? I'll take them when I want to." My friend walked the lengthy distance back to my apartment with me, as I recall. He attempted to reconcile my actions, figure out what was happening with me, and make a breakthrough connection, but certainly to no avail.

A female friend of mine who had been involved in helping with this disaster of events came to my apartment that evening. In almost a maternal way, she allowed me to lie on her lap like the sad toddler I had become while she stroked my hair as I fearfully fell into a heavy slumber. Sleep was good, because at that point, my mind could have used hibernation. Instead, I slept around a dozen hours that night and awoke in time to go to the same friend's dance competition. My parents' objections went unheard as I insisted that I would drive their car to Sun Prairie, Wisconsin, which was a twenty-five-minute journey, in order to attend the event. During the drive, at one point in my never-ending monologue, I remarked that at any moment we could die or something to that effect. I slowly tilted the wheel to the right, let go with my hand, and gave the steering wheel consent to drift in the direction of the parked cars on the side of the road. The smooth Monte Carlo was probably pushing forty miles per hour before I jerked the wheel back to the center of the lane. My roommate, mother, and father were not impressed. Allowing me to drive was like giving the controls of a roller coaster to a five-year-old. Actually, that's not true at all. I knew how to drive; it was a matter of whether I wanted to do something crazy. Despite my confidence in direction and navigation, I got the group lost, and we missed watching her team's performance.

—19—

MINNESOTA NICE

The desperate attempt to escape loneliness at all costs can lead us into unsatisfying and even dangerous relationships, yet it is a sign that we have this sanity hidden within us.

—Karen Kissel Wegela, *How to Be a Help Instead of a Nuisance*

4/2/05: This was both marvelous and frightening to me. For those who do not know, visual hallucinations, unlike the consequence of potent mushrooms on a sunny day, are not a good sign with mania. This might have been "rock bottom," terminal cognitive velocity— or, to put it simply, I had reached the crazy-as-fuck status.

My parents were able to convince me to go back to Minnesota with them that day, and I recall sleeping most of the car ride. This respite was the equivalent of plugging in your phone for twenty minutes; the phone does not get a full charge but gets enough of a charge to keep it running. That year, the University of Wisconsin–Madison spring break, which was in the middle of March in 2005, happened to fall on the week of my temporary retreat in Minnesota. Even though I was not on South Padre Island or in Panama City, Florida, chaos ensued. As usual, when I returned home, congregating with old friends was the norm. This assured several things: there would be a lot of going out to bars, not a lot of sleeping, and a fair amount of drinking.

My parents actively discouraged the prospect of me staying with a friend for the week, so in an act of rebelliousness, I impulsively buzzed all but the center strip of my hair (i.e., I gave myself a Mohawk). The hair was very short, so the style could have been considered more of the European "fohawk." My mother saw this act as the least of the problems occurring. "It's just a haircut," she said to my overheated father. She calmly evened out the strip in the center with scissors per my request. She had cut my hair a hundred times before throughout my childhood and into adulthood while maintaining fidelity to the redundant and conservatively short style of haircut. There I was, back in the same chair of my mother's preferred domain—the middle-class, suburbanized kitchen. My father had a different reaction altogether. He was in a rage due to a sheer loss of control. He was seeing just one more reflection of how unbalanced I had become as well as feeling an internalized guilt over his seeming proliferation of the illness. The first of his progeny to be diagnosed with the lifelong disorder had lost touch with reality.

An altercation suddenly arose. My dad was yelling as I was provoking him, and a thought crossed my mind that he might physically injure me. He threatened to throw me through the window (as we were now standing in the dining room, adjacent to the kitchen), but I did not back down to the man, who was six inches taller as well as sixty pounds heavier. Instead, I exited the home for the day. There is some evidence (mostly anecdotal) that when an individual is experiencing manic symptoms and is proximal to another individual with bipolar disorder, the latter person often begins to have symptoms of his or her own (i.e., my father began to experience low levels of mania because of my anxiety-provoking behavior). The suggestion is that this heightened mood can somehow trigger the other person's state of mind. It makes sense if you consider it in the same framework as a depressed roommate's effect on others in the house. For my father and me, the saying could be "You're really bringin' me *up*" as opposed to *down*. I imagine the phenomenon is also analogous to the way social networks guide or steer each individual within the group—for example, when females who live together begin to synchronize their ovulatory cycles within roughly three menstrual cycles (known as the Wellesley effect). It is not implausible to connect the augmentation of my pheromones during the cellular events occurring throughout the manic phase to communication of my feelings and moods with my father (you can do an online search of "Pheromone Signals Transduction in Vomeronasal Neurons" for more information).

I did return home eventually, and there were some less-than-exciting moments. I went to lunch with family and some friends, but the trip to my father's office sticks out in my mind. The office visit was based on some belief that I could participate in gainful employment—and it was a way for my father to keep an eye on me. Also, my brother was teaming up with my father in the real estate business, sharing an office with him, so I could spend some time with my brother as well. My selling point was that I was bilingual, despite a limited capability to converse in Spanish. These newly acquired foreign-language skills were just some of the parts inside my vehicle of grandiosity and misperceptions. There were a growing number of individuals of Latino descent moving to the South Minneapolis area, and I believed that I could somehow act as a translator or someone understanding of their culture. My father and brother offered little encouragement on this idea, so why not take it to my dad's boss? I actually knew the man fairly well from my years of playing softball on the company's team and from doing work for my father in the office. My entrance was eloquent. I barged into his large wood-grain-filled office, interrupting his meeting, in order to discuss my proposition. Bear in mind, I was dressed informally and had visible tattoos and a new haircut, and he did not initially recognize who I was. Needless to say, there were no official contracts signed that day, and I imagine my father later had some explaining to do.

An old basketball teammate and friend whom I had not connected with in some time purchased a house down the street from my parents' place, so I stopped over to visit him early that week. Later that same night, I went to various friends' houses. Staying in one spot was not an option. I recall my friend stopping at the liquor store with me. I purchased a bottle of Seagram's 7 with a Sprite chaser—a proper drink for a gathering, I thought. After spending a brief time at one friend's house, I let the friends I was with know that I was heading to the prodigious Mall of America to meet this old basketball friend as well as a small group of people from my high school. The friends I was with, cognizant to some degree of how sick I was, did not want me to leave. After a long discussion and a hit of pot, away I went in a taxi. Marijuana and other stimulants do not have a calming effect on the manic mind. For me, smoking pot was akin to an average person doing a line of cocaine or taking some methamphetamines.

Upon arrival at the gluttonous American feed bucket that is the Mall of America, by chance, I ran into some friends I knew who had been in Panama City at the same time I had years prior. This was just the way the universe was working for me; constant connections coincided with the prescience I thought I had about this extraordinarily positive outlook on the world. The "nothing could go wrong" mentality was a strong component of my euphoric yet volatile mood. I often just ran into people I knew. The socialization fed an appetite that was an ever-consuming beast. I went everywhere I could on my own, because fear did not exist. The actions and events of my life were puzzle pieces that always seemed to fit together in my mind. I was earnest with my desires, and introspection was not an existing trait; I made decisions at rapid speeds.

The friends I encountered at the mall that day appeared to think I was drunk based on my uninhibited presentation. The ambiance and aesthetic beauty of the mall (now I am really laying on the sarcasm) were not enough, so my friends decided to enjoy some watered-down beers at the family establishment known as Hooters. I was not prejudiced or judgmental toward this activity, so I decided to enjoy a cold one, which is interesting because my drinking had deescalated at that point. Think about it: if you feel absolutely amazing, with unlimited energy and without fear, an offer of alcohol is like an offer of a hammock. I was swinging in a cocoon-like shell of unadulterated mania, but it was no form of relaxation.

I left my phone number and probably a bizarre new impression with the guys at Hooters and made my way over to a sports bar to find the friends I had initially planned on meeting. I was at least two hours late, meaning they had all been drinking in a steadfast manner during that time. With a disposable camera in hand (don't ask—it was 2005), I snapped a small number of worthless pictures. The reception from these characters whom I had not seen in years was warm but reeked of Miller Lite as well as cigarette-scented clothes. Immediately, I set my eyes on a girl carrying an innocent smile and a soft, persistent gaze sent from classically picturesque (especially for a disposable camera) and relaxed dark-colored eyes. She was a crush of mine from high school. Finding women was my common dominator at all times, but it came much more naturally with inflated self-esteem. Fear is overridden by ultimate confidence, and self-gratification immediately comes to the forefront of mania. Soon we would just be two kids playing in the sandbox.

As it was getting late, we all went back to the basketball friend's new house down the street from my family. It was high school all over again, except there was a flat screen hanging on the wall and a limited chance of parents coming home to break up the party. Not only was I smoking at an alarming rate during this period in time, but I even decided to take a little dip from an acquaintance's Copenhagen tin. At one point I had tobacco in my lip, I had a cigarette in my mouth, and I even had some Nicorette gum in my pocket that I had received in the hospital (it probably has some cancer-causing agents as well). I was armed. We stayed up all night. Well, I did, but most did not finally pass out until the sun was coming up. As Hunter S. Thompson said, "No sleep for the devil." I was not yet demonized, but I had too much stuff to do to waste my life sleeping.

The next night, I found myself congregating with the same group of people at the Annex bar, a dungeonesque nightclub and bar in downtown Minneapolis. One of the bartenders (not a woman you take home to Mom) struck me, and in a cautious but straightforward manner, I attempted to flirt with her. This forward approach was not something I had mastered without the aid of mania in the past. In a flash of brilliance, I slid my empty vodka-and-tonic glass to her with my father's business card as a makeshift coaster. My cell phone number was on the back, along with what I can imagine was a ridiculous comment on it. I turned around for a couple minutes but then came back to the scene for a full investigation. I was fixated and determined. This behavior of attempting to pick up women in a bar was completely unusual for me. I met women through friends and introductions from others. Aside from the occasional flirtatious gesture, bartenders who were *informally* dressed with sadomasochistic outfits that included skirts leaving nothing to the imagination were off-limits in my usual mind. Apparently, my arrogant new persona was intriguing to this individual, and she said that contact would be made. After the thirty-minute drive home, I received a call from a foreign number. It was the bartender, and I was elated. She instructed me to meet her the following night, as I was nowhere near downtown Minneapolis and she would be bartending until late into the night. Let the decadence continue.

If I knew what happened during those days, I would surely write about them, but instead I will just stick to the familiar and somewhat lucid accounts that relate to my disorder. As was my tradition, I had to continue to try to meet with "all of my friends" when returning back home. The following night, a large group of friends from high school—we will say "high school" to simplify things—went to a party near downtown Minneapolis. I was not thinking about anything except for convincing at least one person to go to the Annex that night to see the bartender. My increase in goal-directed activity (in this case, finding the bartender—a goal within a sexual and social domain) met another symptom in line with the criteria for mania. The anxiety in the form of obsessing only differed in this case from the negative, ruminating thoughts that contain one's depression in that the perception was positive in nature.

The large group made its way to a bar named Grandma's near the University of Minnesota campus. I mostly drank Sprite but did have a few beers (they were a dollar each and handed out from packed serving trays), knowing it would be a long night. My friends were concerned, but I do not believe anyone knew how to handle my situation. My mania was the anxious elephant in the room. Eventually, the inhibitions of one of my friends was lowered or saturated to my level from his alcohol intake, and I was able to convince him to take a cab with me to the Annex despite the passive resistance and discouragement that his girlfriend openly exhibited.

The bartender was there, and I immediately grew jealous of the incessant flirtations she received from other men. I was still confident of a positive outcome in my persistent endeavors to seize this woman. My friend and I eventually went back to the house we had originally started from that night. The residents were sleeping, but the synaptic lights in my head were still flickering. I was waiting for the call that the bartender had promised after her shift. I knew the call would not come until almost four in the morning, so I mixed a drink, popped in the film *Heat* (obsessions and emulations of this movie come later in the story), and eventually decided to drink some caffeine. *Don't fall asleep.*

She and a friend arrived in a full-size red pickup truck. We drove to her place and entered a party on the first level of the apartment complex with a small group of her friends. I did not have much interaction with her, but I quickly made friends with the cannabis being passed around as well as with the providers. This was supplemented by some "Bud Heavy" as I referred to it (Budweiser). After an hour or so, she escorted me upstairs to her room and showed me a picture of her ex-girlfriend, and I tried to make sense of this discordant realization. In much the same way the Dude examined the ransom note in the film *The Big Lebowski*, with much positivity, I thought, *Fuckin' A.*

I recall the vertical tattoo of the seven deadly sins written in Chinese characters down her spine. With a salacious grin, she whispered, "You're not gonna get much sleep tonight." I didn't, and for whatever reason, we were up way too early in order to catch breakfast. I do not remember a word that was said, but I do recollect her intently listening to me talk straight through the dining experience. I had eggs for breakfast despite a known digestive intolerance to the food. My disregard for allergies in general extended to cats. For several nights, I stayed at a friend's place that housed a pair of domesticated felines, despite my legitimate allergy. The mind is a powerful thing, and mine was quickly being wasted. That incident was the last I saw of the bartender until I ran into her in downtown Minneapolis about six months later and manic free. All the courage I had was to point from a distance and whisper to my friend, "That's the bartender I hooked up with."

I am not proud of many of these stories or the ones that followed a similar narrative during the week at home, so it is not important for me to produce documentation. The articulation of these events in Minneapolis is in order to suggest that it was one thing for me to be drinking heavily and falling into a night of debauchery with someone, but it was another to be a sober, hypersexual being that was out of control and, from anyone else's perspective, living in an inconsequential fantasy. The progression of the episode had gotten to the point where my unpredictable nature had become so insatiable that I would allow no one to get in my way.

—20—

Parental Control

To maintain a joyful family requires much from both the parents and the children. Each member of the family has to become, in a special way, the servant of the others.

—Pope John Paul II

As my parents were far from the point of tolerance with my behavior, it is no surprise that my mother came running outside in the March chill in 2005 to stop me from taking my father's truck at six in the morning. As she was unsuccessful, I headed toward a gas station, but her threat of calling the police discouraged this decision. Instead, I drove only a few blocks away and considered sleeping in the vehicle for a while. This thought lasted as long as a consideration to go to the bathroom before going to bed. I was afraid that the police would find me, so back to the house I went. Pulling up to the driveway to see a squad car in front of the house produced a feeling foreign to the manic mind—distress. *Be calm. Tell them you just went to the gas station for cigarettes and hope they do not ask for a receipt.* The police officer did very little and instructed me to not do any more driving. I was extremely manipulative and could act aloof when the moment depended on it. This immature behavior was reminiscent of a teenager stealing the parents' car when they were out of town. It was risk taking with seemingly little gain except the potential for someone's notice or acceptance of these childish expressions. I feel a large amount of guilt and responsibility for this on my part, because I still cannot believe that my defiant actions took place, especially those directed at the people I cared about so much.

When the police officer drove off, I made the decision to leave for good, and my father was not going to stop me. His frustration, anger, and feeling of a loss of any kind of control were all warranted. I woke up my frightened and tearful sister and informed her of my departure as well as the possibility of my never seeing her again—a pretty heavy statement to put on a sixteen-year-old. My little brother could not have cared less about my exodus after witnessing the chaos I had created. Things were very different from our Ping-Pong days, and he had become witness to a cinematic disaster that was shredding the film of normalcy our family had once had.

I walked to a gas station fewer than two miles away and, for whatever reason, spent a long time talking with the Kennedy High School (my former school) student running the register. We discussed my ISP group as well as drugs and how I could acquire those drugs from him. The crush from high school eventually picked me up. She had taken me in and rescued me from the subconscious fear that my aloneness late at night would bring. I stayed at her place, and she was extremely generous as well as genuinely concerned for my well-being. We smoked cigarettes in her car, and I purchased milk shakes for us from Denny's on at least one occasion—not an abnormal behavior for me. I was living the American dream—or just a dream.

Spring break came to an end on March 20, 2005, and I elected to take the Badger Bus back to Madison, Wisconsin. My parents unquestionably disagreed with me going back, but I am sure they were sick of watching me destroy myself. Their prayers in the adoration basket at church were not reaching a power that could bring me to my proper senses. Adoration is a form of giving worship to God by entering the names of individuals into a container that is kept vigil twenty-four hours a day while participants come to send loving prayers. Divine intervention, a straitjacket, and a handful of antipsychotics were needed to extinguish the wild fire that was my madness. Taking the bus was an impulsive choice, of course, made at the last minute. My dad agreed to drive me to where the bus picked up students in a neighboring suburb, and for some reason, our interaction in the car was good-natured. We stopped at Walgreens to get me cigarettes and snacks. I convinced my father to smoke a cigarette with me and, of all places, inside his pristine Monte Carlo. He was a former smoker and admitted to me that occasionally, when he was feeling "revved up," he would secretly have a cigarette to calm down. I can still picture him smoking that Marlboro Light with one arm out the window as if the '70s had never left him. Despite my state of mind, this bonding moment with him, in a peculiar way, temporally reenlisted our father–son connection that the recent estrangement had severed. Upon our extremely late arrival to the hub, we had to plead with the bus driver in order for me to get on the bus. To my astonishment, I was able to occupy the lone empty seat, which just happened to be next to an attractive blonde girl. The conversation flowed. By that, I mean my pressured speech was a vocalized version of the archaic writing style *scriptio continua*:

Themindwasmovingatsuchapacethatitcouldnotseparatethoughtsastheycamepouringout.

Four hours later, she invited me to her place and promised to cook me dinner. She was tipped off by phone during the ride by a member of my high school who knew I would potentially be on the bus. It was a coincidence that I happened to sit next to her, as there were several buses going to Madison from that location. To me, this was no coincidence, as my mind was constantly synthesizing the random with the "meant to be."

—21—

MEDICATING BY YOURSELF

People with mania eventually develop insight about the destructive effects of manic episodes.

—Nancy C. Andreasen, *Brave New Brain: Conquering Mental Illness in the Era of the Genome*

I returned to Madison with yet another girl whom I was sure to take refuge with. This girl from the bus had offered to cook me dinner that night, so I went to her apartment, showered, and ate something before attending the local bar scene. After she helped me get hot water in the shower (those dials are tough, but I was convinced the hot water did not work) and we ate dinner, to the bar we went. I was now relying on others for money to buy drinks, but my alcohol consumption was still diminished. With exuding confidence, a mind-set that nothing could go wrong, magical thinking, and the absence of fear, who needed alcohol? This is the temptation of mania that some never get past in the course of their illness, also known as "the highs." It can lure individuals off their medication and back to the euphoria that the mental state bestows.

We went back to her place, but fear and paranoia crept inside the door. *Am I supposed to hook up with her?* I was not really attracted to her, but in order to stay over, I was curious if that was what she wanted. It felt as if she were locking me in; I feared that she was "onto me" or that she was suspicious of my condition. I ran out of her apartment as she pleaded for me to stay. Off to the library I went. Apparently I had some work to do.

I met an individual there who was naive to my condition. He also shared my father's name and a vague physical resemblance. Imagine what that does to the manic mind. He listened to my maniacal discourse and appeared to hold a high reverence for me. The individual was struggling in graduate school, and with my frenetic persuasions, he blew off his late-night undertakings. We went various places in his car, and he helped me out with money. Eventually, I went to my friends' apartment where my belongings were in downtown Madison. I never made it home after the bus ride. These friends knew of the severity that the mania had taken, and since my actual roommates would not stand for any more of my antics (e.g., smoking inside the apartment, staying up all night, having random people over, etc.), I took refuge with them downtown. This was the same apartment where the police would soon be called on the morning of my arrest.

A lot of bizarre events went on that week, many of which I do not recall. If I gathered all of my friends whom I contacted with wild ideas on the phone as well as close friends who actually witnessed the events, I am sure I could add about fifty pages to this section. The reality is that I remember very little up until the night before going to jail. I continued to go out to bars and parties as sleep went from a minimal amount or an occasional activity to a nonoption. I do know that I made many library trips during midterms and ran into people I knew. Conversations usually surrounded what evolved into a pyramid scheme for the Innovated Student Psychology student organization. There was a deeply rooted conviction in my mind that members of the group would propagate across the country, and with a minimal charge, I felt ISP could be a lucrative enterprise.

One evening, I left College Library and got on one of the many buses on campus, smoking a cigarette. Students as well as the bus driver were not exactly tolerant of this activity. The doors opened before my stop. I have never been a full-time smoker but would socially partake in college, which usually meant that as the drinks increased, the cigarettes followed suit. By the end of March of 2005, I was living off of these cancerous agents. Nicotine was the only drug I was taking regularly. It, of course, does not have the mood-stabilizing properties of lithium or other psychotropic medications. My smoking was partially induced by my longtime perception of the activity as a rebellious or rock-star activity. I was the child emulating the deified movie stars who are all too influential. If I had not been manic, at the very least I would have been secretive about the habit. As the going out continued and the nights got later, I witnessed more serious drug use.

I saw pills being snorted frequently, including antidepressants and Adderall. At an after-party one night with a large group of people (filled with unfamiliar, perspiring faces), a mirror was passed around with a trail of white powder that inevitably leads to the pleasure center of the brain. An invitation to another flood of dopamine sat before me. I watched as the mirror was passed around. My heart pounded much like it does when you go around the circle for introductions, just waiting for your turn in an untried group. Thankfully, this was the first and last time I would see cocaine. It was a high-stakes game of poker, and I folded. Instead, I grabbed the lesser of two evils: a large dragon sculpture shaped and carved into a pipe. Marijuana was not good for me, but it might have saved my life. Who knows how high the coke would have taken me.

—22—

CHAPTER 51

The great enemy of the truth is very often not the lie—
deliberate, contrived and dishonest—but the myth—
persistent, persuasive and unrealistic.

—John F. Kennedy

3/30/05 9:31:06 a.m. ID#218492: Being booked in jail must
be comparable to a dog's feelings while being brought to the
veterinarian. Fear and resistance are dragged into a windowless
basement of concrete order. Cooperation is futile when dealing
with a manic mind, so the officers must cage the beast. A locked
wire door allowed me to bark at the enforcers, but the interwoven
holes did not set my insanity free from this holding pen.

At some point during the lengthy manic rampage, I came across a sign at the
Comedy Club on State Street for an amateur night of stand-up. My lack of
any kind of professional comedic experience did not detract me from this
opportunity (although I did go as Jerry Seinfeld for Halloween one year with
a memorized act). In an attempt to separate myself from the other contend-
ers, I left my voice-mail message completely in Spanish. I cannot recall what

I said on the phone message—I called well before business hours—but I did get a voice-mail message back. I am not sure why I did not return this person's call, but I did text all of my friends, telling them to attend the show. This was, of course, the show that I was never invited to perform at. My act was simple, and all of it was in my mind, with nothing on paper. I would go back and forth between a Freudian-like psychotherapist and a manic patient. With an ironic tone, I would say that this was a slight projection and mildly fitting under the circumstances. I inquired about performing when I entered the venue, but the organizers said the event was booked with performances for the night. However, I got lucky. One guy said if there was time at the end, maybe I could go on for twenty minutes. I might have been experiencing the extremes of mania, but I was still nervous. I grabbed a stool and bellied up to the bar next to an attractive girl as I ordered a 7UP. For attention, I methodically placed all of my cigarettes (about fifteen or so) in a line on the bar, along with the other random things from my pocket. This was in anticipation of being noticed as a weird, funny guy. Instead, I am sure I came across as utterly creepy.

Understandably, none of my friends appeared that night at the Comedy Club for my "big break" (which I thought would eventually lead me to a tour in California), and it did not take long for me to leave. I would return days later to this location for one of the most unusual and scary moments of my life, when I was ripe with delusional psychosis.

If not long before, it was now apparent to everyone who knew me that I needed serious help, but no one knew what to do. In Wisconsin, there is a state statute that is informally known as a Chapter 51. This is Wisconsin's law for involuntary commitment to mental health treatment, and it has a number of criteria that need to be met in order for someone to go to a hospital, psychiatric unit, or mental institution against his or her will. A person is considered a subject for 51.15 and 51.20 under the Wisconsin statute if he or she

1. is mentally ill, drug dependent, or developmentally disabled;
2. exhibits a substantial probability of physical harm to him- or herself or others, evidenced by recent acts or omissions, attempts, or threats; and
3. is a proper subject for treatment.

Basically, anyone can create a three-party petition, including family members, the police, mental health workers, or friends who are concerned about the individual's safety or danger to others. The petition is then brought to a judge, who makes a decision based on testimonials as to whether there is evidence for the person to be involuntarily admitted. Usually, the police find the individual and bring him or her to the proper institution. Unfortunately, in my case, I knew these laws, and I was just organized enough to not meet the criteria (I had not threatened harm to myself or others). And even if a petition had been made, it would have been dismissed because of unsubstantiated evidence by the court system. These laws vary slightly from state to state, but the process and results are similar. Deeper into the law, it was certainly true that there was perceived evidence of "impaired judgment, manifested by evidence of a pattern of recent acts or omissions" and "substantial probability of physical impairment or injury to himself/herself." However, the court system is concrete and often leaves others' perceptions out of the picture. These laws are problematic because they are weighted in the direction of the liberties of the potentially sick individual. However, some of these liberties work against the individual in that they end up destroying the person's life under the umbrella of freedom. In that sense, friends and families are left with few options.

Who knows? Had I been committed based on a Chapter 51, it is possible that I would have returned to a hospital. My resistance toward medication probably would have continued. My resistance would have been enabled by the system, because involuntary treatment in Wisconsin (as of 2005) did not permit medication administration against a person's will. Ted Kaczynski, or the Unabomber, is a perfect example of someone who has a severe and persistent mental illness who sits in prison refusing to take medication for paranoid schizophrenia. I listened to his brother, David Kaczynski (who alerted authorities to Ted's possible involvement in the killings), speak about his brother. He stated that his brother told him that he would rather plead not guilty and go to prison than to say that he was insane. Ted Kaczynski is an intelligent man who graduated from an Ivy League school, so despite the severity of his illness, the judicial process as well as the correctional system allows him the choice to imprison his body, which includes his mind. Where is the cognitive behavioral therapy or motivational interviewing? Give me a chance with that guy. The lecture had a profound impact on me in 2006. Afterward, I contemplated what, if anything, could have been done differently in 2005. I ended up in jail during the spring of 2005, but fortunately, I did not send any explosive letters or hurt myself. My alarming and defiant act was what eventually extinguished my liberty.

If this section seems disconnected or all over the place, then I am realistically setting the scene for what happened. It should also exhibit a reflection of how my mind is currently functioning in order to piece this picture together in a somewhat cohesive, linear manner. The last several days in March of 2005, before I was institutionalized, are so disconnected in my memory that they have become analogous to a tackboard of one hundred photographs in collage form. These pictures in my mind cover the duration of only a week, but a mixture of mania and the five-year lapse in time puts a strain on the organizational accuracy. I am attempting to convey the story (memories or events) in chronological order, and one of the aids to this process or adjunct to the long-term memory is a miscellaneous collection of items from two separate years. Amid the personal files at home (e.g., banking information, insurance records, leases, etc.), there are two simple files that unlock the madness I have suffered. One is labeled "Manic 2002," and the other is "Manic 2005." I never had a conscious reason for saving these documents, but it is now abundantly clear. The examination of an item as simple as a metal fork from the psychiatric hospital stay or an exotic drawing created in jail elicits a flurry of memories that can both seize my attention and amplify my heart rate. The recollections that I must retrieve through less-tangible means are more difficult. In addition, I face a struggle of choosing what someone might actually want to read in this book as opposed to the sole significance an event has for me—staying up all night and going to "Smut-N-Eggs" (Bennett's), which serves breakfast with a side of twenty-four-hour pornography; buying a carton of the cheapest cigarettes; suffering delusions related to the new quarters as well as money in general, etc. Therefore, if this is not completely coherent or historically accurate, I apologize. The actual images in my mind are not stored in a filing cabinet of perfected organization. These are not simply snapshots and videos of a time that could be forgotten. Instead, they are the sum of the parts that I hold in order to remember my ability to persevere as well as have a sense of compassion for what I have been through.

An unpleasant asylum was soon to come; I was about to be incarcerated. This would turn out to be the most terrifying encounter of my life, and I do not wish it upon another human being. When you are in such a situation, the enforced pain transports through your idle body with a paralytic wave that pushes against the very walls that contain the hopelessness. The experience can be likened to a torturous burn that, left untreated, can result in lifetime scars. Now owning that emotional anguish, I can empathize with those in present-day detainment.

—23—

Snake Handling

It's like you said. All I am is what I'm goin' after.

—Al Pacino, *Heat*

April 2005: *I do not relate this directly to psychosis, but rather an adaptation in order to survive the unadulterated insanity that imprisonment assures.*

On the last day before going to jail, I remember having a conversation with a friend and explaining that I did not need my glasses—or contact lenses, for that matter—despite a nearsighted astigmatism diagnosed eight years prior. During this ridiculous exchange, in one motion, I took my rather new and expensive glasses off of my face, placed them on the floor next to me, stood up, and emphatically smashed the spectacles with my foot. His verbal and facial expressions were along the lines of "Andy, what the hell are you doing?" I told him and his roommate that I could go a day without glasses and that it did not matter. They stated they were heading to State Street and wore body language spelling out that they were exhausted with me. If you asked most people, there would be a consensus that someone going through a manic episode can be difficult to be around. Incessant talking that dominates all conversations, immeasurable energy, and the flight of ideas wear down the individual or individuals subjected to the behaviors. I followed not far behind them and ended up at the trendy retail store Urban Outfitters. I know, I know—the prices of the merchandise are *insane*. After they left, I decided to try on a belt, tie, and leather wristband. I removed the price tag on the leather band and wore it to the register. I paid for the tie as well as the belt with my credit card, all while wearing the stolen band. It was almost as if I wanted to be caught, based on this petty crime as well as the events later on in the day. The high from shoplifting was just one of hundreds that fed the burning fire of mania.

Later that evening, I wandered back to my apartment. I wore the new tie and belt as well as some outlandish collaboration of clothing items. My fashion sense grew increasingly abnormal as the episode prolonged. While at the apartment, I gathered all the coins I had into a Ziploc bag (about three pounds of quarters, nickels, dimes, and pennies) and then grabbed a small blanket and my three-and-a-half-foot-long ball python. I placed these items in a backpack. My intent was to panhandle on State Street with the snake as the main act. My roommate just wanted to go to a bar and—apprehensively, I am sure—let me come along. Halfway to State Street on the bus, in spite of my intention to be inconspicuous, I showed a group of guys the snake in my bag. They were curious about what my plans were for the reptile. After all, it was still March and not that warm outside. Soon after, I realized that even though I had packed a bag of *very important things*, I had forgotten my wallet. Without any identification, it would be difficult to get into the bar. I decided to walk home from the next stop and told my roommate I would meet him downtown. I started to walk but then saw a guy getting on a motorcycle. Without question, I approached him and asked for a ride. It is one thing to hitchhike but another thing to ask another seemingly heterosexual stranger to give you a ride on his motorcycle. Mania and boundaries are like oil and water. Apparently, it was not that strange to him, and he said he was going to the Regent apartment complex, which was only a few blocks from my apartment. When my private motorcycle transportation was complete, I headed home. This is where the story surpasses intrigue. I came across what appeared to be a bulbous, street-dwelling, crack-cocaine-addicted woman. Instead of giving her a little change from my ample collection, I donated all of the money I had in coin form—approximately thirty to forty dollars. My only request was for her to buy me some cigarettes, as I did not have my driver's license. For some reason, this plan did not work out with the chief convenience store operator of the Open Pantry. Even though I was not the combative type, I had some choice words with him and then exited the store.

As I was walking down the sidewalk—bear in mind, I was lacking prescription eyewear—a large opossum scurried across my path. Despite a later visual hallucination, I can say with confidence that this really did happen. *Hmmmmmm. Opossum and a hungry snake in my backpack.* I began chase and recall getting extremely close to the marsupial in a shadowy area (this was around ten o'clock at night), when it hissed and lunged within inches of me. It was a little scary, but I still released the snake on it. Just to be clear, opossums are nasty, tough creatures that weigh between four and twelve pounds (depending on the sex), and my snake was on a diet of rats. The size of the opossum made me think it could have been living inside the cafeteria at Ogg Hall, a dormitory on campus, for three years, feeding on an ample supply of leftover cheese.

The snake did not stand a chance even if it would have gotten close enough to make a strike. Scaling down the scene in order to offer a better perspective, this would have been like throwing an earthworm into a ring with a hamster. Not surprisingly, the snake retreated out of my visual field, and I did not know where it was. My assumption was that the snake had climbed up through the undercarriage of a car parked on Jefferson Street and taken refuge in the engine. I was not sure what to do except wait. A sidenote: it appears that as my mania progressed, the outer childish expressions tended to behaviorally mature to more dramatic incidents. Smoking cigarettes in front of my mother, running away, defying the religion that my family's morals were founded on, and conducting unconventional experiments with wildlife quickly escalated to petty theft, combativeness, and more irritability, as well as what is to be disclosed in the following accounts. Waiting and mania are almost always mutually exclusive. I headed back into the Open Pantry and blatantly stole a package of Swisher Sweets, which are little cigars (an act reminiscent of being a fifteen-year-old). The cigars were mere feet from the clerk's counter, and with only my back turned as protection from him seeing me, I slipped the container into my pocket. He understood clearly what I had done, but it was of little concern to me. The already-disgruntled employee abrasively demanded my departure.

I walked in a cocky manner back to the scene of the animal crime, emulating Al Pacino's character, Detective Hannah, from the film *Heat*. I felt almost as if an internal semblance had taken place, where I believed I was *in* that movie or had *become* that character. That is the only way I can describe it. I smoked part of one of the cigars and used the burning red ember to try to entice the snake out from the suspected car. For whatever reason, I decided to bury the cigars in the ground, as I thought it was possible that the clerk would call the police. Sure enough, a police officer arrived shortly thereafter. As a matter of fact, it was one of the same police officers who had generously escorted me to the hospital less than a month prior (when I had assaulted my brother and fled his car before eventually being hospitalized). He questioned what

I was doing and even assisted in trying to recover the snake. In addition, he searched my bag for the missing cigars, which he did not find. It now seems that going to jail for petty theft would have been a gift or blessing in comparison to what happened the next morning.

The snake was not recovered, and the officer informed animal control while placing a notification on the car. I suppose this was to tag the car for the authorities as well as warn an unsuspecting driver that he or she might have a python riding shotgun. The police officer eventually left, and I was determined to wait for the animal's miraculous return. After a brief period of time, I felt it was imperative to write some esoteric symbols and ramblings on the flyer that the cop had placed on the car's driver-side window. I slipped the announcement and a one-dollar bill with some more of my delusional writing on it under the front door of the Regent apartment complex, which was across the street. To have insight today about what those actions meant at the time would be remarkable.

I made my way back to the Open Pantry despite knowing the clerk was not going to welcome my company. He was at least five inches taller than I was and weighed about 190 pounds. Whatever words we exchanged transported the conversation outside. It was the closest thing I'd had to a full-on, throw-down fistfight in my life, and nowhere was the presence of fear. I wanted him to hit me. I was feeling so powerful that the fight was just another rush or incident that would not get in my way. As the scene was evolving, two men arrived in a fast, high-end, low-profile silver Honda with tinted windows and expensive rims. Their company eclipsed the dispute, and before I knew it, they were bringing me back to my apartment. During the short ride, they made it known that they had a gun in the car, shared a proclivity for drug use, and were headed to Chicago in the early morning. This news was exciting for me, because I had voiced an interest to many people, including my psychiatrist as well as a friend who lived in Chicago, that I wanted to go stay in Chicago. Also, one of the gentlemen stated that he had bipolar disorder, so there was an instant connection. This seemed to be the perfect situation for me.

We got out of the car in the rear parking lot of my apartment. The gentleman with bipolar disorder talked about how he was also an amateur boxer. As a physical testament or dubious test, I requested that he punch me in the face. He refused at first but then said that he would use his left hand (his predominant hand was his right) and that I would reciprocate after (i.e., hit him back). I closed my eyes, and when he hit me, I felt less of a sting than a constellation of stars that penetrated every thought process as well as bodily sensation. I was transported to a fourth-dimension climax. It felt amazing. These were not the cartoon stars that you see affect Wile E. Coyote when the Road Runner causes him to hit his head on something (e.g., an anvil). It was an internal visual and conscious awareness of this new subjection. I imagine the experience would have been very different if the store clerk had hit me out of anger or if I had undertaken the same activity while clinically depressed. It was my turn next, but I could not bring myself to hit him. Even though he was well versed in having his face assaulted, there was no reciprocation, as it did not feel right to me. Instead, I told them I had to pack up some belongings before leaving. They said they would return in a couple hours to pick me up. It was probably nearing midnight at that point. Night fell fast as I unknowingly had less than ten hours of freedom.

—24—

PLEADING INSANITY

*We knew that we had nothing to lose except our so
ridiculously naked lives.*

—Viktor Frankl, *Man's Search for Meaning*

I quickly loaded my bag with some of my favorite articles of clothing, my iPod, and who knows what else. After all, I was moving to Chicago. In addition, I packed the bag full of prescription drugs. Most of these were not the "fun" drugs one might think of. Antipsychotic and antidepressant medications are not really meant for a wild party.

My delusions and paranoia were really starting to set in. Perhaps the stress of leaving triggered these distorted thought processes. I was fearful of being caught with a large assortment of prescription drugs, so I utilized an unorthodox packing approach. For example, I mixed some of the pills into Yoplait yogurts. That way, the medication would not be discovered by the authorities if the car was pulled over, not to mention the fact that raspberry yogurt blended with Lexapro is just a super start to one's day! The paranoia and unsettled feeling of waiting intensified my need to get out of the apartment. Instead of leaving with my belongings, I decided on a new course of action: take nothing with me. First I would need to cover my tracks, because I was not coming back. Erasing my identity became the focus of my ensuing madness. The night was almost one year to the day after the infamous case of Audrey Seiler (March 28, 2004), a University of Wisconsin–Madison student who faked her own kidnapping, causing a countywide search as well as national news attention for several weeks (she was supposedly suffering from mental health issues during the time of the false abduction). I am sure that case was lodged somewhere in the back of my mind, not to mention the fact that at the time of the incident, Audrey Seiler had been living at the Regent Street apartment complex.

I contrived a suicide scene inside my apartment. I am not sure how convincing it was without a body, but I viewed that as a minor detail at the time. I ripped apart DVD cases, left little notes, and wrote something on the mirror in the bathroom with a bar of soap—a trick I had learned from a friend in Mexico. The idea is that when a person showers and steam collects and fogs the mirror, the soap blocks the fog, which leaves the unsuspected message. The message on the mirror might only have been a reflection of the sheer madness that was taking place.

In addition to these peculiar behaviors, I shaved a male, or horseshoe, balding pattern on my head with a razor blade. This was influenced by Johnny Depp's similar hairstyle in his portrayal of Hunter S. Thompson in the film *Fear and Loathing in Las Vegas*. I used a hair clipper to cut and shave an upside-down question mark (¿), which is used grammatically in the Spanish language, into the back of my head. To complete the suicide scene, I made some superficial cuts on my forehead, which are noted in the police report, in order to have some blood in the sink. I intended the blood to be DNA evidence for the investigators to collect. In one final gesture, I clogged the sink with the water running before I set off out the door into the early morning darkness with a T-shirt, Diesel jeans purchased in Mexico, shoes, and a deplorable haircut.

Relating again to the film *Heat*, this time, much like a metaphorical kid in a costume, I imitated Robert Dinero's character, Neil McCauley, who steals an ambulance in the beginning of the movie. All I needed to do was find an ambulance. I began my journey by going east on Regent Street, heading in the direction of Meriter Hospital. The few possessions I had on my person could still tie me to my identity, I thought, and ridding myself of them would eliminate the chance of someone discovering who I was. Those were the strands of irrational connections that raced through my manic mind. As I continued to walk, I threw my wallet into a bush, pulled out my contacts and flicked the tiny saucers to the ground, and hurled my chain necklace, a gift from my first girlfriend, into the sky. Materially, I was almost as bare as one could get—almost. Once I found the partially underground garage at the hospital, I saw an ambulance. It was wrapped in a long orange extension cord, which was plugged into an outlet, presumably to ensure that the battery stayed charged at all times. There's nothing worse for an EMT than having to get out the jumper cables as a man is having a heart attack in Middleton (suburb of Madison), Wisconsin. The ambulance was locked, and I was wary of the revolving glass door looking me in the face, which was an entrance into the garage from the hospital. *Someone could come out at any time.* I had reached a fearful mental state, lost in an unparalleled reality; it is difficult to understand how it is even possible that I ended up there. My decision to continue disrobing of my identity and clothes was an animalistic behavior that cannot readily be explained. I quickly stripped my clothes from my body and dropped them to the ground on the secluded passenger side of the ambulance. After all of my articles of clothing—and I mean all—were off, I then proceeded to urinate on them. I believed this would somehow cover my fingerprints, DNA, or other tracks. I guess the reason does not matter, because the outlandish behavior fits what was happening both cognitively and physically at that point.

Now naked and unable to get into the ambulance, I decided I would settle for the next best thing: a hospital van. Using a toothpick, I attempted to hotwire the white conversion van. It did not work. I snuck back over to my clothes. This memory evokes imagery of the crouching Terminator played by Arnold Schwarzenegger in *Terminator 2* when he first arrives. With a low track-star stance and a vigilant look on my face, I had to swiftly pass those same revolving glass doors and put the soiled clothes back on. I do not remember feeling disgusted at all or even a bodily sensation of dampness. It was just what I needed to do—part of a reduction to a survival mode that lacked forward thinking other than what I needed to get done. My operating system was utilizing only the primitive levels akin to a lost child. *Why* is not a question I ask myself anymore about these incidents. The *how* questions are more important. How did it all go so wrong? How could my mind fall so deeply into a psychotic trench? There is only one answer: I became sick—really sick.

My path, after a lot of meandering, brought me back to my friends' apartment, where a lot of my belongings still remained. At that point, it was about 5:30 a.m. based on police reports, which are provided in the succeeding chapter. Yet another night without sleep, and I was completely mad. I entered their apartment in order to get a really old laptop (we are talking Windows 0.1) that my father had given me as well as to say good-bye.

My memories are somewhat different from my friend's account, which is reflected in the official police report. I walked in; grabbed a few things; placed a glass ashtray in the refrigerator; took my friend's iPod, as I'd left mine behind; and then went to my friend's bedroom. A psychotic friend, radically changed in both a physical and psychological manner, evoked a visceral reaction in her. The whites of her eyes blossomed in explosive fear as she took in the sight of me. *Wide-eyed* would be a gross understatement. I told her that I was leaving and whatever else. She reacted in the most sensible way: absolute confusion and terror. Feeling the walls closing in, I quickly shuffled down the several flights of stairs. At that point, I am not sure if my other friend was awake and they both followed me, but I reached my exit point. Whether my friend screamed before or after does not matter, but in an instant, I shattered the glass-enclosed fire alarm with my fist. All in one motion, I punched through and pulled the alarm. Both sounds—her scream and the deafening alarm—were piercing, while convulsive displays of fearful emotion elicited her involuntary tears. Only upon reflection in jail and after the episode dissipated could I feel compassion as well as empathy for these friends and all the others involved. The feelings from those moments do not persist, but those traumatic experiences are retained deep in my brain matter. Simply stated, I remember the events, but they do not elicit as stressful of a response as they used to. The story lives on, but my perception of it has been altered.

With no time to act, I dropped the iPod next to the building on the ground and headed out through some backstreets with clusters of apartments to shield me. I had to get out of there. The police would soon arrive at the apartment, looking for answers and desiring my containment. If an all-points bulletin (APB) had been announced for a "white male, approximately twenty-three years old" on the campus of the University of Wisconsin–Madison, there would have been a plethora of false identifications. The crowded State Street offered a temporary sanctuary as I searched for a bus in order to flee the scenes of downtown Madison. At a bus stop, I met a cook from Chipotle (for the number of times that franchise is listed in this narrative, I should partner up with them). His English was about as good as my Spanish, but I managed to trade my 1998 laptop computer that I had procured from my father for his baseball hat and sack lunch. Not a bad deal. The hat concealed my conspicuous haircut.

The delusions at that point were so strong that I believed a secret meeting was going to be held above the Comedy Club, where I had attempted to spout what would have been a tragic comedic performance. This meeting was somehow connected to the capitol building of Madison, which I obsessed over. My mind was convinced that the fire that had occurred in 1904 had been a conspiracy of some kind. Invalid accusations of fraud, government conspiracies, and other theories stretched to the deaths of famous individuals such as John F. Kennedy and Johnny Cochran in my mind during that time. I saw signs and clues *everywhere* as I walked with distorted eyesight as well as visions that a higher-power summit was to take place that morning. Instead of getting on a bus, I proceeded to the last block of State Street and went in an open door. This was off the perpendicular road to State Street, part of the "Capitol Loop." I walked up several half staircases (rising above the Comedy Club) with intense apprehension. I was headed to the roof with ideas motivated by a mind-set or strategy out of a Dan Brown novel. The supernatural meeting was not an *impossibility* in my brain; it was assured. I *was* going to meet John F. Kennedy, among other celestial beings.

Attached to the wall was a short metal ladder leading to a closed hatch. When opened, the hatch would be not only my entrance to the roof but also a portal to an unimaginable world. I paused for an instant. My heart started to race with unadulterated fear. After all, I was about to enter a secret society that would expose me to the living dead or what should have been an inaccessible gateway to a higher state. When I ponder this encounter, I realize that it was the most frightening moment of my life, despite everything I had been through. However, this event that was to take place was conceptualized and created solely in my mind, which elicits the following question: Just what—or, more so, *who*—was I afraid of?

I began my ascent slowly. As I approached, the terror came on in a slow wave. Immense anxiety erupted from the idea that an early morning cleaning person or someone else might see me and disrupt my plan, but also from what I thought I would see on the roof. As I reached the top, I contemplated how I would open the hatch. It was not secured tightly on the ceiling, so there was a small crack of the early morning sunlight breaking through. In a flash, I saw a shadow sweep past the opening. My intellect was too far gone, but the fear that was powered by my "reptilian brain" (exemplified by the primitive fight, flight, or freeze responses) knew this was one of the assembled individuals (e.g., John F. Kennedy). It confirmed my delusional beliefs, and I raced down the steps of the ladder in rapid succession. I hurried down several stairs and collapsed. I cried out in absolute terror and remorse to a god, but not in the way that a person suddenly prays when he or she is trapped in an elevator or when one is waiting for a police officer to get out of the squad car to ask, "Why is your vehicle swerving?" at two o'clock in the morning. This was different. I had seen something, and the evolved subconscious of the human mind tapped into the belief that a fantastical event had just occurred. "I'm not ready!" I screamed as the tears came pouring down my face while my paralyzed body fixed into a fetal position on the floor. My lips shook with a parkinsonian[4] tremor against my will. This was a near-*life* experience with

---

4 I use this as an adjective because the disorder is related to psychosis. Both Parkinson's disease and mania/psychosis are believed—the key word is *believed*—to be due to an imbalance of dopamine. However, these disparities are localized in separate parts of the brain. If you use antipsychotics to *decrease* or block dopamine production over long periods of time in someone who is

God. At the time, what had happened was a modern miracle, and it could not be explained by science or any other justification. I believed this with genuine conviction.

There is a key differentiation that should be made and then interpreted independently. A delusion is a type of fixed belief (usually eccentric and considered false) that is immune to disagreement despite being contradicted by what is *generally* accepted as reality or fact. Delusional individuals will commit to what they believe in, despite facts or presentations clearly acknowledging discrepancies in their certainty. Similarly, a belief is an acceptance or state of mind that something is real or that it exists (often held by a group), especially when based on examination of evidence. The key element here is the examination of evidence. A delusion is a type of believing, and therefore a belief in and of itself can be delusional depending on supportive facts or groups that *believe* the facts to be true.

No one can tell me that this incident did not happen, because it did. The problem, as with other seeming acts of God, is that these conclusions are responses to the unknown. We fear what we cannot understand, but I feared what I thought I actually did understand. One's assumption about the origins of an astonishing event is that there is no other explanation. In my case, the explanation was simple: I was psychotic and delusional. Did I see a shadow

---

prone to mania/psychosis, the person often develops tardive dyskinesia (e.g., tremors in his or her hand). This occurs when the part of the brain that controls motor movement (i.e., the basal ganglia) becomes dysfunctional. On the other hand, it is believed that an inverse situation occurs for individuals suffering from Parkinson's. With an *increase* in dopamine (i.e., with L-dopa), their minds can become manic/psychotic. The globally endorsed dopamine hypothesis of psychosis says that too much dopamine causes psychosis (e.g., in schizophrenia). Too little dopamine can result in motor control problems, such as tongue movements or rigidity (e.g., in Parkinson's disease or with someone who is on too much antipsychotic medication). This hypothesis is beginning to be questioned in terms of whether antipsychotic medications actually make outcomes worse long-term. Is the chemical imbalance *caused* by the drugs rather than originally present?

cross my line of vision? I saw the shadow, but it was because my brain developed that experience. Was it John F. Kennedy traversing the rooftop of a building on State Street? John F. Kennedy was absolutely not on the rooftop (if he was, then like me, he was missing a large part of his head), because my brain developed that narrative around a delusional belief system and, more simply, he is dead. It does not matter completely, because I experienced it.

This was a profound, embarrassing, and informative event when I explored it months later. One fundamental difference between my psychotic delusion and other unsubstantiated beliefs (e.g., Armageddon, the apocalypse, and the rapture; miracles; omnipotent or omnipresent gods; transubstantiation; a heaven with seventy-two awaiting virgins; hell; etc.) is that the latter examples have millions of followers across the world. I am the only one who believed what was going on, and more importantly, I was mentally ill. My aim is to convey that a belief and a delusion are very similar but not in a negative way. Most lack scientifically supported evidence. Using my own religious background as an example, the transformation of bread literally into the body of Christ (i.e., transubstantiation) is not something I *believe*, because I do not have sufficient facts other than what would be considered faith, devotion, or perhaps hope. I remember what I *thought* I saw, which I *believe* was due to dysfunctional activity in my brain. I can say with confidence that another individual present would not have had that same experience. I know I am harping on the issue of religion, but the reason will become evident as I discuss my psychotic nature's shift into a hyperreligious state. In respect of all beliefs, I certainly missed out on what would have been by far the coolest rooftop party on State Street.

After I pulled myself together, my journey steered in the direction of the lawyers' office where a friend's parents worked. I think I might have been in need of some legal advice. Despite my attempt to verify that I knew the lawyers at the firm, the gatekeeper turned me away. My next stop was city hall, which was connected to the police station as well as the Dane County Jail. Was I turning myself in? I went to speak with someone about a "case I am working on with my boss." There was a client in Mendota Mental Health Institution whom I had worked with in the past, and I told a worker that I was involved in that client's case. I am quite sure she did not take me seriously, considering I was completely disheveled and wearing part of a ripped bandana on my bare feet. The bandana was interwoven between my toes, and I was convinced this would be a hot seller on campus one day. *Brilliant idea,* I thought. Grandiosity is a horrible thing to waste during a manic episode. She told me to wait while—I now assume—she alerted the authorities to my presence. It did not take long for my patience to wear thin and paranoia to surface in my mind.

I decided to leave; I walked down the hall to find two police officers coming around a corner. Instantaneously, I was dropped to the floor, handcuffed, and taken into the elevator. After witnessing the locks in the police car go down when being unlocked, I believed that we were descending instead of actually going up to the sixth floor of the building. What would be one of the worst experiences of my existence ultimately saved my life. To be in jail for sixteen days is one thing, but to spend fourteen days confined in a solitary jail cell on the psychiatric unit with one visitor (a public defender) is something else. This was not a DWI charge whereby my parents would come down to bail me out in the morning and I would have a teary-eyed, sad story for my friends. There would be no bail or transport to a hospital. Despite it being the only way back to sanity, it would be an unsympathetic, slow, and painful treatment for the mind. My friends and family could finally breathe a sigh of relief. To them, I was safe—which I was, on a basic, physical level. There was a constant suicide watch, or overall vigilant observation, during my stay by the corrections officers. I do not hold any resentment against the friends and family who fought for my safety and treatment, but to not have any visitors or seeming advocates for my release was heartbreaking. The deprivation of jail lobotomized my vitality and left me with a psychologically broken brain.

—25—

BOOKED

*And if the world refused to square with his version of reality
then it was necessarily an uncaring world, a sour and sickening
world, a penal colony, and he was doomed to be violently lonely
in it.*

—Jonathan Franzen, *The Corrections*

The police report gives a detailed, informative, and fascinating summation of what occurred that morning from the perspective of both the police and my friend (in order to keep anonymity, various names and addresses were omitted). It is a well-documented testimonial. Although not infallible, it is a collaborative voice of some of those who witnessed or interacted with me at the height of my madness.

MADISON POLICE DEPARTMENT

Date of Report: 3/20/2005   **Case No:** 2005-32754 Original

   Ref. No:

Occurred Incident: 65 - Check Personv   **Sec/Area:** 403 Central

Dispatched as: 65 - Check Person   **Grid:**   STATELANGD

Case Offense: **ARRESTED PERSON - FALSE FIRE ALARM**

Addr of Occurrence: _____Apt. 4

Call Date/Time: 03/30/2005 06:08 **From Date/Time:**

Dispatch Date/Time: 03/30/2005 07:59 **Thru Date/Time:**

Reporting Officer: PO Marine _____3697

Special Routing:

SUSPECT   ANDREW JAMES ARCHER

   M/W DOB: 08/24/81 (23 yrs) Height: 5.9 Weight: 155

   Hair Color: BRO Hair Length: SHAVED Eye Color: BLU Build: MED Other Phys Char:

   ARCHER'S HAIR HAD BEEN SHAVED IN THE FRONT AND PARTIALLY IN THE BACK.

   811 GARFIELD STREET, APT.2, H: 612-721-7495

SCHOOL: U.W.

CHARGE #1:   FALSE FIRE ALARM, S.S. 941.13

HOW ID'D: VERBALLY

INJURIES: ARCHER HAS SUPERFICIAL CUTS TO HIS
              FOREHEAD AND THE CROWN OF HIS HEAD

STATUS: ARRESTED AT 7:49 AM ON 3/30/05

VICTIM   CITY OF MADISON

WITNESS   _____

   F/W DOB: _____ (23 yrs) Height: 5.7 Weight: 110

   Hair Color: BRO Eye Color: BLU

   _____

SCHOOL: U.W.

HOW ID'D: VERBALLY

PROPERTY DAMAGE INFO:

Item #1   THE GLASS ON THE FIRE ALARM NEAR THE
ENTRANCE _____

          _____STREET WAS BROKEN AND THE FIRE
   ALARM

   HANDLE WAS PULLED

PROPERTY INFO:

Status Code   Description   Est Value

LOST   2.4" BY 4.1" WHITE $400.00

    IPOD, 40 GIGABYTE,

    MAC AND PC

LOST   ONE ASHTRAY $150.00

OFFICER NARRATIVE:

On 3/30/05 at 6:14 am, Officer _____and I were dispatched to _____Frances Street, _____reference a white male who had pulled the fire alarm at that residence. However, dispatch stated that the resident there told that there was no actual fire alarm and it was because the white male who had pulled the alarm was not mentally stable. Dispatch notes also further described the male as having shaved his head, causing some injury to his head with the blade. While Officer _____ searched the area for the male who had left and was seen running towards Langdon Street from the residence, I made contact with [_witness_].

[_Witness_] stated to me that she had been sleeping at approximately 6:00 am when she had been woken up by Archer. Archer was standing beside the bed and [_witness_] stated to me that his face was approximately 1" away from her face. [_Witness_] recounted that Archer told her, "This is the last day of my life and I need your cigarettes."

While interviewing [_witness_] I also gained more information on Archer's appearance. I relayed this information to
Officer _____ and also stated that the resident at this address believed that Archer may still have the razor blade that
he used to cut his hair off.

I was informed by [_witness_] that Archer was on medication and bi-polar. She stated that she believed he had not
been taking the medication for a period of time unknown.

I learned from [_witness_] that Archer was originally
from Minnesota, specifically Bloomington, where his father, _____, worked at Caldwell Banker. Archer apparently
is a U.W. student but had not gone to class recently due to his
recent decline in mental health.

I asked [_witness_] if she was disturbed by Archer's actions and [_witness_] stated that she did not want to get
Archer in trouble and would not want to pursue any type
of charges. I got no other information from [_witness_]
regarding any type of disturbance Archer may have caused
her. [_Witness_] reiterated that she just wanted Archer to get
some help, specifically some type of mental institution.

I asked [_witness_] if any of the roommates at the resident
had seen Archer and she stated that none had seen him that
morning. [_Witness_] stated that Archer did live at 811
Garfield Street, apt. 2, however, that his roommates and
Archer were in some kind of fight. According to [_witness_],

Archer had damaged some of the belongings of his roommates (see officer _____'s report, case number 2005-
32768). Combine this with Archer's increasingly declining
mental state, [_witness_] stated she had talked to Archer's
roommates and that they apparently did not want Archer
back in the residence with them.

That quote struck me when I first read the police report: "she had talked
to Archer's roommates and … they apparently did not want Archer back
in the residence with them." This was devastating to read weeks later
after leaving jail. I then understood how much I had affected my friends
and family. I wondered if they still felt that way. Were they going to hold
it against me? Had I destroyed relationships with all these individuals?
The guilt was incredible. It took years to get past the notion that it was
my fault.

After Archer had woken up [_witness_], [_witness_] stated
that she yelled at Archer, "No," because she stated that she
did not want Archer to kill himself. [_Witness_] stated
that at no time was she in any fear of Archer assaulting
her physically or sexually. After Archer left [_witness's_]
room, [_witness_] stated she chased after Archer but that
he was down the stairs at that point. [_Witness_] stated
that she did get a visual of Archer as he was at the bottom
of the stairs and that this was when Archer broke the glass
on the fire alarm near the entrance of the residence and
then activated the alarm by pulling it. This action did cause
the fire alarm to activate which stayed active, up to including the time that I was interviewing [_witness_] later on.

[_Witness_] stated that there was no fire at the time when Archer activated the alarm.

[_Witness_] stated to me that the previous night when she went to bed at 1:00 am, that her IPOD was seated on the table in the living room. She stated that there was also a $150.00 ashtray in the living room as well.

The glass ashtray was actually in the refrigerator. I am not sure why I placed it in there, but I am sure that it was for a delusional reason.

She stated that when she woke up to Archer, that she could no longer locate the IPOD or ashtray. I state to [_witness_] that although it was possible that Archer may have taken these items that because she did not see Archer acquire it and because she did not lock her residence to the point where Archer was able to freely enter the residence, that I did not have probable cause to charge Archer with theft of those items.

[_Witness_] also pointed out three bags located in the floor in the living room which she said belonged to Archer. [_Witness_] stated Archer sometimes did stay at their residence in the past and that was why he had his belongings there. She stated that Archer had not been staying there recently though.

I had learned from [_witness_] that Archer had possibly stolen a pet snake from his roommates and that it had not been seen since Archer had been seen. I also learned from [_witness_]

that Archer may still have the razor blade on his person that
he had used to shave his hair. I also learned from [_witness_]
that Archer's medications were located in the three bags which
were now in her living room. Due to the fact that I also could
not figure out what other locations Archer may have fled to and
because I was not sure if Archer had the blade that he used to
shave his hair off with on his person, and because I wasn't sure
if there was a snake in those three bags, I did search the three
bags that were said to have belonged to Archer for any items
that would reveal the aforementioned information.

I received information I needed about Archer and ran it
through New World, where upon I did get his identifying
characteristics and statistics.

The New World mentioned is a contemporary database, which reads like
a tool from a fictional book, that decodes "identifying characteristics and
statistics." It operates as a technological bridge for inter-agency work across
multiple jurisdictions.

I broadcast an attempt to locate on Archer, emphasizing the
fact that he had been off his medications, that he possibly
has a razor blade on his person, and that I did have probable
cause to arrest him for the fire alarm.

I did give [_witness_] a Victim Rights Information sheet
with the case number regarding the possible loss of her
IPOD. She stated that no one had consent to take her IPOD

from her and that she was the rightful owner of this item. She
stated that none of her roommates had this IPOD as well.

After broadcasting the ATL, I did contact Sgt. _____,
who informed me that Archer had attempted to turn himself
in on the 5th floor at the DA's level.

The notation about me turning myself in on the "5th floor at the D.A.'s level"
refers to when I was telling the woman that I was working on a case with
my boss moments before being arrested. The reference in the report that I
was turning myself in is not correct. My intention—whatever it may have
been—was probably an underlying, indirect gesture to confine the madness
and not a waving of the white flag.

Myself and Sgt. _____ went to the 5th floor to contact
Archer where he was placed under arrest at 7:49 am on
3/30/05. Archer was dressed in jeans and t-shirt with no
shoes. Archer had a red handkerchief tied around both feet
but apparently not for protection against the ground.

The concrete description the police officer gives of my footwear is a sane
and humorous comparison to the grandiose thoughts and revelations I had
at the time about the bandana.

The handkerchief was actually part of a red bandana. The thin piece of fabric
had been passed from my deceased grandfather's oil-and-gasoline-stained
hands to my mother and eventually to me thirteen year ago. What once was
an insignificant family heirloom has become a tangible marking point of a
devastating moment in my life. Forty years lying at my feet.

He also had on a hat which covered his new haircut. I removed his hat, searched him incident to arrest and discovered that the front half on the crown of his head was shaved off to the skin. I also did observe small cuts on his forehead and crown consistent with the razor blade shaving off hair. However, I was [un]able to discover the razor blade on him. I was unable to discover any snake on his person as well.

While escorting him down to the holding cell next to the OIC's office, I asked Archer basic identifying questions including his name and place of residence. Archer stated to me that he was, "Under cover," and that he couldn't help me out. He asked me if he could ask me some questions and I stated that I could not have a conversation with him without reading him his rights. At the mention of these rights, Archer stated that his attorney, Daniel _____ should already be on the premises waiting for him. Archer then stated that, "My ass," was in trouble. Archer then stated that, "Demetrius," was also going to help him out with the situation. Archer then listed off several more names rapidly, which I was unable to write down. I found it difficult to follow the vein of his conversation. He jumped from subject to subject speaking of, "Demons and Angels," at one juncture and then speaking of Wisconsin Badger's football coach, Barry Alvarez, backing him up. Archer then mentioned the name of, "Denny Alvarez," but would not go on further.

This notation by the officer is as clear an example as one will find of "flight of ideas or subjective experience that thoughts are racing." The flight of ideas continued to distract me from the present events, but soon the socializing would come to an end.

At no time did I ask Archer questions about his crime or his actions that day. I limited my questions to Archer solely to booking-type questions.

I asked Archer for his social security number for the booking sheet and Archer began speaking Spanish. I understand Spanish only in a marginal way but did understand the he was telling me, "I don't speak English."

Archer asked me what he was being arrested for and I stated to him that he was being arrested for pulling a fire alarm when there was no need to. Archer asked me where he pulled the fire alarm and I stated the _____ Frances address and Archer stated to me that he was not there at all today. Throughout Archer's stay in the holding cell at the Patrol Counter, Archer continued to question why he was under arrest and that I should, "Hurry the booking up so I can make my phone call." I stated to Archer that his phone call would be made once the booking process was completed and Archer denied this process saying he wanted his lawyer. Throughout this time, Archer was handcuffed behind his back due to his mental instability. Archer complained of pain on his wrist which he stated was recently tattooed. He stated that was why he had pain.

Officer _____ then assisted me in escorting Archer to the Public Safety Building jail. Sgt. _____ informed me before I left that Archer's mother had called from Minnesota stating that Archer was mentally unstable.

Officer _____ and I escorted Archer to the Public Safety Building jail where meanwhile, Archer continually speaking of his, "Undercover capacity," and that he couldn't give us certain information.

Archer was placed in the booking area where he stated he did want to talk to me. I began reading Archer his rights from my Department-issued Miranda Rights card. When I asked Archer if he understood his rights, Archer nodded. I asked Archer for a verbal affirmative and Archer then shook his head side to side. Thus, I was unable to ask Archer about the fire alarm pull or the possible stolen IPOD.

In the jail, Archer did inform one of the deputies that he had voluntarily admitted himself to U.W. Hospital for a case of, "Whooping cough." I do recall while searching Archer's bag at [_witness's_] residence, that I found some hospital gown and infection protecting-type equipment.

Deputies informed me that they would like me to retrieve his bags from the _____ Frances address because I mentioned to them that I thought I believed I saw pills of some type in those bags. I left the Public Safety Building in an effort to retrieve these bags. Officer _____ stated that she would attempt to gain the information of Archer's mother from Minnesota and relay it to the Public Safety Building Deputies.

> I retrieved the bag from [_witness's_] residence and returned
> it to the Public Safety Building whereupon one of the depu-
> ties retrieved some of the pills and some doctor's notepads.

> I phoned [_witness_] and she stated that she was willing to
> take the bags back and return them to Archer's residence on
> Garfield Street.

As I conclude reading this report, I cannot help but feel for my friend (i.e., the witness) and what she must have been going through. Her day was no less chaotic than mine. I think about school and movie theater shootings. I think about the overall loss of innocence, and I wonder just where I was headed that day as the memories run through my mind like a movie reel. The face I wore that morning would not be out of place with the likenesses of Jared Loughner (Tucson, Arizona), Cho Seung-Hui (Virginia Tech campus), and James Holmes (Century Movie Theater in Aurora, Colorado) that the media displayed on those horrific days.

If I had not been apprehended on March 30, 2005, then what would have been the alternative ending to the story? Did I have the capability or potenti-ality for violence? Was my mind so far gone that I could have hurt someone? The world had stopped making sense in the way it does now, so I cannot say or imagine what another outcome would have looked like.

—26—

Maculate Inception

The juvenile sea squirt wanders through the sea searching for a suitable rock or hunk of coral to cling to and make its home for life. For this task, it has a rudimentary nervous system. When it finds its spot and takes root, it doesn't need its brain anymore so it eats it!

—Daniel Dennett, *Consciousness Explained*

A person's feelings while being booked in jail must be comparable to a dog's feelings while being brought to the veterinarian. Fear and resistance are dragged into a windowless basement of concrete. Cooperation is futile when dealing with a manic mind, so the officers must cage the beast.

A locked wire door allowed me to bark at the enforcers, but the interwoven holes did not set my insanity free from this holding pen. Eventually, I was booked and photographed. The tattoos were noted, as well as whatever little information I would give them. The picture tells a tale of a deranged individual with a restless mind that had gone too long without sleep. I was no longer a successful, privileged soon-to-be college graduate; instead, I was severely mentally ill—nothing more. The disturbed animation in the mug shot of my profile speaks to the arrogance that was preventing any deep introspection of the events that were unfolding; I was going to jail. The tag of my T-shirt is visible in the profile picture because my shirt was inside out. That was absolutely intentional, as were my many interesting outfits that accompanied me to eventual incarceration.

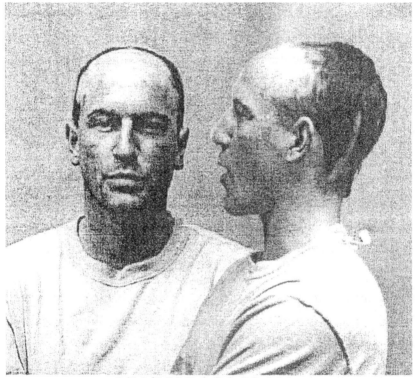

3/30/2005 9:31:06 AM

Before the commencement of this writing project, there were few individuals whom I had shared these horrifying images with. I kept the mug shots dormant in a filing cabinet for over five years. Through this writing process, the pictures have faded in their capacity to emotionally disrupt me. Now the photographs represent a specific moment in time and not a defining representation of who I am.

A social worker reminiscent of Sigmund Freud with his white beard, glasses, and inquisitive as well as compassionate demeanor spoke with me in order to get a deeper understanding and assessment of the situation. My only seeming ally at the time did not foster any interest in my collaboration. Paranoia distances one from any form of authority, and consequently, trust settles within how one's brain is responding and deceiving the person of a consistent reality. I felt I was right, and they (meaning everyone) were wrong. This all-knowing attitude as well as the desire for absolute omnipotence ultimately will lead one to rebelliousness, as it fosters a combative disposition. These descriptions (omnipotence, all-knowing, etc.) help me understand the condition, but I understand that the words are frequently juxtaposed in the context of a deity. Understandably, my godlike feeling and mentality coincided with escalating hyperreligiosity. To put it simply, hyperreligiosity is a state where one develops extremely obsessive thoughts and beliefs surrounding a religion, to the point of delusion that, in particular, impairs aspects of his or her functioning.

My psychosis (e.g., delusions, paranoia, etc.) took hold, and only months later could I understand this as a contribution to the conception of an evolutionary "god" that resides in all of our unconscious minds. The events during my manic episode in 2005 were not deeply religious experiences; rather, they were extreme, grandiose beliefs and sensations of invincibility that confirmed an untouchable and superlative self.

A surreal courthouse arraignment soon followed my booking. An assigned attorney briefly questioned and verified my contact information. He looked like a semiretired ex-Mafia middleman and part-time Florida native with his puffy comb-over, whitening hair, and suspiciously apricot skin tone. The delusional state of mind I was in quickly read into his

subtle reactions: "This is *your* address?" I thought that he knew something important and that we were connected. The nuances in his voice
and facial expressions created wild ideas in my mind that he worked
for the government and was connected to my apartment, based on the
symbolic rose crest on my building and other bizarre conceptions. A
recent ex-girlfriend at the time helplessly watched the hearing, unable
to speak on my behalf. During the inquiry, I was very arrogant and not
worried in the least. *This will all be over soon.* Whether there was an allotted opportunity or not, I spoke into the microphone briefly, and I have
no idea what I said. The time in court was short; my charges were read,
and I was swiftly ushered out of the courtroom.

Eventually, they moved me to a holding cell where my anger became even
more animalistic within my mandatory enclosure. An environment that
forced an inactive life was no place for this infuriated creature; my mind
demanded expansion. Ironically, the jail psychiatrist was my colleague
(she worked part-time there completing assessments for the newly incarcerated). This meant my former coworker was now befit to evaluate
my psychological state. Our first encounter came during some stage of
my devolved, primate behaviors. You see, at that point, I was no longer
around people within a cell that had a large wire door. My chamber was a
panic room with a small window on the door. There was no telephone or
intercom system, as there had been during my hospital stay. The psychiatrist witnessed the angry-child version of me stuffing the suicide smock
that I was supposed to wear, as well as all of my clothes, into the toilet
while continuously flushing it. *Let me out!* This stunt was in the hopes of
flooding the jail, an act that could not be accomplished, but the perceived,
or misperceived, goal of obtaining attention was granted when she came
to the door.

Despite my being nude and psychotic and having a less-than-desirable hair-cut, her compassion and affect did not deviate from her normal, collected presentation. She had seen more mania than the average person has witnessed reality television shows (both types of episodes are seasoned with delusions). Our conversations were never stored in my long-term memory, but she was a figure who momentarily put out my raging flames. I can still see her curly brown hair and tanned skin inside the picture-frame-sized window. My dehumanized world was softened, but her visits were structurally purposeful and efficient while systematically abbreviated. I needed to take medication, and I needed to take it immediately. The new environment placed my body into an embryonic state, and in order to develop or adapt, psychopharmacology was essential. Involuntarily rooted in the purgatory that was this form of encapsulation, all control lost, my mind had consumed itself.

—27—

MENTAL CAPTIVITY

Are you really sure that a floor can't also be a ceiling?

—M. C. Escher

The holding cell was a square dark gray box. I felt as if I were inside an oversized closet on a sinking submarine. The air was confined, and everything was hard as well as cold. Deprived of any stimulation and without a way out, eventually I went to sleep. The image is of a child who throws a tantrum but, when left alone, tires himself out over time and goes to bed.

I have recollections of jail that I cannot bring myself to share with people (maybe I will write a second edition). The memories do not haunt me, but they are so explicit and personal that they preclude me from writing them down. Odd or embarrassing is one thing, but grotesque is another. Fortunately, a lot of the time spent in the holding cell is a blur that is not unlike memories from a long night of drinking. After one or two days, I was moved to the jail's psychiatric unit, which was a U-shaped area from the perspective of the main door. There was a locked central door, and three cells for individuals were on each side, making a total of six. The three cells on each side faced one another, staring across the open space of the U. The bottom of the U, perpendicular to the cells, was a window to the outside world. It was blocked or fenced in such a way that one could not get close enough to look outside. I was convinced that the unit was underground and the window was an elaborate illusion manufactured by the Dane County Jail. In actuality, I now understand we were on approximately the sixth floor of the building.

My new, secluded home was meant to be as innocuous as possible for the sake of my physical safety. However, for my mind, it was the ultimate cause for aggravation. The cell was similar to the one I had been moved from. The cube that would be my habitat for roughly 275 hours was decorated with empty tan-colored walls. To get an idea of how long my stay was, imagine watching the six seasons of *The Sopranos* about four times in a row. A concrete slab that rose to a level of two feet was my bed, and it came with an anorexically thin mattress atop. In addition, a steel sink and toilet combination, a roll of toilet paper, and a steel mirror were the amenities. The room was privatized (except for Big Brother's security camera in one upper corner, facing the toilet and bed), with only a small, square window on the door. It was there that I would spend many full days before getting a phone call or shower.

One of the first things I did was try to map out the dimensions of the small room using the only standardized measurement tool I had: toilet paper. I counted ply by ply. When I was finished surrounding the cell's perimeter and cross angle, a guard came to the window and saw what was occurring as well as the finishing touches: *ISP* spelled out in toilet paper. He told me that the roll of toilet paper was all I was getting for whatever period of time and advised me not to continue the activity. For some reason, my (delusional) belief was that using Pythagoras's theorem for the exact dimensions of the cell would somehow allow me to escape or aid my plan of starting a fire. *Yes, start a fire.* Time is not of the essence in jail. The idea is to get rid of it as quickly as possible. At that point in time, my concrete bedroom contained exactly what I mentioned above and nothing else. No books, US Weekly, Internet, music, pencil or pen, paper—nothing. My free-range mind was limited to the emptiness that disallowed the liberty of expression or distraction. Phase two of my fire-starting mission began. The only thing in my cell that was flammable was lint. With my bare hands, I collected every piece of dust, lint, and hair from within the approximately six-by-nine-foot surface area of the cell floor. This activity was no dirtier than splashing the water out of the toilet in my holding cell a day or two earlier. During my spring-cleaning, I found a clear plastic wrapper, which I used to roll the collectibles, a sufficient assortment of disgusting material, like a cigarette. I then hid the appropriated, dusty joint (as opposed to a joint that causes one to become "dusted"), fearing potential ramifications. How or when I planned to light this fire, I am not sure.

Pope John Paul II died on April 2, 2005 (three days after my arrest), which set off a fury of delusions and "signs" of things greater than the reality most people live in. Based on my previous near-meeting on the rooftop of State Street with individuals who were long deceased, I did not believe that the news was true. Later, I would create some bizarre drawings commemorating the news. The turn of events surrounding Pope John Paul's death elicited an explosion of outrage in me. I was convinced that the pope was not dead and that I should reform my life by returning to my Catholic roots in order to become a priest. The anger of being confined and my overall manic rage manifested in a heightened psychotic state.

The mirror in my cell, as a safety precaution, was made of steel as opposed to the potentially injurious glass. I vividly remember punching the steel mirror, which was held securely to the wall. It moved. The mirror dropped about a foot down the wall, but it was still secured. This was both marvelous and frightening

to me. For those who do not know, visual hallucinations, unlike the consequence of potent mushrooms on a sunny day, are not a good sign with mania.
This might have been "rock bottom," terminal cognitive velocity—or, to put it
simply, I had reached the crazy-as-fuck status. If there had been Wi-Fi in the jail,
I certainly would have made a Facebook post about the event. In *your* reality,
the mirror did not move. However, there is no difference in the senses when
one's brain reports through the eyes that an object did indeed shift downward.
I began punching at the window on the door as well as making as much noise
as I could. I wanted out of the jail cell, despite the fact that the physical walls
were not the true restraint causing my distress. Rather, my racing, animalistic,
unbridled mind that could not be reined in was the force haunting me as the
mechanical system lowered me into physical compliance.

The officers quickly moved me to a cell with a view of the main desk. Whatever
privacy I had just had was reverted back to absolute authoritative vigilance. This
exploitative environment led to the degradation of my human spirit. Between
the video camera in the corner and the large bay window facing the hallway
with a six-to-eight-foot distance from the office, nothing could go unnoticed. I
was a boring but potentially witnessed twenty-four-hour TV station. Paranoia
was a constant, but could you blame me? A video camera and an access point
for observation were two things that were not hallucinations. Whether someone was really watching me go to the bathroom from a security camera or
peering through the window is up for interpretation, but thinking about it now,
the possibility disgusts me. I do not care how crazy one is; nobody enjoys a
witness to his or her bathroom habits. Of course, there was not much else to
see as at that point; I still did not have any writing or reading materials.

The cell next to me enclosed a large white man who supposedly had bipolar
disorder. He was extremely loud, and psychotic rants were common. I tried

to speak to him, but it did not go over well. After all, a literal concrete wall to a conversation makes for a difficult exchange. I believe he had attempted suicide among other things that consequently elicited his incarceration. I did not tell anyone my real name while in jail, both out of paranoia and embarrassment. I wish I could recall the aliases, but I know one was Jameson, which was yet another reference to the movie *Heat*.

Directly across from my cell was a middle-aged black man. I would learn later that he had been locked up for maliciously killing his brother with a knife. Who am I to judge? I took any conversation I could get. He spoke with a speech impediment in which he would stutter frequently, especially when talking to the guards. It was clear to *me* that he was faking it. I thought he was using his alleged speech problems to exhibit some sort of handicap, and the situation reminded me of the movie *Primal Fear*. Conspiracy and skepticism of others superseded rationale during that period of time. The first piece of property I received was a small lead tip from a number-two pencil from the alleged murderer during his one-hour stay outside of the cell in the common area. He was very nice, and this object facilitated archaic forms of entertainment (e.g., making calligraphic notches on the wall). I primarily used the pencil to make lead-based notches on the wall for every one hundred sit-ups or fifty push-ups done. I made the marks very discreetly because I was terrified the guards would see the marks and punish me.

I worked my triceps by doing "dips." The positioning for the workout involved forming a triangle with my body slanted at a forty-five-degree angle to the ledge of the bed (arms perpendicular to the bed, making right angles) with both feet on the ground. Hell, just Google "tricep dips" if this description does not make sense. The exercises were short, because my mind was a pacing animal at the zoo. Despite having all day (minus bathroom breaks and eating) to work out, my anxiety was so high that I was lucky to put in a total of thirty fragmented minutes. Also, my weight had dropped significantly during the manic episode, and the regimented diet of two thousand calories per day was just not enough. This made for a lack of energy and a constant state of unbearable hunger. Meals were all I could look forward to during the day, while my only form of escapism and my drug of choice was sleep. There was an environmentally established proclivity for sleep in jail, which was quite the polarization from the previous four months. There was absolutely nothing to do except for the occasional conversation with the other incarcerated individuals, so I would sleep during the day. The television was on at times, but I could not see it, because I had thrown my contacts away days prior to being arrested. There is only one thing worse than watching daytime television: just listening to the dialogue of the daytime television.

Eventually, a social worker came to offer medications, which I did take. She also gave me some books, including a novel in Spanish that I assured her I could read. The book had an accompanying English–Spanish dictionary as well in order to translate words. The visits with her and the other social worker (i.e., the Freudian guy) were brief. It is safe to say that I was unable to get any reading done. Feeling my life slip away while trapped in a cage was not conducive to sustained concentration. However, after one conversation, a worker gave me a stack of letters previously held by the jail that had been sent from family and friends. I read through the letters as well as some articles my brother had provided. The material was a subtle connection to the outside world and, specifically, the most important people in my life, whom I had all but written off over the preceding months. I cannot imagine drafting a letter to a friend, son, or sibling who is in jail and afflicted with madness. Where does one start? Some of the letters were very descriptive of what was happening. Some expressed how they had been denied attempts to visit me, which broke my heart. All of a sudden, I was an idle and wounded soldier, fending for myself with an uncertain return date.

I used the letters and any other kind of paper that I collected, including the order slips for medication, to produce a formless style of nonsensical ramblings and drawings. The works are littered with references to the pope, John F. Kennedy, ISP, and who knows what else. My copies of the orders that were given to the nurse had an erratic dispersion of symbols and pictures.

"*Tienes llaves?*" loosely translates to "Do you have keys?" The date in the bubble is 11/22/63, which was made famous as the day John F. Kennedy was assassinated. The bow and arrow stuck in the tree might have related to my last name—Archer.

—28—

BADGERED

The dream is the (disguised) fulfilment of a (suppressed, repressed) wish.

—Sigmund Freud, *The Interpretation of Dreams*

I would try as hard as I could to stay awake during the day, because the tireless insomnia during the night was unbearable. These naps during the day only made it worse at night. I could have easily slept all day, but lying awake in the shadowy silence of the night as an alternative was much worse. I could not read the not-so-far-off clock because of my astigmatism, but darkness would finally come around ten thirty at night. I did have a "night-light"—the giant window that beamed fluorescent rays into my cell. The giant, double-stripped institutional fluorescent light microwaved my brain. I would pull the covers over my head in a childish tantrum that almost said to an authority figure, "No, I'm not talking to you." I prayed for sleep to wash over my tormented mind. Sleep did not last long, as the lights and breakfast came around six in the morning. *Food!* I ate all that was edible and even hid or rationed items, such as apples, because the hunger pains continued throughout the day. I needed to restrict the demands of my ravenous appetite. There were no mindfulness or relaxation classes at the Dane County Jail, so simple human needs were the only sources of comfort (e.g., sleep and nourishment). Dehumanization as opposed to socialization was all that was on the menu. I would usually place the apple or orange inside my Styrofoam cup, which changed the color of the water, and my imagination began to convert the liquid into a self-indulgent juice. I would then add the sugar from the coffee in order to make the drink seem as if it were Kool-Aid. I do not relate this action directly to psychosis; rather, I feel it was an adaptation in order to survive the unadulterated insanity that imprisonment assures.

Some of the best meals I have ever had in my life came in that jail. I write this with all sincerity. It did not matter what the meal was. "Cattle hunger," an aged reference that originated from bulimia nervosa, labels the urges an individual has before a binging session. That was how I felt. I tried so hard to not squint at the clock in anticipation. Lunch would finally come, and a bologna-and-mustard sandwich on cheap white bread tasted so orgasmic that my eyes would roll back in my head. Unlike the cinematic representations of prisoners hastily eating, I slowly and mindfully consumed the food, as mealtime was one of three major highlights of the day. Desire for another meal filled the other three slots during the day.

Detection of the individuals distributing the trays initiated mental salivation, as it was a metaphorical tuning fork. I would attempt to make eye contact with the food workers in order to elicit an extrasensory perception declaring, "Throw a little extra my way?" This wishful and somewhat magical thinking did not work. The fine-dining cuisine was eventually delivered to my narrow, rectangular passageway. This impenetrable dog door was used for the presentation of food, the exchange of documents, and the distribution of medications as well as books. In addition, during the one hour of free time when I exited the cell, my hands first went through the enlarged mail slot. The officer applied handcuffs and then opened the door.

Jail is a restriction from society that breaks the individual down, but it is more so a control over the individual's basic human functioning. It is designed that way. There are specific rules and routines. Everything is time-stamped, and there are no exceptions. At what point does systematic regulation imposed on bodily functions, the dissemination of food, how individuals sleep, or whether they are allowed things to occupy their mind become an inhumane force to people's expressive inertia? Mental slavery comes to mind, as basic needs are owned by the regulating agent, except unprofitable employment was never offered, so captivity is a conservative replacement.

Room checks were common, but conversations were not. Some of the guards were more engaging than others. I recognized an officer's last name, Vogel, and remembered a basketball player I'd played against from a neighboring suburb back in Bloomington, Minnesota, who shared the same name. The guard's curiosity revealed itself when I brought this up. It was a subtle, serendipitous interaction, but it was a human connection that I had not felt in some time.

Looking back on my constant desire to eat and inability to live humanely conjures up images I recall from videos of the controversial experiments Harry Harlow conducted between 1957 and 1963. He removed baby rhesus monkeys from their mothers and used two different surrogates: one made of terrycloth and one made of wire (the surrogate that provided food was alternated throughout variations of the experiment). The cloth-covered surrogate monkey gave some sense of security or protection (e.g., when a frightening stimulus was introduced, the monkeys ran to the cloth "mother" whether it provided food or not) as opposed to the wire imitation monkey. The take-home from Harlow's experiments regarding the monkeys' behaviors is that a lack of felt comfort is psychologically stressful.

At that moment in my stay, what I really needed was affection through the form of physical touch (e.g., a hug) and nurturing. My ego was deflated, and I was no longer different from the monkey that was dependent on the cloth-covered, superficial, yet satisfying connection that a perceived loving relationship can give. The breakup with my girlfriend three years prior was the catalyst for revealing this deficiency. She was the nurturing presence that, although not enough to help me grow as a person, had always pro-tected me from the insecurities of being alone. Symptoms of depression and mania had been subsequent to a breakup of another serious relation-ship months earlier (in the fall of 2004). The cycle of dependency, wishful anticipation, and mental health issues was a clear cause of my progression into madness.

After four to five days on the psychiatric unit, I was finally given a chance out of my cell. I eerily walked through the hallways with a speechless guard who escorted me. Every inch of the facility was cold with sterility, form, and redundancy. This rigidity was encompassed in the uniforms as well as the interactions between people—the kind of exchanges you have with someone you do not like but are forced by proximity to intermingle with. I saw empty and colorless walls that fit with the repetitive, mechanical nature of the entire system. My excursion had a purpose. I needed to have some mandatory blood work. A nurse with a demeanor that spoke to a regret for where her life path had taken her extracted the necessary blood. Much the same as countless nurses since, she asked, "Did that hurt?" The question was preceded by a gesture with her eyes at my exposed left wrist branded with the ISP tattoo. I replied with only a precarious grin. It hurt *like crazy* now that I think about it.

The field trip was short but as eventful as it could be for someone who had felt buried alive for such a period of time. Later that day, I was permitted in the common area for one hour. Making a phone call (using another inmate's identification number) to the friend who had taken me in during spring break in Minneapolis was heart-wrenching. Hearing my voice for the first time in days was both foreign and emotionally debilitating. It cracked in a pubescent manner with a slightly deep pain contained by the sound. The accent of an oncoming tearfulness is what I remember, not the dialogue. I had what was a short-lived shower with no hot water available and only the foam pump soap from the wall in order to cleanse my body. I avoided the mirror in my room, because my once-carefree haircut had become a monstrous elixir of anxiety. They did not trust me with a razor or hair clippers, so I was unable to even out the deranged, self-imposed modification. There was nothing to watch on television. The learned helplessness walked me back to my cozy room with my tail between my legs before the allotted hour had expired. I was no longer the once furiously violent new dog at the kennel. Eventually, I became so estranged from the outside world and so overcome with the hopelessness of not knowing when I would be released that I feared leaving the cage altogether.

—29—

Manic Oppression

I find it dull when my heart meets my mind
Though I hardly know you, I think I can tell
These are the reasons I think that we're ill

—Laura Marling, "My Manic and I"

Incident Date: 4/6/05

A little less than a week after being incarcerated, I decided I'd had an adequate amount of detainment. With seemingly no control, late one evening (around ten thirty), I decided to bring the raucous. I called a guard an asshole and said I would kill myself if I were not let out. The tension of not knowing anything about when I would be released congested my brain, which needed an emotional shunt to release the pressure. With this memory, a conception of purgatory surfaces in my mind along with a noncomical version of the movie *Groundhog Day*. The guard stated that I had to lie down on my bed or there would be consequences. The control that I thought I had over the guards gave me pleasure, and all that ran through my mind was *Fuck you*. I had my towel lazily wrapped around my head in a Middle Eastern, turban-like manner while standing on the top of the bed with my arms crossed. The inmate directly across the common area urged me to comply, because he knew what I did not—that a full riot-geared guard raid was what would follow. It did not matter to me what was coming next. *What can they possibly do to me that is worse than my current situation?* This thought gave me a temporary sense of power and disrupted the uniformity of the system.

There were at least six guards in all-black riot gear (helmets, body armor, etc.) and a front man carrying a shield as well as a plainclothes guard in the rear with a video camera (what I would give to see that video). It would be my own personal Zapruder film, except there would be no Jackie Kennedy to rescue my flying brain. I was commanded in an extremely assertive manner repeatedly to lie down with my arms behind my back. *Fuck you.* Fear was replaced with grandiosity and arrogance that would humble most NFL stars. One more warning or chance at compliance was given as the key to the cell door slid in ever so slowly. The overdressed guards were in a forward-facing huddle and in an athletic stance. They were configured both mentally and physically as if they had practiced, orchestrated, and coordinated this mock scenario a thousand times. Despite the seemingly benign target and lack of danger, their bodies were alerted to the potential for danger. *Fuck you.*

Even now as I write this, while I imagine that moment, my body tenses and my heart collapses in my chest. My brain can temporarily forget, process, or rationalize the trauma, but my body remembers. In spite of the psychotherapy—specifically, trauma treatment, which I will revisit later—this memory still elicits tension throughout my spirit and constricts the blood flow in my body. I can still hear the bolted click of the door unlocking, which gave consent for their entry. Under my own recognizance, in the blink of an eye, I slammed to the ground face-first onto my awaiting mattress. It was as if I had landed on a fumbled football, because in an instant, a methodically planned hog pile (sorry for the cop–pig analogy) was upon me. My recollection is that it happened in a second, but in real time, it was probably more like two. I am at a place now in my life where I can remove myself from the situation and look down at what was occurring. My face evaporated into the mattress, so my sense of sight was gone, but I could feel the pressing bodies as they seamlessly began removing all of my clothing and handcuffing me. One guard slid my pajama-like, standard institutional pants down, and I felt the cold air on my exposed buttocks, but more so, I felt the childish shame of being "changed" in public. This experience seems—and felt at the time—almost perverse, but he was merely doing his job. However, for a long-lasting moment, the notions of adulthood and autonomy were stripped from my mind. The physical impression of my previously para-lyzed body was left in the mattress as all sense of dignity exited with the guard parade and the metal slam of the cell door.

It is clear that the guards followed protocol to the system's policy based on the situation, so the story they would tell might drastically contrast with my own. My recollection is from a reflective, traumatizing, and emotional perspective within that moment. The end result was a temporarily naked and reprimanded child, punished for an act instigated only through a sense of abandonment and fear. I was subservient to the weight of the enforcers, who applied a suicide smock and stripped all my belongings from my possession (not much other than pencils and reading and writing materials).

Chastisement and loss override the few instances of the delayed positive rein-forcement. It makes one wonder or question where the line between regulation and madness falls. An army of enforcers cornering a vulnerable, defenseless human being appears on the surface to be a chaotic approach to the sustain-ment of order. Feelings of guilt and sadness as a consequence of questioning the morality of some of my past behaviors would soon devastate me.

—30—

IF THE WALLS COULD TALK

We see this in the extreme pathology of psychosis when people become lost in a private world and are not able to connect very much at all with others.

—Karen Kissel Wegela, *How to Be a Help Instead of a Nuisance*

4/8/05

Two days later, a worker from the jail came to my concrete home to explain the charges based on my alleged antics. Everything had been taken away. I was sane enough to feel scared at that point. *Will my stay be extended?* The accusations against me were based on my following or not following the listed rules presented:

Obey all jail rules
Fails staff direction
Being disrespectful of others
No disorderly behavior
Don't threaten harm to self or threaten harm to others

A right to appeal was granted in order for me to go in front of a committee for a disciplinary hearing to dispute the charges they had against me. Of course, the charges were accurate, but with no legal consult, it was hard to know what to expect. The process began by submission of a written appeal. The consequence of losing the hearing would have been dire (e.g., a possible extension of my sentence). Rather begrudgingly, I decided that pleading guilty was my best bet. Ironically, my pleading insanity in the form of out-of-control, abnormal behaviors was what had finally landed me in jail, but now my insanity was what kept me in. It is interesting that I was in fact being held for a lack of competence to stand trial, but within the jail's proceedings, there was no issue with my mental status in this case. My punishment was eight more excruciating days in a solitary cell on the psychiatric unit.

Being psychotic in isolation is nothing compared to when reality sets in. Introspection and existentialism rear their ugly heads. This was never truer than when a client of the agency I had been working for was locked in one of the cells across from me on the psychiatric unit. Diagnosed with paranoid schizophrenia, he was a friendly and kind man who had made a horrible mistake after an alleged crack-cocaine binge. An individual from our agency who was delivering him his required medication on a weekend morning did not know that he had been panhandling the evening prior and had earned sixty dollars' worth of money for crack. He was not episodic (i.e., experiencing symptoms from schizophrenia), but he was cracked out of his mind. According to the media, when the worker entered the individual's apartment and closed the door behind her, the individual attempted some sexual gestures. Before she could leave, the individual stabbed her, but the wounds were not life threatening.

I had done that job and visited the individual many times under similar circumstances (minus the violence and inappropriate sexual advances). Now

I was sharing a government-subsidized psychiatric unit with him. I saw his case manger come in one morning to visit with him; the case manager was also my coworker at the time. *What the hell is happening?* I thought. I hid in my cell as negative thoughts and ruminations racked my brain. *Is the future I was planning ruined?* The last thing I wanted was for my coworker to see my jail uniform and deranged presentation. It was a nightmare that I could not wake up from. I felt sick, trapped, and absent from the world I had known—and none of those feelings were delusions.

Eventually, my behavior was reasonable enough that the guards permitted me to use a razor and hair clippers. They must have been feeling confident that I would not slice my wrists. My desire to be clean-cut had never been stronger. Acting—and, more so, looking—crazy had gone on long enough. I blindly shaved in the shower, using a cheap, disposable plastic razor and foam hand soap. I then shaved my head in order to even out the stubble that was filling in the bald spot. I recall being very disappointed with my personal haircut, because parts of the sides were cut a little too short or unevenly. *What am I, a seasoned hairstylist?* At least I no longer stood out in a crowd. This was the longest period of time I had spent in front of a mirror in weeks. My perfectionistic tendencies returned, and a negative sense of self entered my mind. A major difference between humans and other mammals is the ability to reflect on the past and project ideas on the future. My restricted environment began to combine the minimal need for higher-level cognition of animals (as I only needed to eat, sleep, and go to the bathroom) with the agonizing suffering of the ruminating human.

Around April 11, 2005 (twelve days since my admission), I was granted my first visitor. It was not my best friend, a family member, or an ex-girlfriend, but it was someone. John T. was the public defender assigned to represent me. He was a large man, to put it lightly. His vintage gray suit approached the divided table with a limp and a cane. The attorney sat slowly with a full-body decompression and a large exhale. John was an American and probably a patriot who most likely had enjoyed years of sensual smoking with a side of red meat. From my brief analysis of his physical and intellectual properties, he was a hybrid of Matlock and the "Fatman" who teamed with Jake in the popular TV series *Jake and the Fatman*. It was clear as he read through the case materials that it was the first time he had done so (after all, he was getting paid little for this work). I wanted to scream through the circular, vented hole in the glass, "Get me out of here!" Instead, I sat patiently, hanging on his every word. Fixated in silence, I felt as if this were my seminal interaction with a human being.

The sole reason I was being held in jail for so long without bail was the fact that I was incompetent to stand trial. This is effectively why jails and prisons have become the longest-lasting mental health providers without the resources to do so. In my opinion, incarceration is one of the great dystopias, as it acts as a social control system that is inappropriate for those with mental health issues. Another reason these facilities provide for those with mental illness is because the symptoms often go unnoticed (mostly among people of color) as convictions walk those individuals through the revolving doors. I was getting little treatment—mainly just medication—but I was provided a regimen of food, water, and shelter. More importantly, jail offered safety and reassurance to my family and friends that I was alive. It would be easy to condemn jails and prisons, but society must work within its means.

Coming off mania cold turkey is like asking a heroin addict to detoxify on Starburst. The paradox is that the allegorical death sentence created in my psyche had also saved my life, which parallels the disdain I feel for the correctional system. My lawyer, John, assessed my condition and could not understand how I was still in custody. I could not understand why it had taken him twelve days to speak with me. He inquired about whether I was taking my medication, which I confirmed. John said he would take the information to the district attorney and get back to me. My fear and isolation projected a feeling that John was inept and should be working harder and in a much swifter manner. He needed to initiate an indirect liberation from the mental grip the jail had on me. On the seemingly barren horizon was a lone prospect of optimism: I was told that I would be moved to a "pod" in three days (April 14, 2005)—three days, three nights, nine meals, and plenty of downtime. The description reads in the vein of an all-inclusive vacation package, except there was no ocean view, the drinks were watered down, and the rooms did not have key cards.

—31—

SELF VERSUS OTHER

The relationship which I have found helpful is characterized by a sort of transparency on my part, in which my real feelings are evident; by an acceptance of this other person as a separate person with value in his own right; and by a deep empathic understanding which enables me to see his private world through his eyes.

—Carl Rogers, American psychologist (1902–1987)

Despite appearing competent, as my attorney had said days prior, it is evident that I was still coming down from the mania. Whether you skydive or bungee jump, in either case, you are still really high before you land; the difference is how long it takes you to fall. I had come down from the clouds but was still on top of a bridge somewhere, awaiting a fall. The boredom was like no other. I occupied my time by exploring, which, in my mind, was a reality rather than a fantasy. Being the musician I thought I was despite the lack of any musical experience, it was clear to me that I could start a band when I was released. The magical number three was still in my head, and I figured an ex-girlfriend and my roommate could join me in a band (three members). Of course, the daydream stretched to the thought of playing at the Memorial

Union Terrace on the University of Wisconsin–Madison campus, among other venues. One song we definitely would play, I decided, was "16 Days" by Whiskeytown, because I estimated that I would be in jail for about sixteen days (and I was ultimately correct). It became my theme song and source of inspiration. I made a couple rough drafts of what I felt would act as a remarkable album cover (I was still experiencing grandiosity). A snake and some other sort of animal are both incorporated into the band name that I have on a saved drawing.

On April 14, 2005—or fifteen days into my stay—I was moved to what is called a "pod." A pod is a four-celled unit with a shared common area. Leaving the segregated psychiatric unit for the pod was akin to being upgraded from coach to the cockpit of an airplane or receiving a complimentary stay in a luxury hotel after being homeless—you pick. The stimulation—and, more so, socialization—was the most therapeutic intervention during my entire time in jail. There was a communal bathroom and shower as well as a stack of books and a television.

When I arrived in the pod, directly across from me in the U-shaped hellhole was a familiar face. It was a fellow inmate I had spoken with extensively during our respective periods of time out of our cells while in the psychiatric unit. It was nice to have someone I knew, even though he was seemingly a con artist with heavily weighted narcissistic traits. You take what you can get in jail. The only other roommate was an African man who had been arrested for disorderly conduct during a drunken stupor. Not surprisingly, there was little intellectual conversation in our pod. Instead, we sat in front of the television all day. I remember being yelled at by one of the guards for having a blanket wrapped around my body. He stated that the blankets had to stay inside one's cell. The pod had a lot of nice amenities compared to my previous dwelling, but it was freezing cold. The cold is my most pervasive memory of distress from the time in the cell. The experience was like sitting in a cold movie theater while watching a really compelling film; you cannot get up and miss part of it, but you are so excruciatingly cold that you want to run for the exit (why do they keep it so cold in movie theaters?). For the remainder of my stay, I felt the kind of cold that gave rise to my hair as well as goose bumps all over my body. It was a horrendous supplement to the emotional pain I was experiencing. I felt horribly depressed despite still unknowingly being in a state of hypomania, but the depression was environmentally based. How someone could not be depressed while in jail is unknown to me—especially a twenty-three-year-old who had always enjoyed the finer things in life. My fear of getting in trouble with the guard eventually faded enough for me to bring the blanket back out by the TV.

One day passed very slowly, and I remember my narcissistic friend telling me a long bedtime story about how he had ripped off his ex-girlfriend and left her broke. I almost had tears in my eyes, but they were probably from the cold air. The chilly night's sleep did not come fast enough. The next day was even longer. Forget the stack of books—I could not focus. I wanted out or at least wanted to know when I would get out. I am not sure what was worse: getting through the endless day or sitting with the ambiguity of my future. That afternoon, I received a phone call from my boss. This was the same individual who had asked if I would step down from my position as he delivered me to my psychiatric appointment weeks earlier.

He filled me in on the legal details, as he had known my attorney, John T., for many years. Most of the words from our conversation do not stand out in my memory, but one statement has been branded deep into the land-scape of my brain. Even now, it is difficult to type his statement, as my body constricts and my eyes fill with fluid. The physiological reaction, to a lesser degree, mimics the suffering I experienced during the verbal exchange with him. My body could only go into survival mode. Fight and flight were not options, because there was nowhere to go and the judicial system was larger than Goliath. My sympathetic nervous system activated my amygdala with a notification that danger was upon me before I fully comprehended the news. All I could do was freeze. Everything stopped. My brain shut down for an immeasurable period of time as he said, "Andy, they are going to have you moved to Mendota." Mendota is a mental health institution. Utterly frozen by the anesthetizing news, the veracity of this terrifying imposition slowly set in. I imagine this emotion is what actors attempt to portray in movies when authorities on their doorsteps give them the news that their loved one has been killed or their son or daughter did not make it back from the war. My boss lowered his military cap out of respect with his brief silence as I raised my hand to firmly cover my mouth as if to hold in the last of the pure oxygen I had before inhaling this toxic news.

Mendota Mental Health Institute is a place where numerous former clients of mine were involuntarily placed into habitation. Although it is one of the finest facilities of its kind in the nation, the glorified "insane asylum" is not a proper place for a human being. Individuals who are charged with a crime but are not competent to stand trial are warehoused at this institution as an alternative to temporary incarceration. *How can I be going there?* My heart rate skyrocketed as my chest caved in. A tingling wave of fear circulated throughout my body. A dense and heavy ball dropped into my stomach; sickness poured through my intestinal tract as the poignancy of the news rendered me a lifeless being. My body soon became overwhelmed with activity, but my mind hardened as the shock set in. I felt as though I were sinking in slow motion through the concrete floor or as though gravity did not apply to my weightless body, which was too fragile for this disturbed world. I could imagine the face of my boss through the phone as I stood rooted in the rhythm of his voice. There must have been a hurt in his eyes from the words he was forced to share with me. The subtle distress in his message was balanced with an empathic tone. I tried not to cry despite the crackling in my voice. My speech was fractured, but a breakdown was not an option.

There was an inverted V-shaped divider consisting of a nine-foot dull-colored wall that separated me from the two other cellmates while I was on the phone. I was not about to emotionally collapse in front of them. I have a clear vision of the moment, as I can now look down at myself within the recollection. My cognitive memory processes scrutinize my disappearing sense of self during the conversation, and my vision is of someone far below. It is an *It's a Wonderful Life* observation far above a topless jail cell, which stems from this emotional disintegration. It could be better described as the type of experiences led by a character from *A Christmas Carol*, the Ghost of Christmas Past. There I am, with my Dane County Jail attire, shaved head, and plastic sandals—cold. My figure is trapped inside a hellish diorama—a window inside my psyche for those moments that lasted centuries.

When the initial anguish subsided, a current of feelings poured over me. Devastation and agony were the first waves generated. My sense of being was forgotten. This was the worst moment of my life. I had been diagnosed with a stigmatized mental illness and on the cuff of suicide from debilitating depressive episodes, and I had seen death and a family fall apart from tragic circumstances, but selfishly, this was the most awful news to date that I had ever encountered. Next I felt an instantaneous melancholy; my senses were diminished in the way that a diet consisting of Styrofoam could dampen one's palate. Nothing would ever taste good again. This feeling quickly segued into a nascent rebirth as who I was became trapped in the idea of being a patient at Mendota. There was no physical or psychological way out. The report that I had heard was not that I was going to be transported to a mental health institution; instead, in a matter of hours, as quickly as I had been born into the world, I would suffer a waking death. The parts of me that had survived the broadcast of my future did not have the strength to go on. Hearing that someone is dying or has died at least gives one preparation for a last visit or a funeral to say good-bye. In so many words, my death sentence was given and executed all at once. There was nothing left.

—32—

The Bailout

There is no meaningful distinction between his biology and his decision making. They are inseparable.

—David Eagleman, *Incognito*

I have absolutely no recollection of the next two hours in jail. I know that I was horribly distraught, helpless, and completely void of hope. These were layers on top of a fear and sadness that encompassed my world. To this day, I cannot discern how it happened—and frankly, I do not care—but when the announcement was made, the earth radically spun in the opposite direction on its axis. The guard told me that I would be released. Just like that.

The polarization of the two events that occurred that day is incomparable. I was elated. In a matter of hours, I would be emancipated from a Hades not soon to be forgotten. The type of anticipation I felt is the kind evidenced by an animal the moment before you set a bowl of food down for it. Perhaps a more appropriate example is when you reach for the handle of a locked cage and the click of the metal catch elicits a perceived sense of freedom before the creature inside has even gotten out.

My mind obsessed over the notion of an exit. I was finally moved to a holding area and then was given my personal items: clothes and a ripped bandana. The jail donated a pair of boots to me, because I had entered without any footwear sixteen days prior. In a flash, the door was opened. I rush through this period in terms of depth and detail because the anticipation needs to be expressed in a way that evokes the anxiety I felt. I could not clearly make out the details of the physical form of a young woman approaching me. As I walked out of the Dane County Jail after sixteen days—fourteen in segregation—with borrowed boots and blurred vision, I was greeted outside by my first visitor. After living in a concrete cage, the feeling of warm sunshine was like the intense satisfaction you feel from a sip of cool water when you're stranded in a desert. It turned out that the individual I had met in Mexico, who had been a helpful friend during the entire process and an advocate for me during the episode, was my first true sight (I still had no contacts or glasses). I could not have been more exhilarated. She was the first friend I had been in contact with since being incarcerated. She was coming to the jail in an attempt to visit me that day. Instead, on April 15, 2005, we left the building together as I noted in a newly learned vernacular that my inhabitation had been "fifteen days and *a wake-up.*"

I called my father from her phone in order to notify him that I had been discharged from jail. It is amazing how much one's environment has an effect on the state of his mood even if the mental illness is for the most part genetically transmitted. Over the duration of just a few hours, my feeling of what seemed to be clinical depression had been transformed to the happiest I had ever been.

This type of pendulum-like mood fluctuation is commonly thought to be bipolar disorder but clearly does not meet the criteria. Bipolar swings are much larger. I remarked with confidence during the conversation with my father that he did not have to worry, because I was just "really happy and not hypomanic." This was an erroneous statement, because my mood had not yet stabilized, and I was running a little high. My state of mind was definitely on the rim of hypomania. My parents made plans to come see me as soon as possible. They drove to Madison the next day, and when they spoke to my friend, they made it clear over the phone that she needed to, for lack of a better term, babysit me.

As she and I walked down State Street, my friend and I went to the student union and found a roommate of mine bartending on a glorious, sun-coated Friday afternoon. My interpretation of his reaction when he saw me was a combination of excitement and nervousness. He was busy and appeared to feel a little uncomfortable talking with me. After all, I looked a little too happy for someone who had just spent over two weeks in jail. His reaction might also have had to do with me blowing off a job opportunity he had put in place for me a month prior. My roommate had worked in the Rathskellar since his freshman year in college, so he knew everyone and had some pull with the management in terms of persuading the direction of the hiring process.

The first week of that March, he had arranged an interview with a manager whom he was well acquainted with. To make things more provocative, let's just say he had relations with her, even though it is not confirmed. I showed up late to the interview but did not rush inside. Instead, the ideologies of "Everything happens for a reason" and "If it is meant to be, it will work out" framed my mentality, which was also peppered with a dash of delusional mania. This mind-set provided me with some extra time in order to chat with a few people, including my roommate. I recall his interjection vividly: "Dude, you're late for your interview!" My behavior obviously could reflect poorly on him, and he was by no way out of line. I moseyed my way back through the offices that were tucked away behind the kitchen and cafeteria. I sat down with a young college-aged woman who had an appetite that was intolerant of my arrogance. Unfortunately for her, that was all that I was serving. One of her standardized questions was to rate my performance or some type of ability from a previous job using a one-to-ten Likert scale. My reply was "Eleven," much to her chagrin. My arrogance and sarcasm in addition to flirtation, lack of punctuality, and displays representing the antithesis of professionalism acquired me a rejection as well as an even angrier roommate.

Back to the day of leaving jail, the first stop of my new life was the student union's on-campus bar, the Rathskellar. I joined my friend and some of her girlfriends at a table in the establishment where I had previously interviewed for a position. I had awkward reunions with my other roommates and friends during that day and the upcoming days. The reality of everything that had transpired had not entirely set in for me. My parents arrived the next day in the afternoon. When they reached my apartment, we looked through my bills and finances on the deck. In her memoir, *An Unquiet Mind*, Kay Redfield Jamison articulates the effects of mania on finances as the "money spent while manic doesn't fit into the Internal Revenue Service concept of medical expense or business loss. So after mania, when most depressed, you're given excellent reason to be even more so." Fortunately, during that period, my parents were functioning well financially. With swift strokes of his pen across checks, my generous father wiped away over $2,000 in credit card debt I had accrued throughout the preceding months. My cell phone bills, which averaged over one hundred dollars each month (very high when you lack a data plan), were altogether absolved. The stock market that my illness had destroyed was quickly reinstated, as these loans came without an expectation of return. I think the fear of my death or otherwise was much harder to overcome than a few thousand dollars for my parents. We did not discuss the falling-out the previous month, the disruptions I had instigated, or my experience of being incarcerated. My mental illness had taken over and gone unnoticed, and they knew I needed help.

Discussing money was always easier than discussing other issues (e.g., emotions, sex, religion, etc.) in my family. I am grateful for the various forms of care my parents provided, but a dialogue as well as follow-up therapy might have been a better long-term investment as opposed to the appropriation of funds that was my fiscal bailout. They could control the money and "fix" that aspect of the situation, so that is what they did. I mentioned to them that in the course on mood disorders I was enrolled in that semester, there were large amounts of evidence proving the efficacy of family-focused therapy (FFT) in treating bipolar disorder. This therapy includes psychoeducation, which instructs the client and his or her family about the nature of the illness. There is recognition that the diagnosed individual cannot be considered an independent unit separate from the family system that contains him or her. Family-focused therapy appreciates the relationships (positive and negative), conflicts, and support from the people close to the individual that affect the outcome of the person's disorder. Resolution and understanding that diminish stress, as well as education regarding "expressed emotion" (critical, hostile, or overinvolved attitudes and behaviors that family members may have toward or act out with the individual), can aid the course of the illness as well. Unfortunately, some studies estimate that only 50 percent of families are willing or able to attend. My family continues to fall into the remaining 50 percent of families who are unwilling, but many have sought out independent treatment. Their response was one of a nonreaction or neutral acknowledgment of what I had just communicated. Basically, their reply was an exaggerated shrug or gesture that they understood what I said, but without dismissal or any real consideration for the idea. This was not the last time my suggestions about family or individual therapy would be set aside.

I denied my parents' request for me to return with them to Minnesota, because in my overly optimistic mind, I simply had to and would graduate on time. I would not repeat what had occurred the summer of 2002 (taking incompletes in my courses and waiting until the following fall to finish). Despite missing at least two months of class, I was determined to get my diploma. The stabilization of my mood was still absent, but one positive aspect of hypomania is that it often grants optimism even though the odds are stacked against the accomplishment of the goals. My parents left, and I went back to class that next week.

My head was shaved and I had odd tattoos, but the insecurity of the upcoming depression had not set in. I was able to get organized enough to speak (occasionally people corresponded verbally way back in 2005) and e-mail with my professors to get extensions for upcoming assignments, make up tests, and turn in some old work. Two of my courses were taught by psychologists, so they were very sympathetic, and the others were as well. However, my ability to sit and focus was not there and quickly got worse. I had friends with ADHD medications, such as Adderall. These medications are frequently misused or abused without a prescription by many college students. This behavior is the academic equivalent of what Lance Armstrong and other cyclers did to enhance their abilities to compete. But students doping with ADHD drugs race to the top of college hill. Ultimately, the drug facilitated the completion of my undergraduate degree by quieting the noise that my anxiety produced.

One evening during this time period emerges from my mind. After studying vigorously at the Memorial Library on campus, a friend called me to get a drink at the Blue Velvet bar as a study break. I obliged and met her there. She drank something out of an expensive bottle, and I had a fountain drink. I can still hear the statement that came out of her mouth: "So do you *not* like your tattoos now?" In a childish manner, I still thought it was cool to smoke cigarettes and have tattoos, so I had not even considered or reflected on the idea. This is one example that leads me to believe I was still symptomatic and a sense of realism had not yet sunk in. She did make me question the eccentric, hurried splashes of visible ink, but I simply said, "No?" with a perplexed expression on my face. It would soon dawn on me that I had made some horrible mistakes. Finally unfettered from the metaphorical shackles of incarceration and the debt of a manic spending spree, I would soon be confined to an internal battle with an unconquerable monster that a depressive episode often emulates.

—33—

SUFFERING

We call it a fall from grace, but is it really a fall from grace? Is grace no more than a well-constructed act we show the world, while our secret life is hidden from those we love?

—Debbie Ford, *The Shadow Effect*

Early on, I discerned that my anger and bitterness were actually above-the-surface depression while the existing mania slowly resided. I did not call for a psychiatric appointment right away, because *Why doesn't my psychiatrist know I am out of jail? He should be calling me!* The depression approached like an unsuspecting thunderstorm in the middle of an outdoor baseball game. I saw it coming and wanted to run for cover, but there was nowhere to go, as it had encompassed my brain.

When I eventually called and saw my psychiatrist, I was in pain. I remember pleading with him to prescribe an antidepressant, but he knew I was not stable enough for that type of intervention. His medical knowledge said that it was too risky for his and my psychological well-being. Another manic episode instigated by an antidepressant was the last thing that I needed. Lithium was unquestionably continued without reservation. However, I deeply desired something to stop the pain before the mental anguish killed my emotional as well as intellectual spirit. The doctor prescribed the drug I despised: Zyprexa. I should note that this reservation is a personal bias against the drug because of the association I have with it (i.e., the sleep terror I woke up to after first taking the drug). With his expertise, he explained that the antipsychotic drug would help stabilize my mood and assist in alleviating the anxiety. The psychiatrist's metaphorical prescription was for Tylenol when I wanted morphine to numb the indescribable suffering that I was in.

Every day it got worse. It was akin to a slowly impending migraine with increasing pressure on my mind; the piercing noise of anxiety perpetuated the throbbing inability to process information. A mental vise slowly tightened my thoughts and squeezed out a disparaging outlook. "I can't handle this," I said to my father on the phone during a late-night walk with my friend's dog—a mere attempt at escapism. Some of the anxiety manifested as a regression to my past fears related to body-image issues. I was underweight in jail, but the Zyprexa quickly helped me gain over ten pounds (weight gain is the most common side effect of the medication) in a matter of weeks. At another appointment with my psychiatrist, through tears, I told him I could not take the drug anymore. He was not completely opposed to this, as I was slowly going back on Lamictal (an anticonvulsant medication used as a mood stabilizer with mood-elevating components for individuals with bipolar disorder) and continued the lithium. Meanwhile, I feared food and exercised as much as I could. I was disappointed that I got winded and had to stop for air during a seven-mile run, which I had done with ease many times before. I absolutely attributed this decrease in athletic performance to the weight gain. Now I credit it to the fact that I drank and smoked cigarettes for six months in addition to being stagnant in jail for over two weeks. Moreover, the anxiety that manifested as ruminations of how my life had changed made it difficult to go on a relaxing jog.

Somehow I completed all of my courses except for one paper that needed to be done for my LGBT (lesbian, gay, bisexual, and transgender) course. As opposed to reading and test taking, writing still came naturally to me. The lengthy paper was not the most difficult task, and the teaching assistant gave me a generous extension on the deadline. The night before graduation, hours from when I was supposed to walk and receive my diploma, I was completing the late paper. I had already decided not to go to the ceremony, but I still wanted to get my last assignment finished. I wrote the paper on a laptop that I borrowed from the library, which I returned because, well, I was finished with the paper—and college, for that matter. However, when I checked my e-mail in order to print out the ten-page paper (thinking it was in an e-mail as an attachment), I realized that the e-mail did not exist. I had never sent the document to myself as an attachment. It was only on the university's laptop and nowhere else. Another *Fuck me* moment occurred. The technicians were unable to retrieve the file, because the computers were wiped of all files after each use. It is not necessary to describe how I felt about this. The next day, I went to the computer lab with a few notes and wrote as I imagine Hunter S. Thompson would have with the correct formula of alcohol, LSD, and cocaine. With a head full of stimulants and an unrepentant attitude for the grade to follow, I ignited my fingers. Unlike Gonzo journalism, I articulately reconstructed my previous narrative in an even more concise manner. I barely stood up during the four-hour writing marathon before concluding my scholastic duties. Grades were posted for my courses (May of 2005), and I received the following:

Spanish - Winter Module Oaxaca, Mexico	C
Geology	C
Mood Disorders	A
Intro Clinical Psychology	BC
Intro Gay, Lesbian, Bisexual, Transgender	A

After completing the paper that Saturday night, and thus fulfilling my bachelor of science degree, I decided to go meet a lot of my roommates from the year prior as well as others at the Kollege Klub bar, a popular hangout for members and former members of the Greek community (i.e., sororities and fraternities). Exactly one month after being released from jail, not only did I dislike my tattoos, but I also hated and was terribly embarrassed by the two "works of art." The remedy I chose to deal with this embarrassment was to wear a heavy black sweater to the bar that evening. Why I chose that of all long-sleeved items to wear into a basement sauna that smelled of yesterday's beer and overweight perspiration, I do not know. The memory of being extremely warm and psychologically uncomfortable is trumped by the encounter I had with a friend of mine. He was fairly intoxicated and welcomed me with a demanding request to see what I perceived as scars (i.e., the tattoos). It was a humiliating moment, but we laughed it off as if it equated to the scenario of taking an exposed tag off of a newly purchased shirt at a cocktail party. However, the physical abnormalities created during the manic episode and the subdermal ink do not come off with scissors or a swift tug. The other significant conversation from that night was with an ex-girlfriend whom I had not seen or communicated with in almost one year. She was not a Facebook subscriber, so how else could I have contacted her? She had discovered my circumstances, and immediately she asked why I had never told her about my mental illness. I offered no answer. If I had been in an environment that was not playing Usher or filled with drunken college students, I might have gathered the nerve to open up and pronounce, "I never thought I had a chance with you in college to begin with. I was insecure and afraid that if you knew about me having bipolar disorder, you might end our relationship or think I was crazy and lose interest. My confidence was near its peak when we were together, so I couldn't risk losing that feeling."

The way she asked me was with a sympathetic tone, but it still seemed as though I had done something wrong or had been disingenuous by keeping this secret. My relationship with her was less than mature in many ways, so this reunion a year later still fueled my desire to either take her home with me or to tell her to fuck off all the same. Whether or not my interpretation of her question was accurate, I have now, and since that occurrence, come to realize that this illness is an important part of my life. Even more importantly, I need countless individuals in my social, familial, and occupational networks who are cognizant of my condition in order to hinder another episode. This means that a significant other absolutely should be informed early on in the relationship. Any medical condition that could potentially be physically transmitted or that could have an emotionally damaging effect on the other person makes self-disclosure vital in a relationship. Divulging that I have bipolar disorder is something that gets easier with each person I tell. My fear is slowly habituated, but it will probably never be completely abolished.

In the same vein as giving a speech or presentation in front of a group, each time you disclose your illness to someone, your feelings of nervousness and anxiety are diminished in comparison to the previous attempt. After completing the presentation or disclosing the fact that you have bipolar disorder, there is a sense of relief. The more people I talk to about my experience with bipolar disorder, the less my mind subscribes to the cultural stigma that is the general public's myopic view of mental illness, including generalizations that people with mental illness are unable to work or are violent and, more so, the idea of invisibility. The illnesses are kept secret out of fear. Stigmas are slowly broken down as individuals with "success stories" as well as organizations like the National Alliance on Mental Illness (NAMI) expand the audience for their message. Happily, I have never had a negative reaction from a girlfriend, friend, or coworker in the ten years since I was diagnosed with bipolar disorder. I have been fortunate to have had many opportunities to share my story with larger groups, which has been a powerful learning experience. The concluding paragraph for my final LGBT paper, "Separation of Church & Sexual State," dated May 6, 2005, echoes these thoughts.

> Ignorance and prejudice only breed repression and fear in people that become aware of internal feelings that would be cast as different. During my hypomanic and manic episode this spring, it was very clear to my parents and then soon after my roommates and friends that I was acting abnormally. To perfect strangers, I just seemed outgoing and friendly or the life of the party. Awareness of what I was dealing with spurred the episode out of control, because of the resistance to sleep, medication, and anything that got in my way. Advocacy and self-awareness are the tenets of understanding of those that appear different to us. The individuals that are against social change and equality are those that have stopped learning about our ever changing world.

—34—

CEREBRAL IMPASSE

When we are being compassionate, we consider another's
circumstance with love ... To be compassionate is to move into
the right here, right now with an open heart consciousness and
a willingness to be supportive.

—Jill Bolte Taylor, *My Stroke of Insight*

The week following graduation in May of 2005, I apprehensively joined three friends on a road trip from Madison down to Tennessee as well as Atlanta, Georgia. I felt like shit, and my self-esteem told me that I should stay and work off the "pounds." The trip was agonizing as a whole. There were a few bright spots in my mind, but I believed that I could not think the way I had before (was this a delusion as well?). I was somewhat inhibited, but most of all, my anxiety was so high that nothing was mentally tolerable. My eating issues were in full force during the trip. I recall stopping at a Denny's for a nutritious breakfast. I did not want to eat a lot, because I usually regretted it and felt overly full, and I was sure it was having a gross effect on my weight as well as body image. The anxiety drove me to clean my enormous plate despite all of my reservations. Indecisiveness at a depressive level is excruciating. The lack of confidence and the fear paralyze the mind's ability to make simple decisions, in direct opposition to the way mania floods the mind with impulsive choices that all carry an equal or indifferent response. Things all happen for a reason during mania, and if something does not turn out the way in which it was quickly planned, then life goes on in the world of psychological invincibility.

Mania is almost an animalistic mind-set, because the stress response to events easily dissipates, as it does with a zebra that is chased by a lion and almost killed. As soon as it escapes death, the animal does not sit among the other zebras in the pack while thinking or looming over the fact that *Oh shit, I almost got killed.* There is no introspection or need for peer support while manic. For the zebra, after the chase, it forgets what happened and eats some grass. Mania is unscathed by stressors in the same way the escaping zebra forgets so quickly (for more on these ideas, see *Why Zebras Don't Get Ulcers* by Robert M. Sapolsky).

With depression, one is in a heightened state of fight or flight; seemingly innocuous situations cause physiological responses equivalent to those in life-threatening scenarios. In other words, the body is convinced it is in physical danger based solely on the person's thoughts or stress (e.g., think about how some people react to encountering a small bug in the house). Alternatively, some go into a freeze mode (e.g., hypersomnia, or sleeping excessively, especially during the day) whereby the retaliation is mental paralysis and overall physical inhibition. My constant anxiety fit into this framework, as the feeling of insecurity, from an evolutionary perspective, was my brain continuously telling me that my environment was not safe. Every minute decision was dangerous. The heightened alert causes hormonal changes in the brain, which amplify the depressive mood. The specific diagnostic criteria for major depressive episodes are listed in the book's appendix.

Once in Atlanta, my roommate and some friends went to a Braves baseball game. I wore a wristband on my forearm—not in the cool way that fraternity guys do, but to cover up my embarrassing tattoo. Despite the intense anxiety, I was back in my element to some degree: drinking alcohol. My anxiety was temporarily dampened, and I felt good. We had favorable seats behind home plate along with a pint of Jack Daniel's that added an amber color to our giant, dinner-priced sodas. The game was enjoyable, and seeing where a fellow man with bipolar disorder resides during the game was exciting. The owner of the Atlanta Braves, Ted Turner, was told by more people than not that CNN, or the idea of a twenty-four-hour news channel, was crazy. At the time, maybe it was.

After the game, my roommate and I returned to his parents' house and sat in the backyard with a surplus of Budweiser. We stayed up late, drinking steadily. I told him that I was thinking about going off of my lithium medication. The short version of my reasoning was that I could not take it anymore. The pain was insufferable, and a feeling of helplessness encompassed every moment of the day. It is said that when you find yourself in a hole, you should stop digging. I felt buried alive. My friend was not thrilled with the idea and did a good job of nonjudgmental inquiry. This continues to be an amazing quality he has with people.

Drinking at the level I did that night did not come without consequences. In the morning, I awoke early, needing to go to the bathroom. I felt as if a truck had hit me, and I was still somewhat drunk based on my unsteady gait. Standing above the toilet, I began to feel light-headed and soon fainted midstream. Luckily, the mat caught my body, and my parasympathetic nervous system turned off the liquid (sorry to be graphic here). It was an eye-opening and completely humiliating event. I relived it in my mind, consumed with self-deprecating thoughts. I showered for obvious reasons and later that day told my roommate what had occurred. This was a problem. The combination of taking my medications and drinking heavily certainly had played a role in how my body had reacted (i.e., instigating a fainting spell). I made the decision to continue my medication and hope for a change.

As soon as I returned to Madison, Wisconsin, it was time to move back to Minnesota, primarily because I did not have any money or prospects of gainful employment. Back in Minnesota, living at home with nothing important to do, I focused on improving myself—not emotionally or psychologically, of course, but physically. The desire for my mood to lift was there, but how to go about lifting it was not clear. My concentration was on the perceived need to perfect my body. I began running between thirty to forty miles per week, and I was not even training for a marathon or other sporting event. I was justifying the calories I ingested; I was like a depressed hamster on a wheel. The abundance of time in my empty days delayed the only thing I really felt I *needed* to do, which was to work out. I was sleeping in late most days, but if one agrees that sleep is cumulative, then I was at least a month or two behind. My mind used everything in its power to delay the mere accomplishment of exercise I wanted for the day.

> *What time should I eat? Just woke up, and it is already 11:30 a.m. When is breakfast, and when is lunch? I cannot run on a full stomach, but I need enough energy. One sandwich or two? Where should I go run? How many miles? I need to be sure to go to the bathroom before. Probably twice. There's nowhere to go once I'm on the path. I will wait until later in the afternoon. Shit! What about traffic if I go to Uptown or South Minneapolis? The perfect time is around 3:00 p.m. Should I take my brother's motorcycle?*

What would I do with the keys, my wallet, and the helmet? When can I get the most sun? I have to get tan to look better, so maybe I should go to one of the lakes where there are hot girls.

The process of these ruminations was just a different kind of madness. My thoughts were moving at a proper rate, but each thought was less productive than the previous. Every idea had a caveat, so there was an unconscious, constant struggle to determine the "perfect" way to do things in order to dampen the anxiety. It was a kind of procrastination that disallowed me to do the thing I felt I *should be* doing, but more importantly, it inhibited me from doing anything. This was every day for me.

Despite a lot of fear, I agreed to participate in a team triathlon with my sister and older brother, which brought my training to a whole different level. I felt an increased obligation to stick to my strict training regimen, as I felt I needed to get a really good time, or fast run, during the event. Skipping ahead to July 16 of 2005, when the triathlon took place, I performed well, but a picture of me running was met with a negative view in terms of my perceived body image:

Examination of this picture now makes me envious and causes wonder about how my mind could have been so distorted. I do not say that in a conceited manner, but one must realize just how out of shape I appeared at the time. I later explored this concept with a therapist, and she documented our discussion in her notes from a session. The piece below was appropriated from when I saw a specific therapist between 2006 and 2007.

> 9/7/06
>
> We also looked at Andy['s] struggle with self-image, which
> he relates to his appearance and particularly his weight The
> self-image issues seem to relate to his perfectionism and self
> consciousness, if he gains more than he thinks he should [...]
> Andy was able to get this in better perspective through the
> use of the cognitive exercises he worked on in session and
> which he will continue to practice.

During the summer of 2005, I did not want to see any of my friends and would go to bed early. I concluded most nights by watching the evening news or prime-time shows with my parents. Not having cable TV probably prolonged the depression. Thanks a lot, Mom and Dad. We engaged in little conversation, and I certainly did not instigate or vie for their attention. What I longed for was some separation from the emotional state I was in. My mind was filled with negative cognitions, but depression locked my jaw when I desired supportive affection from them. A child who could not express his needs eventually, in a somber way, sauntered upstairs to his bedroom in order to read. One of the books I read was Kay Redfield Jamison's *Night Falls Fast: Understanding Suicide*—not exactly a selection from Oprah's Book Club or a suggested read for the clinically depressed. Nevertheless, Jamison still is a hero of mine, and much like those who find faith and hope from a book that reeks of strong themes such as immorality, destruction, condemnation, death, and existentialism (probably just me), her writing and her compassion for those afflicted with mental illness were comforting. To avoid doing anything social and to keep myself isolated, I watched DVDs of the mediocre (at best) but successful teen drama *The OC*. The amateurish program was obviously geared toward the high-school-student demographic, and this piece of self-disclosure may be the most humiliating fact in this book (my deepest condolences to the Fox network).

A positive effect of the self-induced solitary confinement was that I took refuge and immersed myself in Darwinism as well as atheism. Richard Dawkins and Daniel Dennett became heroes of mine. I had long abandoned Catholicism but had only recently changed my Facebook status under "Religion Views" to "atheist." At the time, I believed this sense of nonbelief would fulfill the void of a lost sense of spirituality. I did not understand that one could have a "spiritual practice" (define that as you will) and also not believe in faith, a higher power, or an immaterial soul. I read dense academic books that explained the mechanisms of natural selection, or survival of the fittest, and decertified or debunked the mystical notion of intelligent design. This knowledge complemented my understanding of the hyper-religiosity that had plagued me during the prior manic episode from that spring. The human mind and society construct protective material to deal with the chasms of the unknown. The thought that there was no afterlife, as I explained, boggled my mother's mind and irritated my father. As I pulled away from but continued to challenge their faith, it seemed that they tried to push back or solicit subtle Christian idealistic views. I now understand that the combativeness toward all religion that became a large part of my life was not constructive. However, many of these convictions hold true for me today. My paradigm has shifted from following a religion that is believed to be structured in morality to being a nonbeliever with a "not-self" understanding. This means I try to have compassion for everything as we are all interconnected. More naive then, it was not until four years later that a mindfulness practice would be at the center of my life.

Soon I was feeling a little better about myself and began venturing out. I had been abstinent from alcohol for over a month but had to break that rule. Eventually, one evening, I told my mom that I was going to a barbecue at a longtime friend's house down the street, where a group would be congregating. The feeling of stagnant thoughts prompted me to slam two Diet Mountain Dew beverages before heading over to the gathering around seven o'clock. I thought everyone there would be able to recognize a difference in me. In reality, few people even knew about the events that had transpired over the four months of the episode, and they treated me no differently than usual. The pessimism I had held before the evening was disconfirmed, aided by a cocktail glass less than half empty during the party, and a subtle sense of relief washed over me.

A breaking point that included explosive crying spells in front of my parents in the kitchen led to my first encounter with psychotherapy. I was set up with a therapist who had her own private practice. I recall in detail the first session. As I had acquired my motorcycle permit in order to drive my younger brother's bike, I decided that the motorcycle would be my means of transportation to the session. Those without an official license were not allowed on the highway, so I took main roads, which grossly increased the duration of the trip. I was prepared for this but not for a traffic jam. Despite my inexperience, I made a plethora of illegal passes and turns, as I was terrified of being late to see the therapist. I arrived sweating due to the poorly ventilated helmet, the ninety-degree heat, and the anxiety that excreted through my pores. I was late, but anyone who has been to see a therapist knows that, like most medical professionals, they are frequently ten minutes late. As a clinician, I plead guilty to the pattern of perpetual lateness (as well as insanity). Prior to the meeting, I had written down a list of things I wanted to talk about. It is clear now that she was a very client-centered therapist—or possibly a lousy one—but nevertheless, as I started into the list, which began with my humiliation and shear hatred for my tattoos, I began to cry intensely. A single word escaped my mouth between the full-body convulsions. She was soft and comforting. A cardboard cutout of a therapist would have probably sufficed in order to produce the catharsis and release I experienced. I continued to see her weekly, and when I was finally hired for a full-time job, things started to look up rather than down.

My younger brother graduated high school that June of 2005, and a big party was planned. The whole family was together, and spirits were high in the group—minus mine. We were somewhat "normal" again. I remember helping out on the grill, and for some reason, the interaction with my dad has always stuck with me. I was flavoring the burgers with seasonings by delicately tapping my finger on the end of the bottle, and he said with a sarcastic grin, "Don't be so dainty with it." That grin turned out to be one of the few remaining smiles produced by him for the remainder of the year. I was somewhat irritated by his comment, mostly because of my sensitive mood, but it is now something I always think about when grilling. Only days later, he would change forever, and seemingly insignificant moments such as that one would all but be eradicated. The dust had finally settled after my manic episode, and everything in the family was going well: my brother graduated high school, my sister was a brainchild, and the father–son (my dad and older brother) real estate business was booming. I was still miserable on the inside, but slight changes and adjustments were happening. In an entry to my journal for June 19, 2005, I wrote the following:

> I do not feel like doing anything, but at the same time I feel
> guilty in a small way because I do not make an effort to try
> and interact with the friends that I have here.

Two days later, I wrote this:

> I feel like I am isolating myself away from people more and
> more. I feel that I am living life a little too scared right know.
> Using my illness as an excuse to not take any risks or to go out
> and have fun.

On June 25, 2005 my father had a stroke, which forever drastically changed the dynamics of my family. I was home when it happened. My sister and I were getting ready to be centered at a local Bikram yoga class. The real motivation for me was an attempt at sculpting my body and not for peace of mind. The same day, I planned on attending a bachelor party that I was somewhat concerned about, because it would mean heavy levels of drinking. However, I was also looking forward to it, as my vista of the future was a Microsoft Outlook calendar that lacked upcoming events—or any color, for that matter.

I instantly heard my mother's contained yet urgent plea as I came out of the bathroom. I hurried to the front door, and she yelled, "Call 911! I think your father is having a stroke." Adrenaline pumped through my body, activated by the sympathetic nervous system, as I ran to the phone. "I think he's having a stroke ... Yeah he's conscious ... 10016 Park Circle." My stomach cramps and turns now as I write. Eliciting such physical sensations is something the body does not have time to do when the fight-or-flight switch turns on during heightened perceived danger. It is only now, when the explicit memories surface, that my mind produces aversive stimulation of bodily sensations. Now as I reconstruct the visual of the most powerful and respected man in my life being helplessly lifted by me, my mother, and two EMTs, the image is surreal. What I remember the most and what strikes me most about that incident is how collected and composed everyone was. It was not like a scene in movies or TV shows, where frenetic hands and hostile or disjointed conversations pile on top of one another. The EMTs discussed how best to move my father, where to place the ambulance gurney, and other pragmatic details. I believe the calmness was a result of my mind focusing on the intellectual aspects of what was taking place in order to defend against the emotional devastation surrounding the incident. Any Freudian or psychoanalyst will understand this removal of one's self from a stressful situation as the defense mechanism known as intellectualization.

The story of my father's stroke and its effect on me and the rest of my family would need its own cover, chapters, and careful contemplation, which does not fit into the framework of this prose. What is relevant is the turmoil it caused emotionally. One irony of the stroke was that it did not have a negative effect on my mental state, because as it was all happening, I was focused on working on the internal demons swirling inside of me. As the most tragic incident ripped through our family, I was starting to feel *better*. This was an emotional and psychological paradox, because during the surgeries as well as the recovery process following his stroke, the worst depression in my life was gradually eradicated from my mind.

I was set to start orientation for my new job two days after that dreadful Saturday. I put on my family's metaphorical work boots and attended to business as usual. I recall one particularly haunting aspect of that time period: every time I received a phone call from my mother or another family member, my initial thought was always that my father had died or something horrific had happened. The sympathetic nervous system often produces this type of stress during—and, for humans, after—a tragedy or life-threatening event. In some cases, this can lead to the development of post-traumatic stress disorder (PTSD). The guilt of how much my dad had helped me during the manic episode drove me to visit him in the hospital four to five times per week despite the one-way thirty-minute trip. Seeing the condition he was in made me a stronger person. It helped me to appreciate as well as empathize with his pain and forgive his now often volatile demeanor (a consequence of the stroke). I processed all that was occurring on the front lines, which I believe my siblings were unable to do at the time. When the surgeries were finished and the therapy sessions expired, our family returned to a new homeostasis in which our father was physically disabled as well as cognitively rewired. From a session dated September 28, 2006, a one-sentence summary written by my therapist captured and regurgitated the words I used to illustrate my pain that still existed over one year later:

> He shared how difficult it is to see him [my father] having
> transformed from a very powerful figure to a man with so many
> weaknesses.

I wrote this portion of the book while sitting in a cabin at an ashram in Vermont with a coworker, and he inquired about what I was writing: "A novel or something?" This was an easy way for me to self-disclose my illness. As opposed to past years, I now look for openings in order to tell others in my life about my disorder. I will talk in depth about this in the following chapter to give an understanding of the importance that a safety net provides for preventing manic as well as depressive episodes. There is something to be said about knowing what's wrong with you. Such knowledge provides a remarkable opportunity to migrate in the direction of our "shadow," which includes the unskillful behaviors we try to ignore and things we dislike about ourselves, as opposed to the societal push for avoidance and distraction.

—35—

ABNORMAL CONNECTIONS

The essence of life is statistical improbability on a colossal scale.

—Richard Dawkins

My father's stroke was most likely due to a serious concussion he'd suffered in high school, which had resulted in short-term memory loss. The concussion had altered his structural brain chemistry in such a way that veins were connected to arteries throughout and vice versa. It was a "ticking time bomb," as the surgeon stated. A moment would decide when one of these entangled threads would clot and finally burst. Thankfully, when it did happen, he survived this still-unbelievable event as well as the surgeries that followed. Despite the aftereffects produced from the damage in his prefrontal lobe, including his tendency to be an ill-tempered or cantankerous individual, he is still capable of many things. Throughout his recovery at the end of the summer of 2005, I continued to see a therapist as my mood improved. The combination of therapy and the structure that a job enforces was a facilitator to my healing. In addition, the Lamictal reached a therapeutic range that was optimal for me. The drug must be increased very slowly because, in rare cases, a potentially lethal rash develops, whereby the treatment is ended or restarted at the square-one low dose. I was still taking lithium and began doing a lot more social activities. In November of 2005, I reconnected with and began dating someone I knew from high school. I was always on the prowl for a relationship, and the new relationship increased my self-worth and perpetuated an optimism that I had all but lost over the course of the year. I would like to say that I abstained from drugs and alcohol, but that was simply not the case. I avoided any depressive or manic symptoms, but the anxiety was still there to a lesser extent. I attempted to control my anxiety through perfectionism, and a good example is the way I took care of my car. I would periodically clean it to the exhausting point of eventually using Q-tips as a tool to remove dust from the vents. I also had other obsessions that commanded me to relieve anxiety through compulsions. For example, my obsession with the musician Ryan Adams propelled a need to download as quickly as possible all of the hundreds of concerts posted on the Internet and use a methodic system of filing the music despite listening to a small percentage of the recordings. This in and of itself is not the most debilitating of behaviors, but I was taking risks by doing this largely on my work computer.

The only real depressive episode that occurred was in Hawaii on a trip with my girlfriend a year or so after we started dating (December of 2006). Imagine taking a vacation to Maui, one of the most beautiful places on earth, and hating life. It was a nightmare. There is one moment that I will never forget: while on a whale-watching tour, sixty yards from a humpback whale and calf, I was fighting back tears that could only come from an internally dark place.

Articulating these events and feelings is an arduous process for me. If one has not gone through a depressive episode or does not have a mood disorder, I can only hope he or she gains some insight from this. We want to think or believe that depression happens from the outside in—that it is a top-down process whereby a negative event occurs and we slowly become depressed. This idea is analogous to events in our life seemingly causing us to contract depression. For example, someone dies and we never had a chance to say we loved them or didn't spend enough time with him or her. This belief or idea gets looped over and over in such a way that these ruminations of the past as well as dreadful thoughts of the future manifest into a cyclonic state of despondency (i.e., bottom-up processes). My understanding is that it is not the events in our life that cause depression, but instead how we describe those stories and what they mean in relation to ourselves. With the example of the friend whom you never said "I love you" to, if your reaction was "I'm a failure" or "I'm a bad person," you might perceive that statement as truth through repetition over time. This cyclical process (event > story we create > belief about ourselves in relation to the event) and clogged memory channels make us susceptible to depression or other mental health problems. Insert one of my events or stories from the manic episode in 2005 and you will see it works in the same way (e.g., going to jail > ruined my life > I am abnormal).

Full recognition of this internal progression that creates most depression and how our own schemas feed into it did not come until years later for me. The obsessing and anxiety took full force during my application process for graduate school in 2007. The thought of going back to school for an attempt at a master's in social work was daunting. The rational decision to go to the University of Wisconsin–Madison was solidified both for financial and psychological reasons. I was familiar with the school and the area, there was tuition reciprocity, and I had close friends still living there. The most difficult part of the transition was to stop and realize that I was actually leaving to start the program. I thought about ending the self-induced mental atrophy that was drug and alcohol consumption as well as the perfectionistic tendencies. In addition, my tendency to seek contentment in relationships had resurfaced with a vengeance, which increased my anxiety. After finally conceding to not use any drugs and alcohol, I no longer had an exodus from the fears or concerns that surrounded the change of going back to school. I simply had to face reality.

When I started school, sitting in class for two hours meant that I felt each heavy heartbeat in my chest. These were not rapid heartbeats; instead, it felt as if my core organ had gained weight, and I was cognizant of each pump. It felt as if my heart were a bass drum being hit with a small, padded mallet to a dying pulse beat of "The Little Drummer Boy." This psychosomatic symptom was driving me mad! Increasing the clonazepam (an antianxiety medication) helped, but the drowsiness needed to be combated by small portions of Adderall (e.g., 2.5 mg) in addition to a lot of Diet Mountain Dew.

Depressive symptoms soon followed the anxiety. On October 7, 2007, I wrote the following in my journal:

> I feel miserable, lost, scarred. I have no idea what to do, literally, I can't think of anything that I would enjoy doing right now [...] I feel like crying and I know I should talk to someone, but I can't decide on going through with it. I'm a hypocrite to everything I believe in right now. Really hope that I get in with a therapist soon, but I'm not even thinking about tomorrow. What do I do right now? The fear is overwhelming.

My first experience with mindfulness occurred when my psychiatrist (the same doctor who had treated me during my undergraduate years) said not to fight the anxiety or get mad at it. He said to "go toward it" by allowing recognition and compassion to the anxiety. After that step, he advised me to just "let it go." This approach is also known as "touch and go." With every feeling you experience, pay attention to it and then move on. It was remarkable. My heart palpitations soon disappeared from my body, although the anxiety would reemerge throughout the two years of the program. I know now—but did not want to believe then—that this escalation of anxiety was partially from psychological withdrawals to marijuana. Using drugs and alcohol during the two years between undergraduate and graduate school had been my main coping mechanism for anxiety. I will revisit this aspect of my recovery at the end of the book (i.e., chapter 37).

Working as well as interning for my former employer, the Mental Health Center of Dane County, made the first year of graduate school very tolerable despite the stress and lack of free time. My familiarity with the job, coworkers, and expectations, not to mention the safety net of a large group of mental health professionals who knew my condition and were always available to talk, relieved me. The four semesters of graduate school were part of the most rewarding years of my life, and I could go on and on about the experiences and positive connections I made. However, for this piece of writing, I want to focus on specific times in my life deeply associated with bipolar disorder. What is important in terms of my mental illness is that self-disclosure was helpful. The first group project I was involved in for graduate school turned out to be researching children and adolescents with bipolar disorder. What the hell are the odds? I decided I was not going to spend several months working on this time-consuming initiative with three strangers while biting my tongue. Instead, I used it as an opportunity to disclose my condition to the fellow students. It was a beautiful moment, as the group members began to share their own issues, past and present, with mental illness, and I believe the discussion solidified our relationships as well as the dynamic of the group in a remarkably short period of time. I was happy with my academic performance and had a renewed sense of intellectual confidence. No longer blanketed by insecurity, I spoke out more in class with my skeptical opinions. That spring (2008), after speaking with a professor, I acquired a teaching assistant position for the following fall semester.

In the summer after the first year, I reverted back to spending ample time in bars as well as apartments filled with pungent, skunk-like smoke (I am talking about weed here), which allowed me to avoid the anxiety that resulted from a lack of structure in my daily life. This lifestyle contributed to my falling in love very quickly with a close friend who was living in Croatia at the time and was briefly visiting Madison, Wisconsin. The fast-paced-love-affair weekend was the impetus for an immediate long-distance relationship. This ultimately led me to go visit her one month later. It was a fairy-tale "honeymoon before the weeding." This amazing trip was unveiling itself while, at the same time, symptoms of hypomania were progressing (staying up into the morning hours, smoking cigarettes, acting more extroverted and overzealous, spending money frivolously, abusing prescription drugs, using recreational drugs, drinking periodically, feeling euphoric, etc.).

For part of the trip, we had luxurious waterfront accommodations on Hvar Island, Croatia, which is located in the Adriatic Sea and is just a boat ride from Italy. The majestic beauty was not enough, as I would ingest mood-altering chemicals and would immerse myself in hedonistic activities throughout my stay.

Chasing love across continents is one thing, but I now know that I could not see the forest for the trees. She was not leaving her nomadic career or lifestyle (i.e., the forest). But the strong sexual and intellectual compatibility we shared and the intensity of my feelings (i.e., the trees) blinded any insight. I understood the hypomania only after considerable reflection, and certainly the insight did not occur in the moment. After all, no one wants to equate being in love to experiencing mood swings or being crazy! The realization that I was experiencing depressive symptoms quickly after the hypomania was tapering came months later. The disappointing reality hit me less than a week into the cross-continental trip.

Suddenly I comprehended the fact that this relationship was not going to work out. I became emotionally withdrawn and slept at every chance I could (e.g., on buses, planes, beaches, and boats and even while hitchhiking). My story had changed although the event had not. This event caused me to believe something negative about myself. Perhaps it was "I cannot be alone" or "I was stupid to flip my life upside down to come on this trip." Whatever the belief or idea was, it had not existed a week prior. This extended stay temporarily extinguished the pain of not being able to see her. However, the relationship ended quickly after my return home, and I soon transitioned into another relationship. My dating sagas forever continue.

—36—

Unconventional Wisdom

The fact is, we know too little about what's going on in the cosmos to commit to that sort of strict atheism. On the other end of the spectrum, we know way too much to commit to a particular religious story.

—David Eagleman, *Incognito*

The second year of graduate school was even better than the first. Practicing psychotherapy had been a dream of mine for more than three and a half years, and it was finally fulfilled. I was learning this craft as an intern and devoting all my energy into the mental health concentration that year. This produced an immense amount of learning. At the closing of my master's degree, mindfulness formally entered my life. I went on a weekend retreat at the Sinsinawa Mound Center in Wisconsin. This experience was facilitated by a single Zen teacher with the backdrop of a Catholic monastery. A small group of individuals—approximately twelve to fourteen people—was in attendance. The judgmental part of my mind was filled with preconceived notions. Later, I found out that the older, devoted women, or Dominican Sisters, at this location were some of the sweetest people I had ever met, perfectly complementing the amazing architecture that was to be our brief haven.

The facilitator was clean shaven, tall, and slender, with paper-thin wire glasses, and he had the emergence of speckled gray hair upon his shaved head. My initial thought, judgment, or projection was that he reminded me of a prototypical Western Christian priest. I cognitively redressed him in a seamless white robe (as Christ often wore), and the clerical appearance was uncanny! I had developed an aversion to figures *like him*, as the indoctrination of Catholicism still bred animosity in my adolescent mind. In this setting, he was stoically perched on a metal folding chair at eye level with those in chairs and just above those sitting patiently on the floor. In actuality, the Zen priest was a modern, well-dressed psychologist who had an iPhone and a full-back tattoo. He was a progressive gay man with one of the softest hearts I have ever met. He displayed a supernatural ability for mind–body therapy techniques. Observing him was like watching a magician, except it was anything but bullshit. The experience had a profound effect on me. I was finally compelled to look inward at my internal processes, to stop judging others, and to start viewing my fears, insecurities, and pain. The first night, I broke down mentally in my tiny dorm room. Structurally, the room had many features of the hospital space that had quarantined my fictitious whooping cough four years prior.

I felt caged in. My heart began to race, and a sense of panic reverberated through my body. *I gotta get out of here.* A full-bodied display of crying and helplessness went on for at least an hour before I literally cried myself to sleep. Much like a child, I buried my face in my pillow, subservient to the emotional demands, and begged for mercy from the temporary insanity that confined my mind. Despite the pain I felt, the experience was a tortuous cleansing that needed to occur. Like a person experiencing withdrawal or detox from a drug of choice, I was beginning to see the world without a protective inhibitor, and it made me sick all over. There was no choice or turning back; I would face the dark shadows of insecurity by opening my eyes. The meditation and talks brought to light the disturbances I was having about who I was. In addition, the previously dormant conflicts within the relationship with my girlfriend began surfacing.

The retreat was properly titled "Waking Up and Growing Up," and that night's events captured a piece of the title. It was my first truly spiritual practice since denouncing the Catholic Church, organized religion in general, and especially the belief in a Judeo-Muslim-Christian god. The insights I learned proliferated real-life changes and, more so, the development of a means to evolve as a person. This stemmed from the encounter of a dualistic self. A simplistic description of who I am is not encompassed by one-sided adjectives, such as *happy*, *generous*, *mature*, and *intelligent*. People cannot be reduced to singular descriptions, but we often do this to ourselves and attempt to push down the parts of us we do not want to be. In addition to the above descriptors, I am also often sad or depressed, selfish or greedy, immature and naive. The retreat was both a mental purgatory and an emotional sanctuary. I grew as a person, especially in a sense of the impermanence in every thought, moment, and event and the overall view that we do not have to judge either description of ourselves when these feelings arise.

Whether we know it or not, we all carry a toolbox that holds our resources and skills acquired throughout life. The tools are used to develop self-efficacy—or, in other words, a belief that one can achieve with confidence certain goals. Some of us have access to more practiced instruments that lead to a healthy lifestyle, fulfillment, and contentment. A toolbox is a good metaphor for coping with bipolar disorder. At one time, I felt with conviction that a diagnosis of bipolar disorder was an impasse to achievement that elicited a futile or hopeless existence. These forthcoming anecdotal suggestions should be explored independently by the individual, but I have achieved success through what follows. My life has afforded me the benefit of academic knowledge as well as personal experience surrounding the disorder; however, this is not entirely necessary to live a rewarding life with the disorder. Embracing the belief that we all have the solutions and resources to fight stress and anxiety can help unlock this case inside of us and prevent future mood episodes. The toolbox metaphor can be taken in a lot of different directions, but to simplify, I can visualize my treatment experience for bipolar disorder as a carpenter's square, also known as a steel square. For those not familiar, the L-shaped tool is used to make a right angle, framing, or other measurements. The longer arm of the tool was drug therapy for me, and I continue this devotion to taking psychotropic medication—it is priority one. This has kept my mood stable, especially in the last six years. The shorter arm of the tool in my life was and has been support from friends, family, colleagues, and therapists. It was not until the spring of 2009 that I realized a connection between the two was missing.

A carpenter triangle is united by three arms as opposed to the two-armed, square steel tool. This idea manifested during a walking meditation at a silent retreat in 2009. I had no intention of writing about it at the time. I had a profound realization that since the detrimental manic episode in 2005, my combative nature with religion was extremely counterproductive, though not completely unwarranted. There was something missing in my life that I needed in order to alleviate the distress I was enduring both in life and from bipolar disorder. My outspoken atheistic remarks directed at my family and friends were not helping me to mature as a person or prevent another episode. I needed a spiritual component of some kind. This message is not meant as doctrine for a specific religious practice, a belief in a higher power, Buddhism, or the practice of meditation but as an example of what has worked for me. There is evidence from meticulously studied neuroscience regarding mindfulness and bipolar disorder that I will juxtapose here before my proposed interventions. Manic and depressive episodes can *cause* residual cognitive deficits for the individual. This means bipolar disorder can potentially cause physical brain damage (based on the age of onset and the number of episodes), which may include the following:

> ventricular enlargements, cerebellar vermal atrophy, cortical atrophy, white matter hypertensities (especially in the frontal cortex), greater left temporal lobe quantity, increased amygdala volume, enlarged right hippocampal volume and chemical imbalances. (Bearden et. al, 2001)

Understanding what that means in terms of deciphering the medical jargon is not important in this comparison. What is useful is to know that mindfulness (specifically meditation) has shown the opposite effect on the brain. Depression and anxiety symptoms are often accompanied by a decrease in activity of the prefrontal cortex. Meditation increases activity in this area, which increases compassion as well as empathy. There is a subtle nuance to these two states of mind. Compassion is a conscientious sensitivity for another person's pain or suffering with a desire to relieve it. In comparison, empathy involves the imagination or cognitive experience of what that person is struggling with. There are individualized results of meditation that can also change interpersonal relationships and interdependence. These include improved concentration, organization, and positive affect over time. Individuals practice mindfulness to meet relationships where they are at and subsequently benefit the self. Not the other way around.

The scientific evidence for the changes caused by manic and depressive episodes exhibits diametrical forces of meditation in the same brain areas. Therefore, I have constructed my own theory on ways to live with bipolar disorder using the carpenter's tool as the visual metaphor at the foundation. I already alluded to many of these ideas, but it is important to express the information concretely and in a concise manner. This triangle has become my approach or attempt to live in a healthy manner while having a mental illness. I can only hope my suggestions help others to avoid initial or recurring episodes.

Medication, Support, and Mindfulness

1. Medication

The first line of maintenance for the treatment of bipolar disorder is always prescription medication. I say *maintenance* because there is no cure or blood test, and it is not something to fight. Not everyone takes medication or stays on it, but I strongly believe it is to be considered during an initial episode. The decision to take medication is a way for individuals to return or closely return to their original states of functioning, which is a major goal of the recovery process. Bipolar disorder will always win the war against a passive victim who hopes it will not attack again; thus, a single line of defense is not enough.

In addition, medication does not just come in pill form. Alternatively, proactive acceptance and empathy for both the individual as well as the disorder breed tolerance for maintenance, which includes the often-necessary psychotropic drugs. Certainly there are cases where individuals have successfully managed bipolar disorder without ongoing psychiatric medicine, but

I have not met any of them in my personal or professional life. The need for medication is especially true during a manic break, when talking someone down from the heights of psychosis is pretty difficult, if not impossible. The least-restrictive dosage should be applied and then slowly increased while the person also receives therapy. In addition, the most important medicine for bipolar disorder is sleep. Maintaining a regular sleep pattern is an essential prescription. A routine of going to bed and waking up roughly at the same time has worked best for me. One of the biggest triggers as well as features of a manic episode is sleep deprivation. There is a tendency for people with bipolar disorder, not surprisingly, to go to extremes or opposite ends of the pole when it comes to sleeping (e.g., sleeping all day or not sleeping at all).

This swinging from one side of the pole to the other is a hindrance to treatment of bipolar disorder, especially when it comes to medication compliance. Commonly, individuals take their medication religiously or all of a sudden decide they do not need it at all. With all medications, including those sold over the counter, there can be a myriad of side effects. When people read the side of the bottle, they can get caught up in the fear of what could come or does come with the administration of the drug. This fear can lead to hysterical online searches with worst-case examples and warning signs about the medication. For example, there is the potential side effect of weight gain if one takes lithium. However, it is difficult to say whether individuals on lithium are gaining weight because of the anxiety they might have after being diagnosed with bipolar disorder, a change in lifestyle (e.g., isolating behaviors that lead to overeating), or an increase in weight based on a recent loss of weight during a manic episode. When examining possible side effects, it is easy to fixate on the potential for an unsettling occurrence. Another side effect that might occur with lithium is acne. However, if people are aware of this, the anxiety or worry concerning their skin can itself cause breakouts. It is understandable that no one desires an additional trip through puberty with pizza-faced memories and adolescent ridicule. A fixation on the skin can lead to more frequent touching or scrupulous maintenance, which makes the issue worse. Occasional skin imperfections must be weighed against the life-threatening results of not taking medication (i.e., depression and mania). My approach is to avoid mirrors and utilize digital photograph-editing programs in order to live in a world where pimples do not exist [insert smiley face emoticon to represent sarcasm]. Whoever prescribes the medication should be consulted to determine the risks and side effects of all medication.

Dichotomous, or black-and-white, thinking leads to depression and is also displayed in active manic episodes. Generally speaking, depression inhibits people's desire to do anything (e.g., a person might stay in bed all day) and their ability to take pleasure in activities they once enjoyed, and it also creates a hopeless perception of the world. At the other end of the dichotomy, mania believes, "I can do anything and everything with no restrictions." Acknowledging—and, more so, noticing—dichotomous thinking in certain decisions can inhibit a manic episode. Considering whether or not to completely stop taking medication, emptying one's bank account, or investing an unreasonable amount of money or energy into something are all red flags for a mood shift toward mania. Insight and others around you who are aware of the disorder can help to prevent these episodes from manifesting.

2. Support

Psychoeducation is an essential first step of psychotherapy for the individual suffering from a psychological disturbance. This process includes the family's participation (e.g., family-focused therapy) to understand their roles and to help the individual gather more insight into his or her mental illness. The hope with psychoeducation is that the individual can better accept his or her mental illness. Also, the patient's own strengths, resources, and coping skills are reinforced in order to avoid relapse and contribute to his or her own health and wellness on a long-term basis. The theory is that the more knowledge the patient has of his or her illness, the better the patient can live with the condition.

Based on the last six years, I can surmise with confidence that continuous therapy is vital to staying healthy, but it is ultimately up to the individual. Personally, the trauma I experienced from going to jail needed to be processed during therapy. A clinician in Madison, Wisconsin, administered eye movement desensitization and reprocessing (EMDR) with me during a session. EMDR invokes bilateral stimulation of the brain (interaction between the brain's hemispheres—right to left—that permits the processing of trauma-related memories in a progressive as well as improved way) while the client recounts the traumatic memory. This is done while vacillating from the past memory back to the present moment in order to process emerging feelings that are both physical and mental.

To activate these physiological processes of the brain, in my case, the therapist used movements of her fingers as my eyes followed from right to left. Others often hold sensors that elicit the same response by vibrating intermittently from the left sensor to the right and vice versa. In the future years, I was able to process negative beliefs I had about myself, such as "I am abnormal," that had been embedded in my brain related to the trauma. This therapeutic technique has allowed me to look down as an observer over the experiences of being incarcerated rather than being emotionally overwhelmed while thinking about the situations. From my own observation, wherever one finds a mental illness or disorder, there is underlying trauma. As a consequence of this treatment, I was able to write and share these memories in a more objective manner without forgetting what had happened.

The massive amount of trauma that occurs when one is diagnosed with a severe and persistent mental illness means the person needs an ample amount of support. This is most true following an episode. Confining oneself to an environment that includes family, friends, and mental health professionals will increase one's likelihood of stability. When one is comfortable, speaking about the illness with others can be helpful. The fear of the attached stigma makes self-disclosing to others scary, but the benefit of a safety net of others who are aware is invaluable. Transparency among friends, family, coworkers, and significant others often leads to the detection of symptoms early on.

My close friends and family were deemed helpless during my major manic episode in many ways, but one was the inability to contact my treatment providers. It is crucial to sign releases of information for those who are pre-scribing medications (e.g., psychiatrists or primary care physicians) as well as one's therapist. This enables communication between loved ones and the mental health agents in times of crises. This proactive approach is contradic-tory to the all-too-frequent detachment with those close to the individual with the illness. "I don't have a problem" or "I can do it myself" or "I don't need help" are predictable responses to the disorder that can lead to isola-tion (usually accompanied by depression) or extreme needs for attention and uninhibited socialization (common with mania). Without the releases, friends and family will not be allowed to communicate with the treating pro-fessionals, because of the confidentiality rights of the individual in treatment. This was a major barrier during my manic episode in 2005, because everyone in my support system could see me decompensating, but they were unable to help intervene with my psychiatrist. The consequence is often ultimate isolation, such as jail and or hospitalization.

3. Mindfulness

The new buzzword in the mental health community—among researchers and in numerous self-help books—is *mindfulness*. Religious believers and nonbelievers, despite many profound ideological differences, can both relate as well as benefit from the universal applications that mindfulness practices provide. Mindfulness can be defined in many ways, but essentially, it is a nonjudgmental awareness of the present. There is no denial of sensations, thoughts, or feelings. There is an overall acceptance of the spectrum of pleasure to pain and everything in between. Many of the components are taken from Buddhist practices, but there is nothing dogmatic about this system of living. Buddhism in general does not have a built-in belief system and instead includes a practical, proactive component to meet suffering. My view of Buddhism is an Eastern psychological approach to turn toward rather than avoid the suffering we all face.

Western psychology has a similar aim but with a less-centered approach to the individual and an emphasis on the medical or disease model (i.e., diagnosis and treatment). One philosophy is not better than the other, but a combination is very effective in treating the individual rather than just the psychological disorder. Mindfulness involves one's ability to self-regulate his or her attention to the present moment. There is a suspension of each experience, so mental events and feelings can be processed. An acceptance of these perceptions in the here and now reduces a tendency toward avoidance behavior. Whether it is everyday stress or a pathological state of mind, our thoughts demand us to cling to something, which inhibits present awareness: "Do not dwell in the past, do not dream of the future, concentrate the mind on the present moment" (Buddha, a long time ago).

In the verbiage of Westernized psychology, the themes of *depression* and *anxiety* could take the place of *past* and *future* in mindfulness teaching to apply the notion to mental illness. "Do not fixate on your negative thoughts about who you are and what has happened to you; do not obsess and worry about what is to come. Instead, focus your mind on the present moment" (me, 2010). A real barrier to mindfulness is the abuse of drugs and alcohol. These substances are short-term interventions that give the individual a temporary state of homeostasis. Illicit drugs or ones that are abused are powerfully seductive tools that blunt feelings of the past and present for mere moments of painless bliss. The dilemma with this approach is that the momentary aspect of the drugs' effect on the mind leads to an often intolerable increase in pain during the absence of the drugs. Setting aside the potential side effects drugs cause when interacting with prescribed medication, a true feeling or sense of stability will never occur with temporary, superficial, self-administered drugs. Unfortunately, drugs are a very successful *short-term* intervention for many.

The behaviors that result from misguided cognitions or thoughts (discussed below) enable repressed feelings to surface when we are not ready to handle them. We are constantly trying to bottle up or hold down unwanted sensations, which causes constant suffering. It is analogous to holding beach balls underwater. The more beach balls you have to hold underwater, the harder it is to keep them from shooting above the surface. You can do it for a while, but once a major stressor comes along, you lose the capability or threshold to submerge these feelings, and they explode upward (Chopra et. al, 2010). Alternatively, mindfulness instills compassion, curiosity, and openness in the individual; using the previous metaphor, the beach balls constantly coincide on the water's surface as they are acknowledged but enabled to casually float away. A mindfulness practice reduces stress and ultimately increases concentration. One method that has been efficacious in producing this effect for me has been meditation, but mindfulness is a complex psychological application with many facets. Whether one has a spiritual practice or not, I believe a healthy lifestyle has to include something more than day-to-day life distractions that keep us passing through the Internet and other forms of self-gratification. This just means implementing into life an element that transcends the egocentrism we are often reduced to. The we-are-the-center-of-the-universe outlook, where everything that happens directly affects *us*, is a self-centered distraction. Drawing a distinction, one must take a step back from the self in order to find acceptance. Whether through cosmological laws, Darwinism, Islam, Christianity, atheism, or mindfulness, we all have the ability to meet and tolerate the suffering our giant brains inherently cause. Without the capacity to show empathy for others, it will be difficult to have compassion for yourself and all that you have gone through in coping with a mental illness.

This therapeutic example of what has helped me to cope with bipolar disorder starkly contrasts with my undeveloped treatment plan in 2002, when I was first diagnosed. The potential for my well-being is based on this triangle (medication, support, and mindfulness). This correlates in direct opposition with the following proposed impediments to the process of recovery from a mental illness:

1. perfectionism / dichotomous thinking;
2. isolation and oversocialization; and
3. drugs and alcohol.

I believe these are three pertinent factors that defy the triangle theory I prescribed above. To preface these ideas, it is important to make note that I have been significantly affected and continue to battle these endeavors, so this is not meant to be self-righteous or an act of condemnation of these behaviors.

—37—

DEPENDENCIES

The definition of insanity is doing the same thing over and over and expecting different results.

—Albert Einstein

Perfectionism / Dichotomous Thinking, Isolation and Oversocialization, and Drugs and Alcohol

1. Perfectionism / Dichotomous Thinking

In the early months of 2006, I began working with one of the most empathic psychotherapists. Her soft presence in the dwarfed office included mind, body, and soul. Her gentle affect was both welcoming and emotionally noxious. I was not ready to face some of the beach balls I held below the surface. The confined space and persistent reflections she produced did not make it any easier. Perhaps I was better acquainted with sterile and relatively benign psychiatric sessions: "How's your sleep? Are you having any problems with the medication?"

Our relationship quickly flourished. More than anything, she helped me to gain insight into my obsessive behaviors. I asked her to provide me with her therapy notes after each visit, which she agreed to do. I remember looking at the first note with urgent curiosity: "and [he] is perfectionistic with di-chotomous thinking." I had to look up *dichotomous* in the dictionary, but I understood perfectionism and quickly realized these traits dominated my life. It would take years to make even the most subtle of behavioral changes that deviated from the strict boundaries of perfectionism. These two traits protect against what I believe to be fear—fear of both failure and the relin-quishment of control.

As they relate to bipolar disorder, these forms of thinking can be seen across various avenues. In particular, dichotomous thinking is often applied to the decision of continuing psychotropic medication. As I described above, if one gains weight after a manic episode, the response is often that it is only the medication that is the culprit. Therefore, the individual goes off of his or her prescribed drugs. In actuality, the person may have lost weight dur-ing a previous episode, there is often an initial weight gain that subsides, or the anxiety that is experienced leads to overeating and a lack of exercise. However, instead of trying a different dose or another medication, the idea of following one's prescribed medication is dismissed. This is an example of an all-or-nothing mentality, or dichotomous thinking, that we can each own up to with some familiarity.

Perfectionism is a more specific deterrent to accessing our internal resources, and it precedes as well as coincides with dichotomous thinking. Everything needs to get done *flawlessly*, and in my case, perfectionism manifested in cleaning the house, washing the car meticulously, and maintaining obsessive exercise regiments. Or, on the opposite end of the spectrum, I did *nothing* at all. Often a procrastinator, I would let things go until later—for example, I would blow off exercising for weeks or months at a time. This change would come after sticking to an obsessive schedule for months. An alternative behavior was always inserted in place of the obsessive one. All of a sudden, I was spending every hour a day with a new girlfriend, getting high instead of dealing with life, or drinking every night. This type of behavior became my response to anxiety. I would do it continuously and was unaware that I was neglecting other aspects of my life.

These behaviors manifest in different ways with different people, but once you can identify dichotomous thinking, you cannot *not* see it. As I looked at the child-sized stacks of papers and overall clutter in my boss's office several years ago, he spoke about his "little bit of OCD," or obsessive-compulsive disorder. He said, "You either do it perfectly or you don't do it at all." Similarly, I would either have one or two alcoholic beverages or would leave the car keys at home (assuring I would not drive drunk) in order to drink my memories away. The black-and-white thinking gives you a sense of control, but in reality, the anxiety has it over you. Much like drugs and alcohol, the wave comes over you with increased force when this type of coping skill (perfectionism / dichotomous thinking) is not present. You don't like it. It is just a different type of withdrawal. These counterproductive behaviors act as temporary relief from anxiety across many domains, but they essentially lead to more and more anxiety.

2. Isolation and Oversocialization

From an anecdotal perspective, isolation and oversocialization can be correlated with depression and mania, respectively. A fine balance between the two is optimal. Isolation can lead to loneliness and a sense of apathy for those close to you as well as a loss of pleasure in activities with others. In addition, solitary tendencies are often related to the individual's desire to maintain secrecy of his or her symptoms (e.g., depression). Mania leads to a constant need for socialization, which is often a real sign of emptiness, fear, or a disregard for taking time to be alone with one's thoughts. The outcome of the latter is an excessive need to be the center of attention as well as a constant socialite (e.g., always partying, dressing in unusual manners, etc.). The child within mania commonly overexpresses him- or herself in order to receive this attention. Rebelliousness and the promotion of self-gratification are evidenced as well. Noticing the direction one is leaning toward or falling into can be very insightful when treating bipolar disorder. A balance between isolation and socialization is a clear goal. Friends as well as family members who are aware of your tendencies can offer a safety net when these warning signs arise.

3. Drugs and Alcohol

The polar opposite practice to mindfulness is abusing drugs and alcohol. A quantifiable amount of drugs and alcohol that is not disruptive to bipolar disorder is yet to be discovered. Use at your own risk. Both stimulants, from marijuana to cocaine and even caffeine, as well as antidepressants are good at precipitating manic episodes. The use of these substances can jump-start an episode, so it is worth consideration for those with bipolar disorder. Alcohol is a depressant by nature and also a lousy long-term antianxiety medication. It gives temporary relief to one's anxiety but then exacerbates symptoms when it is not in the body. Much the way perfectionism and dichotomous thinking increase anxiety when the behavior is stopped, with alcohol, anxiety usually increases the same way. This can lead a person to ruminate over stressors that can direct the individual spiraling into a dark hole. Drugs and alcohol are socially accepted, which is part of the appeal, but they can also lead a person into a state of emotional blunting that coincides with an overall lack of compassion for oneself and others. Mindfulness tends to breed compassion for oneself and others. The comorbidity of alcohol and drug abuse among those with bipolar disorder, if research participants were truthful, in my estimation, is close to 90 percent. Statistically, it is closer to 60 percent over one's lifetime for someone with some history of substance abuse (*Bipolar*

Disorders, 2008). I struggled with alcohol and marijuana abuse after finishing my undergraduate studies, despite the notion that it was "just a college thing." On November 1, 2006, my therapist documented the following:

> Alcohol use – Andy volunteered that he got intoxicated last
> weekend for the first time in a long time [...] Andy was hung
> over the next day and had difficulty recalling aspects of the
> evening and shared his regret [...] I reiterated concern about
> Andy's drinking, especially considering the memory lapse,
> which Andy accepted although he continues to decline a
> referral for a CD [Chemical Dependency] evaluation.

I was in denial about my substance problem, and I did not want it confirmed by the evaluation. The results of the eventual assessment (i.e., the CD evaluation) left me with additional diagnoses as follows:

> 11/20/06
> Diagnoses: Bipolar 1 disorder (296.7); alcohol dependence
> (303.9); cannabis dependence (304.3) per CD evaluation.

To put this in layman's terms, I am what some would call an alcoholic, as well as being addicted to marijuana. These diagnoses were based on history as well as the amount and frequency of use at the time. It is a far cry from just partying a little or engaging in the behaviors only on the weekends. This means that I am an addict and that these disorders are as incurable as bipolar disorder. They can be treated and kept at bay, but moderation in terms of drug use would be like saying, "I'll just take a little bit of lithium to treat the bipolar disorder," as opposed to the prescribed dosage. The conclusions were not conjured up in a subjective manner; instead, these results are based on the medical standard for psychological disorders with the use of the *Diagnostic and Statistical Manual* (DSM-IV). From what I can tell, the majority of my friends and some family members meet the criteria for these categories as well. As a sidenote, there is something called a specifier that is often tacked onto the end of a diagnosis. In my case, the current diagnosis for the substance abuse disorders (i.e., alcohol and cannabis dependence) ends with "Sustained Full Remission." In other words, "none of the criteria for Dependence or Abuse have been met at any time during a period of 12 months or longer." It is hard to believe that I have abstained from both of those drugs for over a year. This specifier is an expunging of part of my psychological record.

There is a disposition at the end of the therapist's documentation for areas to continue to work on. It is a simple treatment plan that is repeated in some variation from week to week.

P:
1. Maintain routine, including regular bedtime, eating healthfully, [and] regular exercise, and monitor alcohol use.
2. [Perform] cognitive exercises to support better perspective/reduced perfectionism.
3. [Practice] anxiety management.

This was a treatment plan for me, but it is general enough to be used with many individuals dealing with bipolar disorder. However, the advice is also applicable to anyone who wants to pursue a balanced life. I think (1) adhering to a lifestyle that is beneficial to one's body, (2) being attentive to perfectionistic tendencies, and (3) skillfully coping with stress is a successful regiment for anyone's well-being.

—38—

TRUST IN MIND

*Like the lotus flower that is born out of mud, we must honor
the darkest parts of ourselves and the most painful of our life's
experiences, because they are what allow us to birth our most
beautiful self.*

—Debbie Ford, *The Shadow Effect*

There is something to be said about knowing or understanding the answer to the question "What's wrong with me?" I am glad I do not have skin or lung cancer or diabetes, but if I did, I would hope that tanning beds, Parliament Lights, and Dunkin' Donuts would be desires not fulfilled. The story I have shared and the suggestions I have made will not apply to everyone. The ideas are not meant as doctrine for everyone with bipolar disorder but, rather, as a framework that one individual has found comfort in. Additionally, a crucial aspect that leads one to acceptance of the disorder is separating the disorder from who the person is as an individual. It pains me to hear language like "She's bipolar" and "He's a borderline" or, similarly, the word *schizophrenic*. These words have become shorthand nouns for people. Correctively, "She *has* bipolar disorder" and "He *has* borderline personality disorder" and "They *have* schizophrenia."

The person need not become the illness. There is hope as the proliferation of mental health parity laws grows (i.e., physical health insurance is equivalent in breadth to coverage for mental health treatment). It is imperative for the general public to understand that there is no difference between remarks like "A schizophrenic," "That bipolar person," "He's cancer," and "Wow, check out the cerebral palsy over there!" I have never heard a person say, "Yeah, she was formally diagnosed yesterday, and it appears that she *is* stomach cancer." This language makes it tiring for those individuals with bipolar disorder to realize that they are more than a list of diagnostic criteria—a tall structure that is made up of symptoms and episodes as the individual resides within it. There is so much more to life that one can experience than just "having bipolar disorder." Mental health professionals need to be responsible and have forethought regarding potential negative consequences of this detrimental form of labeling. The vernacular should deviate from this abbreviated and often stigmatizing terminology. One needs to advocate and speak for "individuals with bipolar disorder." Eventually, this kind of language can change the lens through which the general public views mental illness. Individuals with mental illnesses can then become whole through the sum of all of their qualities rather than being trapped within the casing of a mental illness.

Sadly, there are daunting and reliable statistics as to the course of this disorder. The probability that I will get sick again during the remainder of my lifetime is one that any gambler would bet high stakes on. However, clinging to the fear of the next episode is not productive, nor is it enjoyable. This what's-around-the-corner ideology can only become a self-fulfilling prophecy. If you think and focus on the idea of becoming depressed or manic, then you probably will. Practicing awareness and making positive decisions are different from living in a perpetual state of trepidation. Support and trust in one's judgment can help one resist the temptation to believe that every feeling is a symptom. Being sad does not always mean you are depressed, and feeling really happy does not always mean you are becoming manic. It is important to know that the majority of manic episodes occur prior or subsequent to a major depressive episode. Some estimations conclude that there is a 90 percent chance of a second manic episode for those with bipolar I disorder. Roughly 40 percent of people with bipolar disorder have an average of one episode every two and a half years, or four in every ten years. In my case, I have beaten the odds. I have not had a diagnosable manic episode in the last six years, and I have had only minor periods of depression, along with low levels of anxiety. Are there trends of highs and lows as well as periods of intense anxiety? Of course. Over the last six years, have I had more significant symptoms of anxiety and depression than someone without a mood disorder? Probably. The truth is, what has happened in the past does not concern me. The knowledge I have cultivated has made a path to contentment that had been lost in my life. This is the focus of my attention as I hold on to the behaviors that work toward a healthy lifestyle each day.

Not long ago, I heard a wise metaphor describing how humans experience pleasure and pain. The arbitrary numbers are not as important as the message itself. To generalize, as individuals, we all seek pleasure while concurrently avoiding pain. The reality of life is that only 2 percent is pleasurable and painful, while the remaining 98 percent is neither of the two. This means that if we constantly seek pleasure and avoid pain, which includes lacking awareness of the pleasure, we will miss out on life entirely (100 percent). What we can take from this is that in order to experience life to the fullest, we must acknowledge and sit with all the feelings in the spectrum and realize that most of life is neither pleasurable nor painful. In my opinion, the Western world does not adhere to this philosophy. In the United States Declaration of Independence, the goals are explicit: "Life, Liberty, and the pursuit of

Happiness." Perhaps an amendment to this phrase will someday revolution-
ize the language to "the acceptance of all emotions as one, with liberty and
justice secured in evidence." One must accept the dark moments of his or
her life that have manifested through anxiety, depression, and mania. This
pain is what we learn from and grow out of (or write a book about). At the
same time, one must adopt a commitment to skillful behaviors as well as let
go of the counterproductive choices we all make. This is the most successful
way I know to continuously heal from bipolar disorder. These "cures" I have
presented will only last moments; however, acceptance can last forever.

—39—

BIPOLAR TOO

You are perfect just the way you are, and you could use a little improvement.

—Suzuki Roshi

The events in this book are memories that have made me stronger as a person. However, there was one visual reminder that I could not get past. It was not a scar or an imperfection but, instead, what felt like an invasion of privacy. The tattoo on my wrist kept me in a constant state of fear that I would be questioned about its genesis, which would inevitably lead me to *involuntarily* tell the story of my illness to justify the bizarreness of the tattoo. Most days, I hid the ISP/3 tattoo with a watch that had a wide leather strap. I endured immense anxiety when it was exposed, because I dreaded the inquisition that I was certain would happen. There was no appropriate response in my mind that appropriately validated the reason for the tattoo. The worry of that question—"Oh, what does that mean on your wrist?"—caused a constant vacillation between dealing with the pain and subsequent embarrassment of potential exposure of the tattoo and having it covered with another tattoo. This was noted as follows by my therapist in 2007 within a list of presenting problems:

8. Challenges of incorporating diagnosis of bi-polar disorder into view of self, and challenges about how/when to disclose this information to others. Specifically, continuing to accept a visible tattoo that is related to a manic episode. Coming to terms with the tattoo as both a physical reality and as a symbol of having experienced a manic episode.

Originally, I felt that getting a cover-up tattoo was a weak way out as opposed to dealing with the anxiety of being questioned about its significance. When I asked a wiser man than myself about this predicament in the spring of 2009, he put it simply: "Sometimes it's all right to take the easy way." Months later, a feeling of relief washed over me. Finally, I had decided on a lotus flower, which symbolizes development and growth. The fact that these beautiful flowers are erected from small, dirty puddles resonated with me and, more specifically, the events that the tattoo represented. It took four years for the indelible ISP/3 tattoo to be washed away, but it is still not forgotten.

One thing I have noticed is how the new tattoo—like most—has become habituated. Much the same as a person loses the physical sensation of a foreign object when wearing a watch, hat, or piece of jewelry for long periods of time, I forget that it is there. These accessories mold into your body (smartphones might be doing the same), but my original tattoo was a mentally itchy scab. The new *lack* of feeling, or the habituation, is a nice feeling, because it was something that I never felt with the other tattoo. Presently, it is liberating to have some locus of control over the attention the tattoo receives or the scope of meaning I describe it with. It could also just be that a flower is a little lighter to carry.

In the summer of 2010, as I was finishing the first draft of this book, two of my siblings offered suggestions and constructive critiques for the book.

Throughout this laborious process, they attentively read and gave feedback as I shared pieces of the manuscript with various friends and family members on Facebook. However, the arrival of August 2010 brought about ominous changes in these siblings. Signs of hypomania surfaced almost concurrently for both of them. These are incredibly intelligent individuals with knowledge in the area of mental illness and witnesses to my own temporary downfall. In addition, they were reading my graphic depiction of bipolar disorder as they became symptomatic. This is the seduction of mania or hypomania whereby the brain tricks itself into thinking it is operating in a healthy manner. "I feel *fine*" is an all-too-common response from individuals when questioned about their state of mind. The euphoria perpetuates a desire to constantly do things, and there is no time to slow down for introspection.

As a side clinical note, there is an easy test for this faulty biological clock that mania causes. When one speaks to a person who is in a manic state (i.e., someone who is demonstrating rapid speech, flight of ideas, domination of the conversation, etc.), one can ask the individual how long the person believes he or she has been speaking. Manic individuals' concept of time, or orientation, is all too often severely impaired (e.g., a passing hour is judged to be merely ten to fifteen minutes). The notion of losing track of time in the middle of an enjoyable task or on a romantic date is similar to the internal clock of mania. The mind rapidly cycles, but the second hand moves in a stuttered orbit outside of reality.

Writing about past events is one thing, but my siblings' symptoms now forced me to face the memories of my own diagnosis eight and a half years prior through the sounds of my siblings' voices. The pressured speech, euphoria, and frequent phone calls and online video chats were filled with goal-oriented activities and out-of-character personalities. These were more than subtle indicators, but I was hesitant to trust my intuition, for fear my suspicion was merely a projection of my own illness. Reality became an eye examination where disorder and normality seemed to be the difference between "One or two? ... One or two? ... Two or one?" My siblings' senses of normality shifted in and out of focus between these lenses while I was forced to determine what was *abnormal*. My knowledge of the nature and course of the illness made it extremely difficult to determine an appropriate role. An intervention was needed, but I had to remove the therapist within me in order to be a compassionate and supportive brother who also has bipolar disorder.

After medication and therapy sessions, their words and sentences soon had appropriate pauses. Their moods were once again stable, and the predictability of their behaviors was reinstated. Unfortunately, the inevitable depression set in for both. Their saddened dispositions quickly manifested in behaviors comparable to a young child's indecisiveness and need for comfort. I could not hold my siblings together or extend a hug through the digital screen that enabled yet limited our connection. A heartbreakingly slow polarization occurred as I was forced to witness a severely wounded animal struggle to maintain its balance. I found myself walking a thin line between wearing my therapist hat and just being there for them as an empathic brother. This may read as cliché, but all I essentially wanted to do was take their pain away. The pain was from my remembrance of being diagnosed in 2002. I used that grief constructively by staying with it, and as a result, I remained present with them during our conversations. It is never possible to know exactly how someone is feeling, but the interactions with my siblings were as close as I have come. Thankfully, months later, their adjustments were starkly disparate from my own hard battle with bipolar disorder. My optimism and intuition tell me that they will not have enough of these gut-wrenching stories to produce a book of this kind.

Bipolar disorder is not an illness that resides merely in the bowels of poverty. This hereditary condition is not prejudiced; it infiltrates across race, socioeconomic status, and gender. If one hundred people read this book, then statistically, one to two of those individuals either has bipolar disorder or will develop it in his or her lifetime. This story will help people understand bipolar disorder from another perspective, and hopefully it will comfort those diagnosed. Perhaps it will lead to interventions with those afflicted by bipolar disorder (in a similar way that I was able to assist my siblings) before tragedy can strike. I have lectured on bipolar disorder and the stigma of mental illness at the University of Wisconsin–Madison and presented as a member of the National Alliance on Mental Illness (NAMI). Additionally, I taught at Minnesota State University, Mankato in the fall of 2012. I taught a clinical course titled "Advanced Social Work Practice with Individuals." Speaking publicly for the first time about the illness, my sibling joined as a guest lecturer on the topic of mood disorders. The graduate school students heard a success story about an individual with bipolar disorder. Their responses included comments like "I will always remember this," "I wish more people would be willing to discuss their mental health issues," and "Your family story definitely was the best learning experience and something that cannot be learned from a textbook."

I expect to continue these dialogues with those who are interested. Bipolar disorder no longer needs to be a closeted, scary illness that is shaded in our family trees. It is merely an extension of the highs and lows we all face in life. Everyone wants to feel good or happy, but in reality, as with bipolar disorder, finding a sustainable middle ground in life is the protective balance that keeps us on our feet when the unexpected life stressors aim to push us over the edge.

My current contentment in life—or sanity, for that matter—led to my decision to finally sit down and write this book. At various points during the reprocessing, this narrative transported me through a spectrum of emotions, which included the extremes of my feelings. Some of the memories were emotionally nauseating, while others opened into a refreshing catharsis. The writing and organizational process of this story has cleared my head. Consequently, there are brief moments of psychological equanimity. This long journey has built a confidence within me and altered former beliefs. I am a realistic, organized, and disciplined human being who is strong enough to take on immensely emotional, physical, and time-consuming tasks. Writing this book was only a dream of mine or, at best, a possible project for the future. Now an amazing and fulfilling accomplishment has not been a means to an end but instead has unlocked doors to continue to share this story with others. The progress I have made to accept this disorder has enabled me to become a present-focused, insight-oriented bystander of this story and no longer a victim of the past.

—40—

My Sane Asylum

A series of psychological studies ... has revealed that after
spending time in a quiet rural setting, close to nature, people
exhibit greater attentiveness, stronger memory, and generally
improved cognition. Their brains become calmer and sharper.
The reason ... is that when people aren't being bombarded
by external stimuli, their brains can, in effect, relax ... The
resulting state of contemplativeness strengthens their ability to
control their mind.

—Nicholas Carr, *The Shallows*

Pleading Insanity is an opportunity to see the nasty insides of a manic episode, including the destruction, but ultimately the hope for some semblance
of recovery from bipolar disorder. This book is a reminder of where I have
been, where I am going, and where I will never return to. For what it is worth,
this piece of literature enabled me to observe a transformation over the last
six years as well as the framework for how I arrived at the gentler shallows.
I experienced alterations of both mind and body that gave me the strength
to repeatedly view the darkest times of my life. Similar to the reintroduc-
tion of an animal into the wild, the writing of the first draft was a frenetic

release of information that had been confined in my brain for too long. The feeling of relief this caused allowed a new sense of worth to fill my spirit. I then read and reread the story and read it again. I gained new insights after each read-through. The process repeated over and over as additions, subtractions, reviews, and edits were made both by me and other dear friends. It is a wonderful thing to invite others to hold the tragedies that have weighed you down. The dispersal of my illness through narrative is a type of sharing that reduces the magnitude of bipolar disorder in terms of who I am and, as a result, fosters an infinite potential for the future.

The traumatic elements of the episode in 2005, including my admittance to the psychiatric wing of the hospital, my damaged family relationships, and my incarceration, are important for others to read. Throughout the memoir, those aspects were the areas I hurried to get into. I never intended the book to be an autobiography; I wanted it to be more of a snapshot of in-your-face mania. It is so challenging to capture in words just how scary it is to see a seemingly healthy person morph into a high-speed, feverish, bizarre, and extreme version of him- or herself. My goal is to help others cultivate a non-judgmental understanding for the morphing process of bipolar disorder.

A major struggle I had with writing this book was my impulsive nature to write in the moment from that time frame while adhering to fundamental writing styles. The emotional and traumatic memories fueled a form of writing that was primal, free of consciousness, and tangential. I tried my best to keep the bursting ideas within a linear narrative, but the text resembles a middle-school collage. At times, this was appropriate for how I felt in those chaotic moments. Proper grammar and formal English writing courses fought against the flights of ideas. The rational part of my brain kept cohesion, overall organization, and precise methodology throughout the tiring project. I believe this to be a beautiful union that has organically created a writing style I can call my own. As I wrote, the trauma and emotional memory that had been dormant in the amygdala of my brain were all of a sudden wrestling with my prefrontal cortex for authority. This rivalry in the brain is analogous to a pair of self-entitled junkyard dogs fighting over the same scrap (in this case, a scrap of information). The descriptions of the events in the book are very loose, flowing, and abstract, so inevitably one will encounter legitimate written errors. However, in some cases, my aim for stylistic prose overrode traditional grammar in order to establish the momentary feeling (i.e., the amygdala's real voice) of the situation I pulled from long-term memory. The visceral state I wrote from did not always make sense, because a lot of the *real* story did not either.

I moved to northern New Hampshire to accept a job at a nonprofit mental health center in 2009. Fresh out of graduate school, I was ready for my dream job. This opportunity came with a small caveat: I would be living in a town consisting of fewer than two thousand people. To give a better perspective, franchises included, and were limited to, Rite Aid and a triplex gas station: Subway, gas, and Dunkin' Donuts. The emptiness became a sanctuary, but at times, I felt caged in. The writing of this book is one of those Bon Iver stories, as I became reclusive in a log cabin on the outskirts of the town during its production. At least three days a week, I regimentally devoted countless hours at an empty, Internetless bakery with my oversized laptop. There is no way to be certain, but had I stayed in Madison, Wisconsin, or gone to a large city, I believe *Pleading Insanity* would not exist. Not now. The stillness and slow pace of life that occupies less stimulation enabled me to focus as well as look deeper inside myself while analyzing the world I live in.

I continue to receive my own therapy to grapple with issues that inevitably arise, I have abstained from drugs and alcohol since the end of 2010, and my mood is stable. My practice as a psychotherapist continues to improve, and in September of 2011, I became a licensed independent clinical social worker (LICSW) in New Hampshire. In the beginning of 2012, a new job brought me back to the Midwest. I obtained a LICSW to practice in Minnesota and continue to practice psychotherapy.

There are moments of stillness that last a little bit longer each day. Whether it is practicing a sport, learning to play the guitar, or living with a mental illness, one can always improve. Although a plateau does not exist, there are resting points as well as flashes of serenity. Transposing these stories and ideas from the complex neural network of my brain was a learning experience in many ways. I dream of one day becoming a writer and after three years, I figured out what my intention has been in writing this book: I just wanted to share this story.

Appendix

The diagnosis below is what I was given, and it is just one example of criteria for "296.4x Bipolar I Disorder," which is based on the most recent episode. The others include *Single Manic Episode* or *Most Recent Episode: Hypomanic, Depressed, Mixed,* or *Unspecified.*

Diagnostic criteria for 296.4x Bipolar I Disorder, Most Recent Episode Manic

A. Currently (or most recently) in a Manic Episode.

B. There has previously been at least one Major Depressive Episode, Manic Episode, or Mixed Episode.

C. The mood episodes in Criteria A and B are not better accounted for by Schizoaffective Disorder and are not superimposed on Schizophrenia, Schizophreniform Disorder, Delusional Disorder, or Psychotic Disorder Not Otherwise Specified.

Diagnostic criteria for 296.89 Bipolar II Disorder

A. Presence (or history) of one or more Major Depressive Episodes.

B. Presence (or history) of at least one Hypomanic Episode.

C. There has never been a Manic Episode or a Mixed Episode.

D. The mood symptoms in Criteria A and B are not better accounted for by Schizoaffective Disorder and are not superimposed on Schizophrenia, Schizophreniform Disorder, Delusional Disorder, or Psychotic Disorder Not Otherwise Specified.

E. The symptoms cause clinically significant distress or impairment in social, occupational, or other important areas of functioning.

Criteria for Manic Episode

A. A distinct period of abnormally and persistently elevated, expansive, or irritable mood, lasting at least 1 week (or any duration if hospitalization is necessary).

B. During the period of mood disturbance, three (or more) of the following symptoms have persisted (four if the mood is only irritable) and have been present to a significant degree:

- Inflated self-esteem or grandiosity
- Decreased need for sleep (e.g., feels rested after only 3 hours of sleep)
- More talkative than usual or pressure to keep talking
- Flight of ideas or subjective experience that thoughts are racing
- Distractibility (i.e., attention too easily drawn to unimportant or irrelevant external stimuli)
- Increase in goal-directed activity (either socially, at work or school, or sexually) or psychomotor agitation
- Excessive involvement in pleasurable activities that have a high potential for painful consequences (e.g., engaging in unrestrained buying sprees, sexual indiscretions, or foolish business investments)

C. The symptoms do not meet criteria for a Mixed Episode.

D. The mood disturbance is sufficiently severe to cause marked impairment in occupational functioning or in usual social activities or relationships with others, or to necessitate hospitalization to prevent harm to self or others, or there are psychotic features.

E. The symptoms are not due to the direct physiological effects of a substance (e.g., a drug of abuse, a medication, or other treatments) or a general medical condition (e.g., hyperthyroidism).

Criteria for Hypomanic Episode

A. A distinct period of persistently elevated, expansive, or irritable mood, lasting throughout at least 4 days, that is clearly different from the usual nondepressed mood.

B. During the period of mood disturbance, three (or more) of the following symptoms have persisted (four if the mood is only irritable) and have been present to a significant degree:

   • Inflated self-esteem or grandiosity
   • Decreased need for sleep (e.g., feels rested after only 3 hours of sleep)
   • More talkative than usual or pressure to keep talking
   • Flight of ideas or subjective experience that thoughts are racing
   • Distractibility (i.e., attention too easily drawn to unimportant or irrelevant external stimuli)
   • Increase in goal-directed activity (either socially, at work or school, or sexually) or psychomotor agitation
   • Excessive involvement in pleasurable activities that have a high potential for painful consequences (e.g., engaging in unrestrained buying sprees, sexual indiscretions, or foolish business investments)

C. The episode is associated with an unequivocal change in functioning that is uncharacteristic of the person when not symptomatic.

D. The disturbance in mood and the change in functioning are observable by others.

E. The episode is not severe enough to cause marked impairment in social or occupational functioning, or to necessitate hospitalization, and there are no psychotic features.

F. The symptoms are not due to the direct physiological effects of a substance (e.g., a drug of abuse, a medication, or other treatment) or a general medical condition (e.g., hyperthyroidism).

Criteria for Major Depressive Episode

A. Five (or more) of the following symptoms have been present during the same 2-week period and represent a change from previous functioning; at least one of the symptoms is either (1) depressed mood or (2) loss of interest or pleasure.

Note: Do not include symptoms that are clearly due to a general medical condition, or mood-incongruent delusions or hallucinations.

- Depressed mood most of the day, nearly every day, as indicated by either subjective report (e.g., feels sad or empty) or observation made by others (e.g., appears tearful). Note: in children and adolescents, can be irritable mood.

- Markedly diminished interest or pleasure in all, or almost all, activities most of the day, nearly every day (as indicated by either subjective account or observation made by others)

- Significant weight loss when not dieting or weight gain (e.g., a change of more than 5% of body weight in a month), or decrease or increase in appetite nearly every day. Note: in children, consider failure to make expected weight gains.

- Insomnia or hypersomnia nearly every day

- Psychomotor agitation or retardation nearly every day (observable by others, not merely subjective feelings of restlessness or being slowed down)

- Fatigue or loss of energy nearly every day
- Feelings of worthlessness or excessive or inappropriate guilt (which may be delusional) nearly every day (not merely self-reproach or guilt about being sick)
- Diminished ability to think or concentrate, or indecisiveness, nearly every day (either by subjective account or as observed by others)
- Recurrent thoughts of death (not just fear of dying), recurrent suicidal ideation without a specific plan, or a suicide attempt or a specific plan for committing suicide

B. The symptoms do not meet criteria for a Mixed Episode.

C. The symptoms cause clinically significant distress or impairment in social, occupational, or other important areas of functioning.

D. The symptoms are not due to the direct physiological effects of a substance (e.g., a drug of abuse, a medication) or a general medical condition (e.g., hypothyroidism).

E. The symptoms are not better accounted for by bereavement, i.e., after the loss of a loved one, the symptoms persist for longer than 2 months or are characterized by marked functional impairment, morbid preoccupation with worthlessness, suicidal ideation, psychotic symptoms, or psychomotor retardation.

ACKNOWLEDGMENTS

Kay Redfield Jamison continues to be a major inspiration in my life. Her courage to reveal (in *An Unquiet Mind*) publically in 1995 that she has "manic-depressive illness" has made her a pioneer in the fight against the stigma of mental illness. My dear friend Matthew Patrei was another major influence. Reading his master's thesis was a major impetus to writing this book. The articulate, emotionally infused autobiographical account of his childhood experiences went beyond expressions of self-disclosure. I aspire to one day write in the same league or at the caliber of his brilliance. There is a long list of writers whose thoughts and works have influenced me. These include but are not limited to Jonathan Franzen, David Eagleman, Jonah Lehrer, and the late David Foster Wallace.

I am thankful for everyone who has supported me in my short existence, but especially over the previous eleven years since I was diagnosed. Without the help of my close friends and family, I would never have achieved the expensive diplomas, licenses, and professional dreams. I am forever indebted to those individuals. In addition, I am grateful to the numerous mentors who supported me through the years as an undergraduate (Lyn Abramson) and graduate (Donald Coleman, Peggy Sleeper, and Flint Sparks) student. These distinct souls have made me a better writer, practitioner, and human being. Whether they knew it or not, their compassion erected my self-confidence to a level that enabled me scholastically, professionally, and spiritually.

Equally important are all the colleagues in my various occupational ventures who have listened to my concerns with nonjudgmental ears and kindhearted eyes. I will shorten this list by referencing only Journey Mental Health Center, which is formerly known as Dane County Mental Health Center. During my time in New Hampshire, Judith Houghton supervised me in every sense of the word on the path to my LICSW. She kept me healthy with genuine empathy and love during our time together. This also goes for the agency—Northern Human Services—as a whole, which taught me an invaluable amount of clinical skills. From the professional secretaries all the way up to the directors, the staff quickly treated me as one of their own. They neither ignored nor were alarmed by my illness. I miss the community of Colebrook, New Hampshire, which accepted me into their family from 2009 to 2012.

Anne Kubena undeniably deserves my singular praises both for being a close friend and collaborator on this project. In spite of our friendship often being disconnected over the last decade because of distance and separate paths, she has always been there for me.

The countless mental health workers I have been in treatment with—from psychiatrists to therapists—who have saved my life are not to be forgotten. If medication and talk therapy had not been prescribed, I can definitively state that my death and epitaph—not this book—would have been written. Sometimes it is difficult to see a cause and effect with psychotherapy. However, it is no accident that drug abuse is gone from my life, I have fully processed the trauma, and my relationship dynamics have changed in healthy ways.

I am astonished, flattered, and honored that in our hectic, digital, and split-focused era, a person would take the time to read this story (especially the acknowledgments section—no one reads that!). This has been a fairly anonymous read, so I won't list names. However, I have not forgotten the people who experienced this story either firsthand, through these words, or by listening. Everyone has been selflessly reassuring when I asked for help.

The book would not have been possible without the support and encouragement of my friends and family who countlessly agreed to read through the book with each draft. I am grateful for my mother's edits, accolades, and earnest enthusiasm about me publishing this book. My father gave me guidance in writing the sections of the narrative that I was barely sentient for. Having siblings who believed in me during this adventure made a difference that I cannot articulate, not to mention the family as a whole, who carried me when I faltered over the years.

In addition to all of the individuals mentioned above, this book is dedicated to the people bearing the undeniable suffering bipolar disorder can produce. All of us must *acknowledge* and understand that it can get better. Thank you.

NOTES

ABOUT THE AUTHOR

Andrew James Archer is a licensed independent clinical social worker (LICSW) practicing psychotherapy in Minnesota and serving as an adjunct instructor for Minnesota State University–Mankato. He has been an academic guest lecturer across the United States, including as a presenter for the National Alliance on Mental Illness (NAMI).